P9-DBP-129

Advance Praise for
Mexico, A Love Story

"Twenty-two distinctive and unique voices sweep the reader through an exhausting and passionate range of emotions. The book is alive with love and laughter, tears and tenderness, death—and voices from the spirit world. Reading it is like inhaling a culture in all its dimensions. Like the richness of Mexico, the book sizzles with the heat and heart of the Mexican people and pulses through women in love."
—Rita Golden Gelman, author of *Tales of a Female Nomad*

"This insightful collection of stories is filled with vivid descriptions and engaging characters. Women write about their love affair with Mexico and reveal a complicated lover imbued with beauty, passion, danger, and excitement that will lead them to a transformative experience."
—Rose Castillo Guilbault, author of *Farmworker's Daughter: Growing Up Mexican in America*

"Nearly two dozen American women wander into the vast world-next-door that is our neighbor to the south. With equal measures of curiosity and courage, they journey to sunny resorts, grim penitentiaries, and time-challenged villages. Like them, you will be enchanted and amazed."
—Héctor Tobar, author of *Translation Nation: Defining a New American Identity in the Spanish-Speaking United States*

"With open minds and hearts, these writers engage Mexico in all its sensual, spiritual, confounding glory and emerge transformed."
—Gina Hyams, author of *In a Mexican Garden*

"This wide-ranging collection of gringa experiences in Mexico shines a light upon, and becomes a part of, one of the most charged cultural conversations on earth: that between North Americans and their southern neighbors."
—Tony Cohan, author of *On Mexican Time* and *Mexican Days*

"In this book, a love of Mexico flows from many springs. An L.A. teenager goes 'home' to Oaxaca once a year. A woman goes on vacation and stays seventeen years. Some fall in love with colors, food, the sea; some discover themselves in their interactions with the people they meet. What is common to all their stories is an openness to experience, an eagerness to transcend the familiar self. Sometimes there's hurt, too, because real travel, like real life, is not covered with a warranty. These wonderful myriad voices remind us that getting away is sometimes the real route home."
—Sandra Scofield, author of *Gringa* and *Occasions of Sin: A Memoir*

Praise for
Italy, A Love Story

"A multifaceted look at the charms of the popular Mediterranean country through the eyes of twenty-eight noted women writers. They contribute appealing personal stories of their travels to various parts of the country."
—*Santa Barbara News-Press*

"In this thrilling and layered new collection, women . . . explore and describe in loving prose individual infatuations with a land that is both complicated by and adored for a rich tradition."
—*Sun Journal*

"Camille Cusumano has assembled a unique cast of women writing about their encounters with Italy. Together, they come close to defining that indefinable something—the people, the culture, the fit of people and culture with their landscape—that draws the traveler again and again to this land."
—Lawrence DiStasi

"When I first discovered Florence, with all the bridges except the Ponte Vecchio still destroyed, I fell in love. This proves the experience of loving Italy is not confined to women. But the women in this book offer a useful perspective, highly flavored, with engaging, erotic implications. . . . The book is great voyeuristic fun."
—Herbert Gold, author of *Haiti: Best Nightmare on Earth, Bohemia, Fathers,* and *A Girl of Forty*

Praise for
France, A Love Story

"This is a very readable collection. . . . Tales are alternately loving, witty, nostalgic, and, yes, occasionally swooning."
—*San Francisco Chronicle*

"The heart of this book is in the maturity of its voices of experience."
—*Boston Globe*

"In this beautiful collection, women share their experiences first-hand, reflecting on the ways France's unique culture has enriched and enchanted their lives."
—*France Today*

"This book is an evocative gathering of short pieces from twenty-five female writers. . . . This is a collection that will be appreciated by the Francophiles among us."
—*Toronto Globe and Mail*

Mexico,

A Love Story

Edited by
Camille Cusumano

SEAL PRESS

Mexico, A Love Story
Women Write about the Mexican Experience

Copyright © 2006 by Camille Cusumano

A version of "The Food of Love" originally appeared in *Elle* magazine and is reprinted with permission of Laura Fraser.

The recipe for Mole Amarillo copyright © 2005 by Restaurante el Naranjo has been adapted and is reprinted with permission of Iliana de la Vega.

Some photos and illustrations are used by permission and are the property of the original copyright owners.

Published by
Seal Press
An Imprint of Avalon Publishing Group, Incorporated
1400 65th Street, Suite 250
AVALON
publishing group incorporated
Emeryville, CA 94608

All rights reserved. No part of this book may be reproduced or transmitted in any form without written permission from the publisher, except by reviewers who may quote brief excerpts in connection with a review.

9 8 7 6 5 4 3 2 1

Library of Congress Cataloging-in-Publication Data
Cusumano, Camille.
Mexico, a love story : women write about the Mexican experience / Camille Cusumano.
p. cm.
ISBN-13: 978-1-58005-156-9
ISBN-10: 1-58005-156-1
1. Mexico—Description and travel. 2. Mexico—Social life and customs. 3. Women—Travel—Mexico. I. Title.
F1216.5.C87 2006
917.204—dc22
2005037673

Cover and interior design by Domini Dragoone
Printed in Canada by Transcontinental
Distributed by Publishers Group West

Para la gente de Mexico

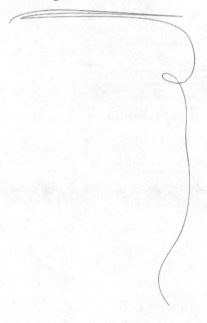

Contents

Introduction

This collection, the third in a series of "Love Story" anthologies (following France and Italy), started life as a two-dimensional outline. The diverse geography and rich culture of Mexico, I thought, were all the framework that was required to inspire a template of themes that would render a fleshed-out portrait of our southern neighbor.

But the flesh, I found, came in a less formatted, more organic way. It came from the living people who inhabit these essays and the people who have written them. As I read through hundreds of stories, seeking one to fill every laboratory-tested theme in mind, I realized the soul of the book, like the soul of any place in the world one visits, resides in its characters and narrators. It's through these individuals—backpackers and teachers, fishermen and priests, mothers and artists—that the country's storied landscape, history, society, and customs come to life. The result is a far more heterogeneous, resonant, and complex text than the one I originally imagined. For just as the whole moon may be reflected in a tiny dewdrop, each personal story that follows constellates a Mexico bigger than itself.

Thus, for example, Kathy Jo Brisker's account of her pilgrimage to Oaxaca to honor her late mother on the Day of the Dead is much more than a sociological portrait of that famous holiday. Tenderly, sensually, Brisker guides readers through the savory feast and its ritual altar-building, and through her mother's passion for the city and its riot of color. And, though it takes place in the same state as Brisker's story, what a Mexico apart we find in Tania Flores's story of visits to her father's village, where the fourteen-year-old author finds a "sizzle that penetrates all the way to my blood, a feeling of *this is where I'm from.*"

Or take Laura Resau's "Bees Born of Tears." This timeless account of a woman's visit to a *curandera* for a spiritual cleansing quietly unravels the Mexico many of us long to see—one in which untrammeled pre-Christian beliefs survive. It is formidable to be led by Resau, through the lens of her need for healing, while she is ushered into the homes—and hearts—of the Mexican people.

These are all love stories, in the most humanistic sense. Karin Finell's saga "El Greco in Mexico" is romantically bittersweet, whereas Susan McKinney de Ortega and Reyna Lingemann offer us fairytale endings. All are as powerful as the myth and religion that drive our modern—and ancient—psyches.

They all revolve around personages you won't easily forget—or want to forget. As our contemporary body of so-called travel literature grows and evolves, I for one am more and more intrigued and enlightened by the character-driven travel essay—and this anthology features twenty-two marvelous examples. They make this collection a virtual "talking" companion for anyone on a voyage south of the border. I found myself wanting to find those two astonishing women in Chiapas who lovingly "kidnapped" Linda Grant Niemann, or to track down Marisa Solís's Ensenada house and meet its friendly ghosts.

After reading Kathleen Hamilton Gündoğdu's fiasco in the dressing room, I imagined myself in Acapulco, cackling among the women who all pitched in to size up the breasts of one timid gringa for her first bra. And where in Paraíso might the parishoners of Katherine Hatch's typical Mexican imbroglio be lurking? Sondra Ross Hines's portrait, of a middle-aged mother of four who yearns for yet another child, lays bare the glaring differences in the North American and Mexican senses of womanhood.

There is some edgy (and edge-of-your-seat) love here, too. Mary Ellen Sanger's haunting tale unveils a nightmarish scenario that had me biting my nails, wondering whether she would escape or succumb to the vagaries of the country's penal system. In Chris Scofield's steamy, erotic tale, the danger is carnal and the payoff is vulnerability; her Mexico is the crucible that melts and reforges our very souls, and her visceral writing makes one feel less like a voyeur than a participant—although that is perhaps true of each personal account here.

I could not have imagined two more irresistible "love" stories, both rooted in Tijuana, than those by Suzanne LaFetra and Sophia Raday. LaFetra takes us inside the prison where she teaches, bringing light and life to her male students, and Raday's lesson in love and perseverance unfolds amid the sordid environs of a metals recycling plant.

Yet even at a typical tourist-resort destination, true "love" can develop—as it did during Charish Badzinski's annual visits to Cozumel. She and her husband strike up an uncommon friendship with a hotel worker—a relationship that can await other visitors who might dare to open their minds and hearts to Mexico.

Clearly, this crosscultural dialogue can exist for any of us, just as it has for the twenty-two women who contributed their personal journeys into the soul of our southern neighbor. For Mexico and the United States are joined at the hip—we share a 1,950-mile border that was so aptly described by Katherine Hatch as "a scar." These are tales without borders. When you delve into them, you do what every narrator has done—fly beneath the radar of the perennial chatter in American news with regards to Mexico: the Minute Men vigilantes, amnesty for illegal aliens, improvement of border security, and the effect (whether positive or negative) immigrants have had on our economy and society.

If these essays by women distill a certain feminine sensibility about traveling, it is not at all to dismiss the masculine, which liberally and lovingly inhabits these tales. Rather, it is to show the reader glittering facets of the lessons we've learned as women living, loving, and traveling alone—or following lovers and ideals deep into cities, mountains, or coastal towns, with Mexico as our teacher. Mexico has left a mark on our lives. And I trust that every one of these stories will leave a mark on our readers.

Camille Cusumano
April 2006

Laura Resau

Bees Born of Tears

Sonia shifts her baby to the other hip and tosses me a stick. "Here, Laurita," she says, breathless. "For the dogs."

The main street of Huajolotitlán ("Turkeyland" in the language of the Aztecs) rises at a forty-five-degree angle, so steep you want to use your hands to crawl up. Brutal midafternoon sunlight glares off the pavement. Low buildings—cement and adobe shops painted pastels and stained with urine—line the street. I catch a whiff of fresh blood from a pink *pollería,* with its plastic bowls of goopy, featherless, dead chickens. Other shops sell only a handful of bare necessities—tiny packets of chili peanuts, toilet paper, cooking oil, Coke, warm beer—all neatly lined up on shelves behind the counter. Shop owners peer out of the cool interiors; a man in the shadows hisses at me, *"Güera, güera"* ("White girl, white girl"). Sonia and I walk in silence, keeping our mouths closed to seal in the moisture.

We are on our way to see María Chiquita (María "the very little one"). All I know about her is this: She is tiny. She is nearly a century old. She is a *curandera*—a traditional healer.

I've been staying in a nearby Mixtec town in Oaxaca, where I lived and taught English to college students two years earlier. This summer I'm visiting villages, talking to women and healers for my master's fieldwork. Sonia, a former student of mine with family in Huajolotitlán, has offered to take me to María Chiquita.

Two years ago I would have been bursting with the anticipation of meeting this *curandera*, but now my forehead is furrowed and my eyes sting from the dry heat. Despite the constant presence of people, I feel alone, an observer of life more than a participant. I have just turned twenty-seven, and nearly every woman my age here has several kids already. During my interviews, women shake their heads and cluck sympathetically when they discover I have no children. Around me, despite poverty, people are having families, living their lives.

On this trip my former students, who haven't seen me for two years, seem worried about me. You look different, they say, pale, thin, sickly. A poet friend said with deep concern, "Laurita, you seem *demacrada*." I'd never heard that word before—it is a poet's word, not something I could pick up on the street. "Something is missing," he explained. "Your *chispa*," Your spark.

I tried to joke about it. "Oh, it's the bad food up North. No fresh mangoes and chilies and tortillas."

He didn't laugh.

I finally said, in a naked, shaky voice, that the two years with Manuel, my ex-boyfriend, were hard, very hard. The six months since the breakup had been just as hard, in a different way. Manuel's words come back like a curse, each syllable punctuated in precise, Spanish-accented consonants: "You will never be in love again."

Sonia and I veer onto a dirt path, where turkeys peck at old plastic bottles and silver potato-chip packages.

"We're here," she says, motioning to a small reed hut with a woven palm roof. It is a quaint, lopsided structure, suggesting the home of a witch, a fairy, an elf, some otherworldly creature. A horde of dogs guard the dwelling, their skin stretched taut over the ribs, sparse fur standing up angrily. They begin a cacophony of barks and growls, which makes Sonia's baby wail.

Sonia quickly pulls the blanket over her daughter's head and whispers, *"Ch-ch-ch, m'hija,* don't cry." There is urgency in her voice. I wonder if she worries that her daughter could get sick from *espanto* (fright) because of the dogs. This belief is so pervasive that even miniskirt-wearing, web-surfing, twenty-one-year-old Sonia probably feels it in her bones. When a person is frightened, her spirit separates from her body; at that moment, the spirit-owner of the land captures her spirit and holds it prisoner. The person grows ill and could even die unless a healer performs a ritual to retrieve the spirit. Most people I know here say they have been afflicted with *espanto* at one time or another, often from encounters with the ubiquitous vicious dogs in Mixtec communities.

I wave the stick in the air like a sword, and the dogs keep their distance. Sonia and I huddle in a sparse bit of shade under a mesquite tree, waiting for someone to call off the dogs. She murmurs under the blanket all the while, into that intimate space between baby and mother.

After the conversation with my poet friend, I looked up *demacrada* in my dictionary. Emaciated. What he meant was spiritually emaciated. I tell myself that life is a series of little deaths and rebirths—part of your self dies; a new part is born. But what if some essential part of your self disappears and there's nothing to replace it?

Maybe the heat is making me delirious, launching me into the dreamy beginnings of heat exhaustion, but something odd is seeping into this scene in María Chiquita's yard . . . the ancient, musty odor of a folktale. A wanderer approaches a hut, thirsty and exhausted, having climbed a nearly endless hill and having confronted savage beasts, hoping to see the mysterious wise woman who will bestow upon her. . . . For a moment, life takes on the crystalline structure of a myth, the pattern of a snowflake, the spiral of a shell. Everything is part of the movement drawing me closer to the center, closer to some truth.

Two girls—about three and eight years old—appear at the door of the hut and walk toward us. They're wearing jelly sandals and well-worn dresses a few sizes too big. Their brown twig legs are scaly with dust.

Sonia shifts her baby to the other hip. *"Buenas tardes, niñas.* We're looking for Doña María Chiquita."

Whispering together excitedly about *la gringuita,* the girls lead us to the door of the hut, protecting us from the dogs with well-aimed stones, and call out *"Tía!"*

A tiny woman appears at the door. She barely reaches my shoulder, which would put her at about four feet, four inches. She wears a pink polyester dress, a blue-checked cotton apron, a red cable-knit cardigan, and a heap of tangled necklaces—plastic pearls and gold chains and leather strings, each holding its medley of saints and crucifixes. A round pair of glasses with thick lenses, '80s-style, covers much of her face. Intricate networks of wrinkles spread out from her mouth and eyes, like the dried-up, folded skirts of mountains. Age spots a shade darker than her brown skin speckle her face. Her thick, muscular hands seem out of proportion to her birdlike body.

"¡María Purísima Santísima!" She smiles a toothless smile and gives me a tight hug saturated with wood smoke and copal incense.

Sonia glances at me with raised eyebrows and a shrug that says she has no idea what's going on.

It *is* strange. María Chiquita had no way of knowing we were coming, yet she acts as though she's known us all our lives, as though she's been expecting us. She is overflowing with something, exploding with it, even. No doubt about it, this woman has *chispa.*

"¡Ay, muchachita!" she says to me. "Come in, come in! Sit down, *m'hija,* my daughter!" Her voice is nasal and urgent.

I duck through the doorway and follow her into a dark, windowless room with parallel slivers of sunlight spilling through the walls onto the dirt floor. There's an altar to the right, a wooden table crowded with candles flickering in small glasses, and a multitude of framed saints and Virgins amid vases of carnations and daisies. A clay incense pot with the charred remains of pine and copal holds a lingering smell of smoky resin. A few *petates* (woven palm mats) are rolled up in the corner. Clay pots, their bottoms burnt black, hang from the wall. The only furniture is a small stool and two wooden chairs. The air smells cool and earthy like a cave.

María Chiquita gestures to the chairs. "Sit down, sit down, *muchachita!*" She is barefoot. Her century-old feet are caked with dust and are dry as leather, rough as hooves.

Here in the Mixteca, people tell a story of a spirit woman called the *bandolera*, a beautiful lady with the feet of an animal—in some versions, she has turkey claws; in others, the hooves of a burro or horse. She lives in a cave full of candles, each representing a life. The short candles are lives about to end; the long ones, newborn babies. In my favorite version, she brings certain people to her cave to teach them the secrets of life and death.

A woman appears at another door that opens to a dirt courtyard, where people are milling around, engaged in various tasks. The woman is middle-aged, a bit taller than María Chiquita and much wider. She introduces herself as María Chiquita's daughter, visiting from Mexico City. "Fidelina Lopez Martinez. *Para servirle.*" Light from the doorway illuminates her face, round and damp with sweat from some exertion in the courtyard.

The girls carry in an extra chair—a plastic one with a Sol beer logo—and a bottle of Coke. The older girl pours me a glass, and the little one offers it to me with both hands. "Here you are, *gringuita.*" The warm syrup feels sweet on my tongue, the bubbles sharp.

Now Fidelina and María Chiquita let the questions fly. Where are you from? What are you doing all the way out here? Do you like our food? Do you like our village? Where is your mother? Are you married? Do you have children? The women send out wave after wave of sheer giddy exhilaration. The air is electric.

Fidelina tells us that her mother doesn't hear well, so I talk loudly, imitating Fidelina's loud, slow voice. "I'm from the United States," I say. "Maryland." I translate the state's name as "Tierra de María."

"*¡María Santísima Purísima!*" María Chiquita shrieks. "You traveled far!"

I answer the rest of the questions, explaining that I haven't lived with my mother for nearly ten years, that I like spicy food, I like "Turkeyland," and that I'm an old maid, childless and husbandless.

As we talk, bees spiral and dip around our heads, attracted, I guess, to the Coke. Sonia shoos them away from her baby, who has fallen asleep. I move my head around in a dance to get out of the bees' paths. The last time I was stung, years ago, on my finger, my entire hand ballooned up. María Chiquita and her daughter let the bees land on their shoulders, rest in their hair.

"And what are you doing all the way out here, *m'hija?*" María Chiquita asks.

"Sonia tells me you're a *curandera.* I wanted to meet you."

"Ah! So that's why!" Fidelina shouts. "My *mamacita* is ninety-six years old! Can you believe it? Ninety-six! And look! Still strong, isn't she?!"

María Chiquita nods vigorously.

She does look strong. More than strong. The whirlwind inside her nearly lifts her small body off the floor. There is something I can learn from this woman, with her candles, with her secrets of life and death.

Fidelina turns to Sonia. "Who is your mother?" she asks, trying to place her in the web of families of Huajolotitlán.

Sonia tells them and adds, "My mother brought me and my sister here when we had *espanto*."

"Ah, yes, *muchacha!*" María Chiquita says. "I remember you."

"What gave you *espanto*?" I ask Sonia.

"Some dogs." She kisses her baby, who is asleep now. "They scared me, and after that I couldn't sleep. I cried a lot. I didn't feel like eating."

People say that unless the child is cured, she might die, or continue to live in a weakened state, missing the essential part of herself. I wonder if you can get used to living without parts of your spirit, like someone who's missing a finger and compensates with others. How many bits of my spirit have I lost over the years? Is my spirit scarred and mutilated, with chunks missing here and there? Or have they grown back, like the arms of a starfish, the tails of lizards?

One day, when I was nine, I was roller-skating in the alley near my house when two Dobermans—trained attack dogs—were let out of a car parked by a garage to enter their kennels. The dogs bolted toward me and pounced. I clung to a splintery telephone pole as the dogs tore into my upper arm and thigh. The owner retrieved them and, ignoring the blood and tears, told me to go home. "You're okay," he insisted, probably afraid of being sued. I skated home in shock.

That's when I started acting weird. I was terrified of any door clicking shut, convinced I would get locked in. I refused to be left without an adult for even a minute. I tolerated no dark corners and frantically turned on all the lights in the house. My weirdness tapered off after a year, replaced by occasional dreams of wandering lost in a labyrinth of alleys. They were eerie dreams, very real, as though some part of myself were stuck amid the trash cans and wire fences and weeds poking through cracked concrete.

Today I wonder whether my nine-year-old self needed someone to retrieve my spirit and return it to my body—literally or symbolically, it didn't matter. And now, after this relationship with Manuel has left me *demacrada*, I think my twenty-seven-year-old self needs a ritual, too. A part of me has gotten lost, and I need to find it.

María Chiquita must notice that part of my spirit is missing, because she announces, "I'm going to give you a *limpia, m'hija*." A cleaning.

"Good," I say. "I need one."

Sonia stares at me. "Are you sure?" She lowers her voice. "You know what she's going to do to you?"

"*Más o menos.*" More or less.

"But Laurita, your clothes will get soaked. You don't have to do it."

"I want to. Really." Anyway, Fidelina and the girls are already spreading out the *petate*.

"Take off your clothes, *muchachita*," María Chiquita orders.

This is an unexpected twist. I hesitate, trying to remember which underwear I have on.

"Down to your underwear!"

I take off my sandals. At least my clothes won't get wet this way.

Sonia bites her lip and watches, amused.

Voices float in from outside, where men and women are doing chores in the dirt courtyard. Hopefully they can't see me undressing.

I strip. My underwear turns out to be an ancient pair—once white, now grayish, mismatched with a grubby, frayed bra. I sit like a skinny plucked chicken on the *petate*, goosebumped and shivering. The dried palm itches my thighs. I wonder if tiny bugs live between the fibers.

María Chiquita pulls a bottle of neon-green liquid from a crate in the corner. I've seen *limpias* done with clear mescal, but I don't recognize this stuff. *"Agua de Siete Machos,"* she calls it. Water of Seven Macho Males? She holds it under my nose. It smells like cheap cologne. I sneeze.

Fidelina hurries out the door, returning moments later with a handful of fresh *sauco* leaves and handing them to her mother.

María Chiquita prays at her altar and then rubs the herbs over me, in my hair, my shoulder, arms, back, legs, the soles of my feet. The *sauco* smells fragrant, potent. She prays to God, the Virgins, the saints, punctuating her chanting with "Laura." My self-consciousness fades, and I focus on her voice, on the leaves' friction over my skin.

Then she murmurs, like a stage direction between prayers, "Take off your glasses, *muchachita*."

The older girl carefully takes them from me for safekeeping.

"Close your eyes." María Chiquita whispers.

I obey. I feel the shock of cool alcohol spat onto my skin. It is a jarring sensation, pulling me out of a certain dullness. I imagine all the *mal aire* (bad air) blown away with these great bursts. I imagine my spirit, something iridescent and alive, something like a blue butterfly, flying through the door and into my open chest, nestling into where it belongs.

When the spitting ends, I open my eyes. The girl hands me my glasses. I look down at my ratty underwear, now spotted with lime green. I shiver and smile at María Chiquita, her eyes huge and wild behind her thick lenses.

I'm fully clothed again. The bees seem even more attracted to me now that my skin and underwear are covered with the neon-green stuff. I'd like to stand up to have more space to dodge the bees, but in a gesture of politeness typical in Mixtec villages, Fidelina insists I stay glued to the chair. The bees zoom around my head. I pray they don't sting. Who knows whether the local hospital is stocked with epinephrine.

"Don't mind the bees," María Chiquita says. "They are good, these bees!"

The bees are buzzing around our heads like crazy now—two bees in particular—circling each other, spiraling around each other as if dancing. I duck out of their way.

"Don't worry," Fidelina says. "They won't sting you."

"But I'm allergic."

"Look! Look how those two bees are staying near you and my *mamacita*."

Sure enough, the two bees seem to be doing figure eights around María Chiquita's and my heads. Urgent, frenetic spirals.

"The bees are your spirits. See, they have met before, your spirits. They met each other first and they led your bodies together."

María Chiquita nods.

The wings inside my chest move, I can feel them. They move with a thrill, a sense of discovering layers of meaning like ribbons intermingling in the wind. They move with the sudden knowledge that the world is a strange, deep, rich place.

Sonia's baby starts to fuss, and I realize it's nearly dark. "We should go, Laurita," Sonia says.

I hand María Chiquita 30 pesos—about $3—her charge for a *limpia*. She hugs me hard and grasps my hand, unwilling to let me go.

"You'll come back tomorrow, right?" Her eyes are full of tears. Her grip is as powerful and genuine as a three-month-old baby's.

"In a few days," I promise.

"Last night," she says, "I was kneeling in front of my altar, crying because of how we suffer. Because we are poor, my family. I asked *Nuestro Señor* to look after us. *Señor Jesús, ayúdame*, I prayed. Help me! And in my sleep, a baby came to me. A fat white baby in green clothes. Really fat, and really white, like your skin!"

There is a framed picture of a fat white baby in green on the altar, I notice. *El Santo Niño*, the holy baby Jesus.

"And he told me, *María, m'hija, have faith. Just wait until tomorrow.*"

She looks at me dramatically. "And today, you come to my door, *muchacha!* He was right, *El Niño Jesús!*"

I think about the $3 I gave her—possibly enough for a small sack of beans, some eggs, dried corn—enough food for a few days if they really stretched it. Is that what she means? Or is she referring to our new friendship involving bees and spirits, a friendship with its own momentum that won't let a seventy-year age difference and thousands of miles stop it?

A few days later I'm back in the hut, on the plastic Sol chair, with bees once again circling my head, although I don't mind them as much now. Since the *limpia*, I've felt elated. I don't care exactly how the *limpia* worked. I simply enjoy the feeling that my *chispa* is returning.

"You remind me of the gypsies!" María Chiquita announces. "They traveled from far away too." She turns to her daughter for confirmation.

Fidelina nods. "*Muy buena gente*, the gypsies, really good people."

"They don't come anymore!" María Chiquita's eyes fill with tears. "Ay, how I miss them!"

"Your skin is white like theirs," Fidelina says.

"And you speak our language in a strange manner too!" María Chiquita adds, giggling. Her fluidity of emotion amazes me, how she cries at any hint of sadness and laughs heartily at the smallest joke.

"And you're so tall!"

Reminiscing about the gypsies inspires María Chiquita to tell us her story. When she was about six years old, a gypsy woman read her palm and predicted she would live to be a very, very old lady. Soon afterward, María Chiquita came down with a severe and sudden sickness.

Fidelina jumps in. "She died, the poor thing."

"What?" I thought I'd mastered my verb conjugations. "Who died?"

"My poor *mamacita, pobrecita.*"

I turn to María Chiquita. "You died?"

María Chiquita nods solemnly. "I died."

The family mourned her and put white candles all over the room as villagers came to pray and cry over her. In the midst of the darkness and smoke and tears, a drop of candle wax fell onto María Chiquita's arm. She flinched. She woke up. People say that her experience with death gave her the power to heal.

She doesn't remember what happened to her while she was dead, but I wonder if she met the spirit woman of death and life inside her cave of candles. Maybe she taught her how to heal. I imagine each of us with our own cave of candles, parts of ourselves burning down to wax pools, dying, other parts of us just beginning, the candles freshly lit.

It is nearly dark, time for me to leave. I tell María Chiquita and her daughter that I won't see them again for a while. In a few days I'll be heading back to Arizona to finish grad school.

From her altar, María Chiquita takes a photo of a statue of San Sebastián and puts it in my hands. He is dressed royally in a sequined, flowered outfit of turquoise, red, and gold; draped with gold chains and bracelets, flowers and ribbons. His arms are tied to a lopsided cross flanked by two small, dark-skinned Jesus cruci-fixes. Small daggers pierce San Sebastián's throat and limbs, and his wounds drip blood. Fidelina's reverent look makes me realize this is a very special thing her mother is giving me.

Suffering saints usually frighten me a little, but this one doesn't look in pain so much as wistful. No, this tortured saint is not creepy. It is oddly comforting, actually, to see how he endures his suffering, trusting that his pain will be a flash in eternity, know-ing that his wounds will heal, with only flowers and sparkles and ribbons remaining.

I think about all the prayers focused on this photo, all the energy directed to it. It is a sacred thing, a thing of power for María Chiquita, and she has given it to me.

We hug. She cries and moans and sobs and chants and prays, making small crosses over me with her hands. *Que Dios te bendiga, muchacha,* may God bless you, girl. Over and over and over again, for a long time.

I'm embarrassed by the attention, unsure how to respond. Not even my own mother has ever given me such a farewell. Then I realize that neither María Chiquita nor her daughter can read or write, so letters won't be possible. She has no phone. She has no money to visit me, no visa. And she is ninety-six years old. Of course she's worried this is the last time we'll see each other.

I am used to traveling, meeting people, saying goodbye. I naively believe that we will see each other in a year or two.

Within days of my last visit with María Chiquita, I get an email from Ian, the man I've known for years and will eventually marry. Our relationship is a stream that surfaces, goes underground a bit, and resurfaces. His email now comes after years of little or no communication, since Manuel discouraged our friendship.

Ian's email is three lines. It says he has been remembering the way sunshine smells on my skin. I imagine my spirit, a velvety bee, flying up to Colorado to confer with his spirit. I write back to Ian, and we arrange for him to visit me in Tucson. The following year, we are living together, engaged, in Colorado.

Bees, I discover, are associated with gods of love—Cupid among the Greeks and Kama among Indians. The Welsh believe that bees came from paradise down to earth to give humans gifts of wax and honey—honey to nourish them, and wax to make candles for altars. A bee entering the house is lucky, and one flying around a sleeping child is a sign of a happy life to come. And in Egypt, bees were born of the tears of the sun god, Ra, and symbolize the afterlife and rebirth.

A year and a half later, Ian and I walk up the hill in Huajolotitlán, just at dusk, when the air is blue and magical and tinged with sadness. We have heard from Sonia that María Chiquita passed away last year, although Sonia is not completely sure; it could be a rumor. I remember how María Chiquita defied death as a six-year-old. I hope it's another mistake.

I pick up a stick to fend off the barking dogs. Someone is walking toward us, a stout woman. Fidelina.

"*¡Jesús María José!*" She hugs us, moaning and crying, and then leads us to her siblings, who have come from other villages. They know my name, although we've never met, and hug us with the same force that Fidelina does.

"How we prayed you'd come!" she says. "My poor *mamacita* always remembered you!"

It turns out we have arrived precisely on the night of María Chiquita's *cabo de año*—the one-year anniversary of her death, when family members and friends spend a week mourning her. I can guess Fidelina's explanation—that the spirit of her *mamacita* buzzed up to the United States to invite my spirit to the *cabo de año*.

Fidelina ushers us into the hut and gives us sweet cinnamon coffee and sugary pastries.

The altar is overflowing with carnations and roses. The light from the candles is stronger than that of the bare bulb dangling overhead. In back of the hut are shadows of people milling around, talking quietly. Other relatives wander into the room and greet us.

They have heard of me, María Chiquita's dear friend from the United States. They have heard how our spirits flew together as bees.

The sugar, the caffeine, the shadows, the candlelight—they lend a surreal quality to the night, and I can almost see, in the midst of so many flames, a tiny body laid out. I tip over a candle, let a drop of beeswax fall, and wake her up, knowing that resurrections happen all the time.

Chris Scofield

The Net

Walking into town from the posada where I live, on the Pacific coast of Oaxaca, requires that I watch every step for the rocky depressions that break through the sandy dirt and the stagnant green pools of piss, dust, detergent, dirty well water, and gasoline. I keep an eye out for easily startled pigs and cringing dogs; the shy children, the more confident ones; the old men, the drunk men; the fishermen with bright plastic tubs of fresh tuna balanced on their shoulders.

It's hot, on the cusp of the rainy season, and time is slow. The air is thick, and every step is a chore, every interaction short and concise, as if saving energy for the first muggy downpour that will signal release.

I'm meeting a friend for a cappuccino at the café with wrought-iron chairs and the best view. From the patio, you can see taxis, *collectivos*, and rusty buses that regularly rattle into town, expelling gringos with backpacks, and the local women, balancing live poultry and cardboard boxes secured by twine while their small, obedient children chase them.

I walk on the bay side of the road, a comfortable distance from the local navy base. At the entrance to the complex are three palm trees: two ribbed with tumorlike growths, one scarred with diamonds and chevrons like a giant argyle sock. On the flat, second-story roof of the barracks where he hangs his uniform to dry, a handsome young sailor in an A-shirt smiles down at me.

The three palm trees remind me of the three exposures left in my Pentax, and of last night's conversation (if you can call it that) with my inebriated husband, who, after an hour of chasing mescal with beer, prattled on how the number three was the manifestation of the Holy Trinity, and how "The Three Bears" was a Christian metaphor, even as he insisted, "We're not too old, we could still make a baby." But he'd had too much sun and booze to hold the thought, let alone me.

Initially, six months in southern Mexico sounded like a godsend: a chance to get out of the rat race; to sleep, read, and take pictures; to get acquainted with a town too small for a McDonald's, or even a decent hotel. To slow down and reassess my priorities. Four months later, I'm tan and thinner, but restless and homesick and tired of being a conspicuous outsider.

In the few minutes it's taken me to walk from the posada, the townspeople have melted into the shadows with long-necked bottles of beer or fallen into hammocks for their siesta. Caucusing chickens dust their feathers. A pig shares a shady hole with a dog fiercely scratching his fleas. I pass a woman fanning herself at her kitchen table; across the room, a barely audible soap opera flips and rolls on a tiny black-and-white television set. Beyond that, all that breaks the humid stillness of my stroll into town is the sound of my flip-flops, a boat motor some distance away, and the lapping of waves on the jellyfish-strewn beach.

The damp hair on my neck corkscrews in the humidity while sweat runs between my breasts, down my belly, into my shorts. The lightest clothing feels like arctic gear. The sun burns my skin on either side of the camera strap through my light cotton blouse.

A boy appears before me, walking my way. He's tall for coastal Oaxaca. Fourteen, maybe older; a child. I smile. As he nears me, he mutters something in Spanish. I don't know Spanish, but I recognize the intimacy of the tone. On a man it would be sexual, guarded but intent, but on a boy? He slows his gait, raises himself to my height, and looks at my eyes, my breasts, my crotch before returning my glance. When he passes, he wolf whistles. Quietly, but clearly.

"Wait . . . " I say, suddenly angry, *"por favor."*

I hear him stop behind me, and I turn to face him.

"Did you *whistle* at me?" I say. My tone is impatient; I feel the heat of the day behind it. *"¿Hablas inglés?"*

Back off, I tell myself. *Relax.*

"Un poquito," he smiles, and holds up his thumb and index finger. He's a kid again, a young teenager feeling his oats, that's all. I take a deep breath and look at the ground between us.

"Never mind," I say. *"Lo siento."*

"Señora," he begins haltingly, "is beautiful woman." He looks around him nervously and asks, "Your husband, he love you?"

Oaxaca bores my tall, blond spouse. He's grown impatient with its pace and inconveniences and, as the months have passed, impatient with me too. "Of course," I say without thinking. Then, "Wait a minute . . . *what* did you say?"

The boy looks away, then points at the dirty white house behind him. *"Mi casa, señora,"* he says. "My house." He walks toward it when a man suddenly appears on the porch.

I've seen the man before, stocky and dark, mustached, smoking a cigarette. The man who threw an inky octopus over his shoulder and dashed up the rainy beach while I watched from my window. The man who catches my eye every time I pass this place and once touched my arm and smiled when I literally ran into him en route to *el baño* after too many beers at Tito's. Self-conscious and embarrassed, I'd glanced first at his deep-set eyes, then at the black mustache hairs that covered his top lip. He'd walked me into the courtyard and, in English, instructed me, "Through the kitchen, past the hen yard, the wash basin, the clothesline, over there . . . *sí*, keep going," and smiled again. Back at the posada that night I imagined him pressing me against the wall of the courtyard: I ride his knee, fall into his mouth, melt on his tongue.

In the dark doorway behind him, a tiny girl in a stark white dress corners a whining puppy. When she sees me, she runs into the house.

The man doesn't see me when he flicks his burning cigarette into the dirt and steps off the porch. He speaks angrily to the boy who hurriedly explains himself in Spanish.

I look at the boy's broad, muscled feet. What was I thinking? I overreacted. I don't want to get him in trouble. *"Con permiso,"* I inter-rupt. I look at the man; he doesn't seem to recognize me. "It was nothing, just talk. Everything's fine. No problem, really."

I walk on, trying not to show how embarrassed I am for blow-ing my cool. I know better too: I'm smiling and I'm American, and that combination, so say the countless travel books I've read, encour-ages male attention. I resolve to keep my eyes straight ahead and not talk to anyone until I reach the café.

I feel the man's eyes on me as I hurry away, the broad, burning heat of the day on my blushing neck, the sweat making a mess of my clothes. When I get to the café, I'll order a glass of *limonada;* I'll even ask for ice *con aqua purificada.* Did I bring my cigarettes? I stick my hand in my pockets. Good: lipstick, extra film, cigarettes, money.

I quicken my pace. My flip-flops stir up small plumes of dust.

I hear footsteps. *"Señora,"* the boy calls out. He's following me.

"Adiós," I say, over my shoulder. *"Por favor,* I need to go. *Restau-rante . . . mi amiga."* God, my Spanish sucks.

"Señora," he repeats. "Please, lady."

"Yes?" I stop, determined to be pleasant this time. *"¿Sí?"*

He hands me a package of Chiclets. "Sorry," he says.

"It's okay." *Do* not *smile,* I tell myself.

The boy points at my camera, then mimics holding it to his face and snapping a picture. "You want photo?" He gestures for me to fol-low him up the hill. "Come. Is okay. *Playa,* ocean, for you take photo. Is beautiful. Come. Is okay, lady."

I stick the gum in my pocket. *Stop being suspicious,* I tell myself. *He's being nice.* And if he expects a tip for showing me a great shot off the beaten path, well, you can't blame him for wanting to make a little pocket change off the tourists.

"Photo?" I feel my heart opening. I remember the exposures in my camera. *"Three* photos," I say.

The boy leads me off the road, up the rocky footpath and past two small houses, a stone well, and a small corral of goats; through the snagging scrub brush and the trees with the yellow peeling bark that our landlord calls "gringo nose." Occasionally the boy smiles over his shoulder at me in encouragement. "Photo," he repeats. His eagerness to please makes me feel guilty. When I pass a woman washing clothes in a bright plastic tub, I cry *"¡Hola!"* and wave. She smiles and waves back.

Two scabby dogs stagger up the hill after us but run off, cowering, when the boy picks up a stone. He disappears briefly, then reappears further up the trail. The trek is steep but quiet; all I hear are my footfalls and labored breathing. When we reach a high, narrow outcropping and a plot of thirsty corn plants, I stop to catch my breath and look around.

It's beautiful up here, with a view of our small fishing town that I've never seen. I take photographs: one of a black smoky plume of burning garbage, fish, and tires snaking through the exhausted brown-gray vegetation; another of a chicken pecking at a rotting goat carcass teeming with maggots and ants; and one more, from a kneeling position. I point the camera down an irregular corn row, and a donkey wanders into frame; behind him, the rugged descent of stick houses and tile roofs empty into the brilliant blue ocean.

I've finished the roll; the film automatically rewinds.

When I stand up again, I feel relaxed and centered for the first time in months. I take a deep breath and smile. Why have I photographed faces when there's so much to see in the quiet complexity of everything else? I turn around in place, further grinding the grit under my heel. A musky wind blows up from the beach below, inflating each brightly colored plastic bag tied to the dead tree nearby with a crisp snap. The sound scares off the bare-necked chicken pecking for bugs in my lengthening shadow.

I love this place, this moment, opening a door inside me. A door I want to remember, a place I want to return to. My secret place—until someone runs me out anyway. Listen to me, another goddamn colonialist! Does everyone fall in love with Mexico, sooner or later? I stand on my tiptoes and stretch, raising my arms over my head, smiling into the burning sky.

Up ahead, my guide enters the ruin of an adobe farmhouse. Pigeons, startled off their roost, dart through the roughly hewn window. When the boy pops his head out the door and calls, "You want me wait, lady?" I answer no, and he waves goodbye, running past me down the hill.

I dig a new roll of film out of my pocket and look toward the adobe; I'll change the roll inside. I check my watch too: ten minutes. I can be ten minutes late, even twenty. My friend will be curious about the photographs and, after our coffee date, will walk me to the *farmacia* where I'll have the film developed.

I hurry into the adobe. It's dark and still inside and smells of damp straw and yeast. I press myself against a wall and open the back of my Pentax. When I tuck the used film in my pocket, I sense someone watching me.

"Hello?" I say into the dark suspense. "*¿Hola?*"

A man steps out of the shadows and into the slatted light of the naked timbers overhead. It's him, the man from the road below, the fisherman with the octopus, the handsome mustached man who touched my arm at Tito's. The man my husband nicknamed Zapata.

The light stripes the man's face and infuses what I see of his dark eyes with a chestnut cast. "*Hola,*" he says calmly. "I hope I didn't scare you."

"You did," I say, walking toward the door. The room is warmer than it should be, given the cool of the adobe and the shade of the deciduous trees surrounding it.

"Wait," he says, and I do. "My son, Oscar. He has big mouth, señora."

"It's okay," I stammer, and close up the back of my camera. "The pictures will be worth it. It's beautiful up here."

"I'm glad you like it," he says. "Some people just see the sun."

I feel myself blush. Until ten minutes ago, that's all I saw too.

The man steps closer. I smell cigarettes and a hint of cologne. And it dawns on me: "Did you follow me?" I ask. My heart is in my throat. I shouldn't be here. "Did you know I'd be alone?"

I visualize the way down the hill, the hole in the brush that empties onto the path, the stone well, the goats, the cactus. . . .

The man steps back. "I follow Oscar," he explains. "You take pictures, I tell him, no money. Be nice to señora, I tell him, no money for pictures."

Shit. "Of course," I say. "Sorry," and shake my head. "Thanks for . . . looking out for me." I thread the camera strap over my shoulder and prepare to leave. "I need to go."

The man takes another step toward me, dissolving into the darkness of the room again. I look toward the doorway, which is burning with afternoon sun.

"Oscar bad mouth to gringas sometimes. I tell him no. He . . . flirts, I think."

"He's young," I say in the boy's defense, forgetting how angry I was moments before. Are the man and I really *talking?* Are we sharing parental insights? I'm probably his age; he'd expect me to have children. "Everyone does foolish things sometimes," I say.

Though I can't see him, I feel the man draw closer.

I flush with fresh heat. Five weeks from now, my husband and I will be back in the States. Five weeks from now, this man, and the feelings that being here with him arouses in me, will be a memory.

"What did Oscar say, señora?"

I see him now. He's three feet away, almost at the end of my arm.

"Nothing, really. Something about . . . I don't know . . . the way I look, I guess. And being married . . . I'm married, you know."

Oh God, why did I say that? I look away, embarrassed.

I feel him smile, his face soften, the corners of his mustache turn up. "You live at *la posada* too," he says, "and walk by my house. Remember Tito's *por comida?* You ordered my *pulpa*. In the courtyard, I help you . . . maybe you drink too much tequila. . . . "

"Actually, it was beer. Listen, I'm meeting a friend at the café."

"Sure, you go, señora. But Oscar's right. You're beautiful woman."

He isn't three feet away, or an arm's length. His hand is on my waist, scooping me up, pulling me toward him, collapsing the air between us. I gasp with the suddenness of it. The broad, pulsing strength of his hands on my back beats through my blouse. His muscles taut, his breathing concentrated, he draws me in, hand-over-hand, fist-over-fist, like fish line.

With his warm breath on my face, his mustache on my cheek, I rock in the warm Pacific waters of his caress and moan. I moan. It isn't loud, maybe he doesn't hear it, but *I* hear it, I hear *me*, and I stop.

He brushes his lips on mine and releases me slowly, stepping back further into the fractured light of the room. When he wipes his mustache with his dark fingers, my heart skips with the earthiness of it: I'm delicious, a morsel to be savored.

"Go," he says, clearing his throat. "Don't be afraid. I won't stop you."

He looks up, suddenly aware that he's spotlit by a shaft of sun breaking through the rotten timbers and *palapa* fronds overhead. He pulls up his shirt collar, takes a cigarette out of his back pocket, lights it, and poses. "James Dean," he says.

I smile nervously.

A donkey brays nearby. The man looks at me self-consciously, cancels the cigarette with his tennis shoe, and nods at the camera still hanging on my shoulder. "Take picture."

"That's okay," I mumble.

"You want campesino, or," folding his arms across his chest and cocking his head, "lowrider in *Estados Unidos?* Postcard, señora, postcard." He takes a step toward me and stops. He's angry. "Maybe you

32

want beach-boy lover. You want one-night stand? I'll be your beach-boy–tamales–Santana–one-night stand, señora."

I look down, I look away, I wish myself invisible. I want to go but don't, can't.

"Zapata? You like Zapata, *sí*? Gringas love Zapata."

Zapata, my husband calls the handsome mustached man. Zapata, the revolutionary on horseback in the turn-of-the-century sepia print hanging over my computer at home: striped pants, boots, chaps, bandolier, and pistols. At his side is a paternal Pancho Villa, also on horseback, and in the background, rifle teepees and smoking campfires, a blur of moving hooves, a locomotive coming into view, and a pregnant young woman standing beside the horse of another mounted revolutionary, her small hand on his pantleg. A moment in time ninety years ago, a cause I've only read about in books, a language I don't speak, under a sun that's too damn hot in a land I'll always be a stranger to.

Yes, I want Zapata. Yes, I want this wild alien country. Yes, I want . . . "What's your name?" I ask, stepping toward him. "Who are *you?*"

"Tomás," he says, straightening up. A wounded pride remains in his voice. "Who are *you?*"

The quiet makes things equal. Dust motes and cobwebs bob in the air between us while the man remains center stage, bathed in the lacy light.

Down the hill, the naval base sounds its 3:00 PM siren. Within minutes, two columns of trim, uniformed young marines will march single file through town, one brace of men going north, the other going south, on either side of the street.

"Who am I? I'm a gringa. Remember?" His hesitant smile becomes sober. He listens. "And you don't know how I feel about Zapata, or Oscar, or you, or *this* country, or *my* country, or anything else." I'm confident but pissed and somehow holding my temper. "For all I know," I say, "you run this routine on every gringa you and that boy manipulate into coming up here."

I want Tomás to see me this way. I want my restless anger in his face as much as I want his righteous indignation in mine. We've earned it, both of us.

He walks toward me, tentatively, and smiles.

I fold my arms across my chest. "I won't be here much longer," I say. "Five weeks." I look at the door and sigh. "Listen, I don't blame you for being sick of us. We smile when we shouldn't . . . we don't know your language . . . we're loud, we're pushy," my emotions are catching up with me. "And honestly? Oaxaca is beautiful, but we don't have heat like this in Oregon. . . . "

The man stands directly in front of me now. "Please, señora. . . . "

"Chris," I say, blinking back a tear. My racing heart is the only thing keeping me erect. "My name is Chris."

"Chris. I want you see *me*. Not Mexico, not vacation, not beach boy." Tomás moves closer and smiles. And pulls me in. Into his eyes and this moment, into the quiet warm Pacific waters lapping the beach below. Hand over fist, he rolls me into his net, into his arms, his mouth and eyes, his world, again.

A chalky narrow of light falls across his face and highlights a purple streak of sea snail dye in his hair. My bones soften in their skin. I put down my camera and lean my back against the wall.

"You look at me," I say.

"It's okay?"

"Oh, yes," I say, sighing when he touches my face.

"Don't . . . close . . . your . . . eyes," he says, so slowly each word dissolves in the heat between us before he speaks the next.

He presses me against the wall and rests his open mouth on the nape of my neck. His thick flat tongue takes measure of it and, with its point, flicks my earlobe, sucking a small beaded earring into his mouth before freeing it again.

Down the hill, past burning heaps of rubber and dusty gray-green vegetation, fresh tuna is unloaded from a rusty wheelbarrow through the front door of Tito's del Mar. Two horny dogs chase a bitch in heat past the café where my girlfriend sits alone, sipping an icy cappuccino on the shady porch. She smokes an American ciga-rette and swings a long tan leg to keep off the flies. She leans out of her chair and peers down the road looking for me, avoiding the ready smile of a teenage boy sitting nearby.

Tomás samples the lip of sweat at my collarbone where it tips before spilling down my chest. Then stops and asks, "Okay?"

I whisper my consent.

He watches me, with measured confidence, while unbutton-ing my blouse; pressing each button through its tiny cotton mouth, slowly, one after the other, finally leaving my blouse hanging loose against my chest. He steps back, and raises the broad cupped palms of his hands, chest level, like he's modeling clay or catching the head of a newborn. My breasts swell to fill them while the rest of me waits, limp, empty, gasping for air against the adobe wall.

I travel his brown muscled body with my eyes, stopping at his mouth, his eyes, his crotch. I touch his shirt and whisper "Come here," pulling him toward me, falling into his thick, sturdy strength, his mouth, and the concentric pools of his eyes that empty somewhere on the other side of the world, a different time, a different country where no one knows either of us. No husband, no children, no fisherman's life.

Where exactly did I step through a portal into this stolen perfect present, a dark room where everything is visible?

Kneeling before me, Tomás finishes the salty trek of his tongue: refreshing himself from the pool of sweat at my belly button, traveling the tender vacancy of my belly to the lush oasis where a greater thirst is quenched; a warm lagoon where I stand thigh-high in ocean water while tiny fish nibble my legs, and he kneels before me, feasting at my center, and I come, sending electronically charged ripples across the placid face of the pool.

When I put my mouth on his penis, I taste the ocean and the sand, the rocky climb to our adobe nest, the pulse, the blood, the hot burned earth underneath it. Buried inside, where my barren wildness meets his tropics, he knows my country too.

Later, I remember it episodically.

The room eclipsed by his eyes and mouth. The cry of a peacock in the bushes outside that made us both jump. The shy sound of my zipper, and his groan as he pushed his hand up the leg of my shorts, past the damp trim of my panties, through my hair and soft wet lips, to the inside of me.

A dream I'd been having all my life; a memory finally realized. Is it still there on that steep hillside, somewhere in that crucial obscurity of time? Does it smile at me from a window, or stand in a lacy spotlight under rotting timbers? Does it remain in the molecules of the adobe room where each sex-sweet touch smoked and spread across my burning skin like a hot pan?

I'll wonder how it ever happened.

How at the café my patient friend was only on her second coffee and third cigarette when I finally arrived. Or how, that afternoon, the earth had shifted on its axis, and I dug a hole all the way to China and dove in head first, but no one noticed.

How after just one of his kisses, I would *always* be tangled in his net; always passionately conflicted, torn between mortal life and dreams.

How in my dreams, I'm pushed against the wall and his muscular knee pulses rhythmically against me while he holds my ass and sucks my breasts till I push him away. There in the room, where I meet his hunger by thrusting myself at his mouth and hands like a voluptuous figurehead on the bow of a storm-tossed ship. Digging my nails into the chipped adobe, hanging on as if *some* thing, *any* thing, could save me from my determined exile to that warm, still, quiet room where my body runs with sweaty juices, and I feel myself dehydrating, but never come up for air, never never, amen.

How after hearing his laugh, surprisingly light and innocent, I hear it buried inside each one of mine.

At home in America, I'll wonder how Tomás and I passed through that same portal three more times while I lived in Oaxaca. Three: the holy trinity, the eternal triad with its flawless configuration of equal angles.

I'll wonder how I live a day, a week, a month, a year, a succession of years without my lover's tongue, his sculptor's hands, his thick brown penis like a forearm balancing my drunken innocence or searching my bright blue ocean for his dreams.

Linda Grant Niemann

A Tale of Two Mexicos

My decision to learn Spanish started with a $200 round-trip fare that Betty, my cop girlfriend, spotted in the Sunday paper. A romantic vacation at the beach was one of those things we had never done and probably wouldn't do, since we were on the verge of breaking up. The big drawback for her was that she couldn't take her gun. For me, it was that she wanted to take her gun. I had no idea at the time that the trip would open a door into an unknown Mexico, or that I would fall so in love with it that I would spend the next fifteen years returning.

Betty and I flew to Mexico City, our first stopover on our tour of the country. "Wow," Betty said, "you can buy tear gas here." Her mood lifted noticeably.

In Betty's view, the world was divided into criminals and potential criminals. It's not that I disagree with this, but I've had the luxury of distance. Unlike her, I could walk down a street in San Francisco without knowing that a slasher had ripped up two children in the apartment on the left. And I didn't have nightmares about trying to stop him.

The slogan on her City of San Francisco badge read *fiero en la guerra, oro en paz.*

"It's Latin," Betty said. "They told us at the academy."

"*Pax*," I said, "if it was Latin. *Paz* in Spanish." I could tell she was shocked, but after all, California was part of Mexico when the city was founded.

"Sometimes you look street smart and tough," Betty would say, "But other times I look at you and think *gosling*."

Not understanding Spanish, Betty relied on her other heightened senses to detect danger. Every stranger got a scrutinizing stare. It soon became clear we were not going to do much socializing on this vacation—but we would survive, that was the important thing. The beach at Chankanaab lagoon in Cozumel loosened us up. We put on snorkels and fins and bought chunks of bread to feed the fish while swimming. Although they looked peaceful from the shore, the fish—electric blue ones with brilliant yellow dots, queen angelfish, long thin barracuda hanging around like dope dealers at a high school football game—all knew what to do when bread appeared in the water: They attacked. I felt fifty fish lips sucking on my bare skin, and I quickly let go of the bread and ducked. Resurfacing, I saw Betty shoot out of the water, a thrashing cloud of fish behind her.

"The bread," she managed, as I joined her under the *palapa*. "It was in my pocket, and they found it. Promise me you'll never tell anyone about this."

"I swear," I said.

"You know," she said. "A police horse is trained to lead you out of a crowd if you grab hold of its tail."

Before we left, Betty read all the guidebooks and decided we would rent a car and drive to Chichén Itzá.

"Fine," I told her, "But you have to drive. I don't want to drive in Mexico."

No problem. She was butch. But after three days in Cozumel, Betty came down with the flu. She still wanted to see the ruins, so we decided to stick with the plan. However, it turned out that car rental rates were astronomical in the nearest town, so we headed for Cancún on an hourlong bus ride. The local bus was actually a minibus; we crammed our packs under the seat and waited in the terminal for thirty minutes while the bus filled up. Betty had the aisle seat, which meant that she got to ride with someone's penis rubbing against her ear. Not her favorite thing, I could tell.

In Cancún, we managed to rent a diseased Volkswagen. Betty had now come down with a sore throat, so I agreed, apparently not gallantly enough, to drive. I could have been more solicitous, I suppose, but I was busy keeping my death grip on the wheel. Every mile or so, we would hit an unmarked *tope* (speed bump), which would knock us into the roof. Moreover, small children holding items for sale would rush out in front of the car, forcing me to brake for them. I was also occupied with dodging head-on collisions with tourist buses that tried to pass each other on their way to and from the ruins. Terrorized, I'd decelerate and pull to the side of the road and see the sleeping white faces pressed against the tinted air-conditioned glass as the bus passed within inches of us. At some point, it dawned on me that Betty had ceased talking to me. No, not just because of her sore throat; now I was on the other end of that detective stare.

The Hotel Hacienda Chichén was a worthy journey's end, with flamboyant trees, cool verandas, manicured gardens, and guayabera-wearing Maya waiters bearing mango-hibiscus coolers in iced glasses. But it was all to no avail; we ate in silence, no doubt both wishing that the other women we were secretly dating were there instead. Unfortunately, the frequent trade-off for having a vacation with sex is having the Big Fight. And what more dramatic setting is there than the middle of the jungle?

"I should have known better," Betty hissed, "than to go to the jungle with someone who doesn't care about me one way or the other. Even when I'm sick."

"I care enough to show you ordinary courtesy," I snapped, the Pasadena priss showing through. "I care enough not to try to ruin your vacation."

But she was sick, and I was through driving, and so I apologized—repeatedly. And although she finally allowed me the excuse, it was clear that part of her just couldn't believe that I had been scared to drive.

I could practically hear her thinking *gosling*.

The blowout was patched for the time being. We were the first at the ruins the following day. Despite all the guidebooks and scholarship explaining pre-Columbian life, there remains a sense of mystery. Betty and I stood in the ruins of the ball court looking up at the impossibly high ring on the wall through which the heavy rubber sphere had to pass for score. *Kind of like having a relationship,* I thought. *Equally impossible.*

The next ruin on the schedule was Palenque, and to get there, we flew from Cancún to Mérida, where we spent one night before flying to Villahermosa the next day. Since Villahermosa was a humid, Gulf Coast oil town, we were off the tourist trail and had to rely on our wits. Out taxi driver pulled the "no change" routine on us at the bus station, and inasmuch as I was more or less speechless, he sped off with our $2.

"This place is a black hole," Betty said as we quickly put our extra money in our socks.

At the station, I was totally focused on hearing the word "Palenque" over the static on the bus station's public address system. I was sitting next to a Maya couple, so I tried asking them about the bus. They both laughed so hard that they almost fell off their plastic chairs, flashing gold teeth and clutching their sides. Then they pointed toward a door leading to buses bearing destination signs. We found the bus marked "Palenque" and joined the other people waiting in line. It was hot. We were glad we had our purified water.

After waiting twenty minutes, a bus driver approached our bus. He had black wingtips, navy slacks, and a thin belt with a Ray-Ban glasses case attached to it. He opened the door to the bus, and a little ripple went through the line, a shuffling of packages. But he ignored us all. The bus door closed behind him with a whoosh, its big glass fish-eyes bubbling out in front of us. Cocooned and impervious, he bent forward slightly and combed his hair in the rearview mirror. He wiggled his mustache, extracted a tie from behind the seat, and tied it. Then, deliberately, he reached up and turned on a small personal fan and sat down in the driver's seat—all alone in his bus—for seven minutes.

Since at this time I was working as a passenger-train conductor, and in spite of the sweat dripping down my nose, I had to admire his style.

In Palenque, we found the Maya Tulipanes—a bare-bones motel with working air-conditioning. I loved the motel, actually, but Betty found it lacking the proper pizzazz for her last few days in Mexico. Since I was going to be going off on my own for two weeks to San Cristóbal de las Casas when Betty returned to San Francisco, I agreed to move to the Meson Palenque, a ritzy, hacienda-like hotel with a swimming pool, a jitney to the ruins, a Maya falconer, a gift shop, and a guard at the gate. Betty told me that when she backpacked through India, she would occasionally check into a hotel like this one to regain sanity before returning to the street, a reminder that she was an American and always had an exit card.

In its strange way, Mexico did not disappoint me in its reminder that there is still a hell ready for those who have a visa exit card— even if you're willing to spend the money, you're not necessarily guaranteed a better time.

It became clear as soon as we tried to check into the Meson Palenque that the desk staff was unaccustomed to foreign travelers on their own. The place was a hostelry for the tour-bus set, who usually arrived herded by a bilingual guide. It wasn't that I spoke no Spanish—I had managed to check us into the Maya Tulipanes, I had managed to get us on a bus—but when I tried to put our passports in the hotel safe, we hit a language wall.

Leafing through the dictionary, I found *"seguro"* (safe) and asked for one. Reluctantly, the desk clerk produced an envelope, which we signed and put our passports in. Now we needed change for a cab. Nobody at the front desk, the gift shop, or the bar could cash the equivalent of $10 so we could take a cab from the Meson Palenque. Finally, we refused to leave the desk until change appeared and, of course, it then did.

On our last day together in Mexico, since we both had early morning buses, it seemed prudent to check out the night before. Where was our stuff in their *seguro*?

The *seguro*, it turned out, was a safety deposit box with a key, and we couldn't have put our stuff in their *seguro*, or else we would have a key, wouldn't we? I noticed that Betty was about to erupt. It was just what she thought; we were surrounded by practicing criminals. At this point, another guest rushed up to the front desk, announcing that he had been robbed while taking a shower in his room. Betty threw her wallet on the desk, flipped her badge out, which thankfully was in Spanish, and went into cop mode.

"Either our passports get here," she said, "or I call the police."

Miraculously, our manila envelope turned up.

Returning to our hot room, Betty set a chair in front of the door with a glass of water resting halfway off its seat.

"So we'll hear them in the night," she said, and promptly fell asleep.

I wasn't so lucky. My thoughts kept taking a paranoid turn. The Meson might not be a hotel but a prison of some kind. I doubted they would let us leave in the morning. With these dark thoughts keeping me from sleep, I spent the night reading in the toilet and listening to the normal sounds of the hotel rustling and squeaking in the humid night.

We left at dawn like refugees, having been lightly breathed upon by an evil we did not understand. I kissed Betty at the bus station as we set out in our different directions, in Mexico and in life, as it turned out.

Mexican buses are all named and decorated by the driver, and my bus was called "Escaleras al Cielo," or Stairway to Heaven. *Heaven would be a nice change*, I thought.

I took my window seat on the bus as it filled up with Maya on their way to the high country. The wall of jungle beside the road seemed impenetrable, yet as we climbed, people emerged from it and waited for the bus. The men carried machetes and plastic water bottles; the women had children wrapped in *rebozos* (shawls) and large bundles tied together with rope and carried with a trumpline. Fascinated, I realized that I was regaining my own point of view, that the suspicious nature of the world had vanished with Betty.

At a mountain town called Ocosingo, the Maya men getting on the bus wore handwoven white shorts and shirts, and the older men's legs looked like manzanita wood, twisted and muscular and dense as iron. I was the only gringa on the bus.

It was a Sunday morning, and as we descended into a valley, church was letting out in a town called Oxchuc. It was the first time I had ever seen an entire town in native dress—in this case, handwoven white cotton tunics decorated with broad, colored stripes. Because of the altitude and the bright sun, the white walls of the village and the shadows of moving clouds, it was as if a flock of birds, not people, had suddenly flown by.

In San Cristóbal, I stayed at Na Balom (House of the Jaguar), the home/museum/library of photographer Trudi Blom. But Na Balom was also a guesthouse and a San Cristóbal institution. Trudi and her husband, archaeologist Frans Blom, had devoted their lives to researching, publicizing, and protecting the Lacandon rainforest and the unconquered Maya who lived there. Scholars and artists from all over the world came to use the library or live-in residence. The Lacandon Maya were also welcome to stay whenever they made their way to town. Passing a Lacandon in the street was a ghostly experience; with long hair and simple, sacklike tunics, they walked silently in a way that urban or even pueblo people couldn't do. You got the feeling they could dematerialize if they wanted to. Trudi had sheltered them, visited them when the only way to get there was on horseback, and championed their fight. She was in her eighties, an institution herself.

But now Trudi was, in the spirit of the Day of the Dead, dancing with death. Her blue-lidded raptor eyes were raccooned with mascara. Huge glass rings dwarfed her fingers. During my stay, I had heard her after midnight wandering below me in her garden, accompanied by her vicious dog and entreating in a ghostly voice, "Vill nobody answer me?" Like a crocodile, she floated on the threshold between the worlds, waiting for silence or fresh blood.

In a room full of trekkers, she was dressed for a ball. We were

all Pips to her Havisham, and she, alternately making pronouncements and abusing us, held court at the head of the table when we
gathered for lunch. The two women her age who joined us for lunch
on that first day seemed like Ariels in comparison. They too had a
quality of body grown translucent to the spirit, but their spirits were
benign. They introduced themselves as Marcey Jacobsen and Janet
Marren. Marcey was a photographer, and Janet was a painter, and
they had been living together in San Cristóbal for forty-five years.
Their clothes were clean and pressed but well worn and accented by
Maya textiles. Their eyes were radiant, and they had strong opinions
on politics and art. It struck me that I had not been in the company
of such interesting and powerful women in a very long time.

After lunch they bundled me away, both of them excitedly turning around to look at me in the back seat of their car. The moment
turned pink, as if someone had filled the car with bubbles. We had
all fallen in love at exactly the same time. Janet reached over the
seat and gave my hand a conspiratorial squeeze, her artist's hands
surprisingly strong.

"We're kidnapping you," she said.

I remember thinking, *I can't do this. They are eighty years old and
they live four thousand miles away. How will I come to see them?* They
only lived a few blocks from Na Balom, and in a few minutes we
were in their home overlooking the city. I tried to imagine what it
would have been like to come here forty-five years ago and stay.
Marcey told me that when they arrived, there were only five cars in
all of San Cristóbal.

As we sat in their living room, I told them about my life on the railroad, about Betty, about my writing and what I had seen from the bus. They told me about their work and how they came to live here. Their community of artists, anthropologists, and revolutionaries was unique in Mexico, and I could see that this interaction between art and the community was for them a rare gem. Janet's paintings were all over town; Marcey's photography shows attracted her subjects and their families. They also told me stories about Chiapas.

"Oh yes," Janet continued, "we warned that tourist not to go hiking in the villages, but he was German, and he wanted to go out alone. Apparently, he touched a child."

"What happened?" I asked

"They beheaded him," Janet said matter-of-factly. Then she added philosophically, "The stranger the story about Chiapas, the more likely it is to be true."

It was so late when I left their house to return to Na Balom that I took a stick of firewood with me to ward off the drunks who careened through the streets after midnight. I felt I had seen in Janet and Marcey's home a vision of what my life could be.

"Join us," Janet had said. "It is such an exciting time to be living in Mexico."

When I left Betty at the bus station, I wondered whether I would be lonely wandering around San Cristóbal by myself, the way I often was on solo trips in the United States. Women don't often travel alone in the States, and connecting with the ones who do is hard. In our cars, hotels, and unsafe streets, strangers are wary of each other. In Chiapas I met solo female travelers everywhere. They came to see the local craft of weaving and were willing to join others to travel to the villages. I had never seen anything like Chiapas Maya weaving. It was austere, intellectual, and transcendent. Done on a back-strap loom, the panels were parts of clothing, but if looked upon separately, they resembled paintings. It was immediately clear that they were books: A woman's *huipil* (blouse) or a man's *camisa* (shirt) could be read for meaning, as well as for beauty. Meaning was embedded in all the daily textiles.

"How do you know what to weave?" I asked a woman in Tenejapa.

"I weave my dreams," she answered.

The Tenejapan weavers had one of the most organized cooperatives, with a storefront near the square and prices they considered fair for their work. The weavings—*huipiles*, bags, sashes, and individual panels—had an ochre or maroon field with black designs and subtle color placement. They were fine art.

I was in the workrooms, in the back of a church, where two women were hand-spinning wool thread from the dyed skeins drying on racks. They used a hand spindle and bowl to unravel the wool and asked me and the woman I had met in town to sit down and learn. They showed us the weaver's calluses on their fingers from resting the spindle there. I showed them the calluses on my palms from gripping the handrails of railroad cars and the callus between my thumb and forefinger from playing the flute. I became aware of how much pride I had in the way that work had written itself onto my body.

As we rode the local bus back to San Cristóbal, I watched the driver's young son collect money on the bus—that had been my job at the time on the San Francisco commuter trains. I realized that I was identifying with the way people worked here much more than I ever did in the States.

You could say my work was archaic, but it was the way I had chosen to live: first with a cabin in the woods heated by a wood stove, then dealing at flea markets, playing music in a street band, pumping gas, clerking in a liquor store, and finally working both passenger and freight trains. After getting a PhD in literature, I had avoided as much as possible the world of offices and institutions. On my tourist card, I had checked the box for chauffeurs. I suppose most Mexicans did not see many working-class American tourists. My fellow railroaders were basically suspicious of travel across the border, as Betty had been. They wanted to vacation with all of their expensive travel-trailers and other recreational equipment, which often was stolen or broken into. They went to bars and got into fights. They were monolingual. They would never be here on this bus with a companion they had met hours ago in the town square. They often resented the Mexican workers they encountered in the United States.

A week later, on the plane home, I was aware that we were flying through much more than time zones. I knew I was going to learn Spanish, no matter what. I knew I would someday live in Mexico and that it would be a welcome home. The plane was filled with Mexican Americans returning to the States from visiting their families. The border was just a line in the sand to them, and I had started to see it that way too. There it was, below us, looking like a rail or a river, something to cross.

Fran Davis

Silver Rings

It took us two days that semester break to get as far into Mexico as we wanted, driving our cars day and night through a desert lined with cacti like petrified men. We crossed the border at Sonoita, the *aduana* (customs) no more than a shed in a wilderness of broken lava and creosote bush. The guards laughed, peering in at us, three girls and four boys driving a 1960 Ford station wagon and a Corvair with smoking brakes. They said we needed birth certificates to get a tourist card. A driver's license proved nothing; we could be citizens of Brazil. Case and Miguel offered *mordidas,* thinking bribery was the right thing, the authentic Mexican touch. The guards must have thought they were crazy—that big, blond Dutchman, Case, speaking Castilian Spanish, and Miguel with his Chicano slang. They turned their backs on us and went inside. Maybe the *mordidas* weren't enough? We drove on anyway, full of ourselves, as brash as rumrunners.

We camped with fishermen on the beach at San Carlos,

huddled against a wind that drove cold sand between the folds of our blankets and spit pebbles into our hair. Miguel and Jenner stayed up drinking with Lupe, the head fisherman, who told them that once he'd killed a man. When Case stumbled up to pee almost pure tequila, he impaled his hand on cactus thorns as big as nails that left weeping stigmata for which we had no medicine, only more tequila. At dawn, when the sky over the gulf split like a blood orange, Jenner and Miguel went out in the fishermen's rickety boat and came back as wrung-out rags, with blisters on their hands from hauling nets.

Only Jenner and Cheryl were a pair. The rest of us were suspended, waiting for the catalyst of Mexico to create romance. We shared beds like brothers and sisters. In Hermosillo I slept between two men, David and Case, telling each that the other was a friend, only a friend.

In Guaymas we stayed in the biggest hotel in town, the Casa Grande, discovering too late that it was also a whorehouse. The evidence was in the leftover pitchers of screwdrivers on the bedside tables and in the eyes of the women we met on the stairs—hematite eyes staring from faces like blackened roses. We didn't belong there—Cheryl and Sandy and I—with our high breasts and young swagger, trailing an odor of Coppertone. We stepped aside, refusing the essential recognition, refusing to meet their eyes.

Roaming the night in Guaymas, high on marijuana the guys had scored, David and I kissed in the plaza's gazebo while the wind thrummed the gingerbread struts like the wires of a cage. "¡Son amigos enamorados!" Case shouted when he found us. The night was full of wind, and we were scattered like ions, we were everywhere, electrified, running hand in hand through the charged darkness, the narrow streets, with Case following, a twisted shadow between buildings, crouching like Quasimodo so as not to be seen. *"Hace frio,"* a señora scolded, pointing at my bare arms and David's T-shirt. But we were warm where we touched. And what did we know or feel? With eyes wide from sweet marijuana and blood running hot for each other and the night and the endless need to explore, to look, to find, grabbing every minute like a toy.

We ate as if we'd never tasted before: chorizo and eggs, Mexican chocolate, and coffee with milk and *pan dulce*, taking enterovioform antibiotics twice a day to kill off the bugs. We avoided gringos and sat at outside tables and spoke only Spanish, our faces tilted to the sun. We drank cheap beer and ate goat stew and *burritos de puerco*. We thought the vultures hunched on the church steeple were authentic, picturesque. We thought they were *México*.

We drifted where the gravity of individual wills pulled us. Case wanted Alamos, a silver town in the mountains, so we went. At the Hotel Enrique, they showed movies in the courtyard, and to climb the outside stairs to our rooms, we had to sneak behind the sheet where film stars danced and swayed and the audience watched us, because maybe we were the better show. A tiny *abuela* worried and sputtered, brought pitchers of cold water to our rooms, and hugged us over and over, offering through her touch a kind of Catholic palliation. David stole into my bed at night and woke me with kisses, his breath like Chiclets, his hands a revelation.

Men befriended us in that town: the *fiscal*, a district attorney who walked with crutches and always dressed in maroon and navy;

the *arqueólogo*, who could speak the Yaqui and Mayo dialects and who told us he was related to the Obregons and thirty-three generals. The men discussed philosophy and archeology and politics with Case and Miguel and Jenner—never with the women. They told about Villistas, the Yaqui Indian village up the hill, the new jail, and the old graveyard.

"*Voy a la iglesia,*" I said finally, putting on a scarf.

"*¿Es católica?*" the *fiscal* asked as I walked away.

I wondered how Case would answer, because I wasn't Catholic. I wanted to flee that round of macho talk, and the church was a place for females, with its dense and plaintive air, its lugubrious Marys, a dark haven.

Later, in the walled cemetery, David, Case, and I walked among broken sepulchres and scattered bones, gazed unflinching at the empty eye sockets of skulls. But we stepped lightly around the children's graves, smoothed over with pink and white lime like sugar frosting that crumbled away at the scrape of a foot.

Outside the cemetery, a man invited us into a house made of sticks. Daylight shone through the walls—like a *chamisal* (brush corral). We stood on the beaten floor and blinked at the cutting light while a silent woman patted tortillas between her palms, ignoring us, the curious *norteamericanos* with our roving eyes and stench of good health.

The day the archaeologist drove the others into the hills for a fiesta in Cuchefauchi, David and I stayed behind. Half drunk on sun and freedom, we wandered the cobblestone streets with linked fingers, looking in silver shops at jewelry we couldn't afford. We ate by a courtyard fountain, shelling out our dwindling pesos for the guitarist to play a song we loved, "Camino de Guanajuato." *"La vida no vale nada"* the refrain went—life is worth nothing—which we believed, all the while sucking at it, gulping it down like new wine. When we stood to go, a girl brought out white bowls containing golden rings of pineapple and said, *"Su piña,"* as if we were forgetting the most important thing. But what I hungered for were the silver rings in the shops.

On Saturday night we went dancing at a cantina full of workers. I danced with a *trabajador* who held me with hands as rough and heavy as slate, even after I pointed to David and said, *"Mi novio."* He didn't even glance at that thin gringo by the bar, but gripped my arms with his flinty fingers and stared into my eyes, willing me away from that sunny place, to its underside, to the stones with their cold veins of silver.

After ten days we came undone. In Ciudad Obregón we flew apart, spinning off from one another like sparks from struck metal. I watched David and Case drive south in the banged-up Corvair that Case was sure he could sell in Belize. Jenner and Cheryl beat the desert and the drive and the boredom by catching a plane to San Diego. Miguel, Sandy, and I made the lonely trip north, which passed in a silent haze because we were no longer going anywhere, only home.

In the morning, Sandy and I walked across the border at Tijuana, saying we'd only been there overnight because we still didn't have those tourist cards. Miguel drove through alone, while we watched, wondering what the customs officials thought about those two suitcases full of women's clothes. The border guards took us aside, patted our pockets, rifled our purses, scolded me for not declaring a tube of Nivea lotion with a Spanish label. What did we think we were doing, anyway, two young women, staying overnight in Tijuana and hoofing it across the border like field workers? They shook their heads at the shame of it, girls with no business in that shifty town, girls gone bad.

For me, the view backward is foreshortened, the past a play of shadows like the movie characters superimposed on our bodies as we climbed the stairs to our room back in Alamos. I can see our faces, the swing of arms and legs, even our smiles, but I can't hear voices or read intentions. I don't remember what we were thinking those days we wandered the sun-cracked ribs of the Sierra Madre like a tribe of lost children. I can't guess what thoughts went through our minds as our lips formed another language to speak to a people we didn't know. Did we think we were the first? Did we think we'd discovered a new world?

Suzanne LaFetra

El Otro Lado

I step over the jagged edge of a broken bottle, as indigenous to the terrain as the rest of the debris and grit that litters my daily commute. I walk through the dirt toward the gates of the Mexican prison, the backs of the visitors coming into focus. Faded *rebozos* (shawls) and looped black braids and worn T-shirts block the view to the world on the other side of the fence.

Some of the visitors know the routine: A hunched man pokes a rolled bill through the fence, a mother momentarily drops the hand of her toddler and passes a creased document to a guard. Most wait patiently, fingers curled around chain link. Visitors tote baskets of food or nylon gym bags or greasy cardboard boxes. A few come bearing gifts that cannot be seen, clandestine treasures that will be delivered only after the visitor is safely inside.

Overhead, muffled static crackles from decrepit loudspeakers. On the inside, runners move from the visitors waiting at the fence into the belly of the Mexican prison, exchanging whistles, unintelligible yips and shouts, in one of the many coded languages at La Peni, short for *la penitenciaría*.

The visitors will wait, but I can't say for how long, as I am never made to stand at the front gates of La Peni. I am ushered in quickly; no need to haggle with the runners or interpret gestures from the inmates the way the other visitors do. I always walk past the small, fenced-off area to the right side of the main gate, where guards search suitcases and purses and bodies. A mustached man with reflective sunglasses waves me right through with a gold-toothed smile, *"Pásale, maestra."*

I am a teacher at the Tijuana State Prison.

My proposal to the bigwig prison officials was to provide basic literacy courses in Spanish to the female inmates. A gringa from *el otro lado*, the other side, teaching the prisoners to read and write? "You're from the other side, teach them English," the warden said, eyeing me from behind his massive desk. A month earlier, I had turned my golden tassel and spurred my gray Honda south to the brown hills of Tijuana to work for a nonprofit organization. Armed with the militant knowledge of a recent college graduate, I fervently believed that literacy was the most powerful weapon in the fight for social justice. I cited academic evidence, trying to prove that literacy would lift the women from their plight. To my sermon he responded, "They can get jobs if they speak English." Finally, we compromised; I agreed to supply an English teacher if he'd let me teach the women to read and write in their native language.

On the first day, I arrived fresh-faced, with packets of sharpened pencils and notebooks. I brought with me the promised English teacher, a coworker named Bonnie who worked mornings teaching women about community gardening for the nonprofit we both worked for. She wasn't crazy about teaching in the prison, but she had afternoons free. Bonnie and I passed through the inspection area and met up with Señor Pacheco, the education coordinator, who edged us away from the northern side of the prison, away from the women's section. "You're going to be teaching on the men's side," Pacheco announced flatly as we walked through the compound.

"No, I'm here for *las mujeres*, it's all set up," I protested.

"They don't want the classes," he snapped, "so you're teaching on this side."

My mouth pressed into a thin line. It had taken weeks of maneuvering with the glacial Mexican bureaucracy to arrange the classes. Damn this macho *cabrón!*

We passed a man squatting and smoking a stub of cigarette; his eyes followed us as we were led deeper into the prison. Bonnie gave me a pleading look. She was skittish and jumpy, and she looked so young walking across the soccer field, arms folded across her small breasts, long skirt blowing in the dusty breeze as all those brown eyes noticed her.

Pacheco fished an enormous set of keys from his pocket and opened a barred door. "Here's your classroom," he motioned with a sweep. In it was a large chalkboard and some desks. The tang of fresh paint lingered in the small room.

I figured that helping some men out of the dark hole of

illiteracy was better than nothing. I was twenty-four; it seemed as good an adventure as any. *"Vámonos, pues,"* I said. Well, let's go.

La Peni didn't look like the jails on TV; there were no American-style cellblocks, electronic gates, or orange jumpsuits. It was a large, walled compound about the size of four city blocks. Gun turrets and watchtowers perched in the corners, but everywhere else it seemed like any other Mexican village. A soccer field took center stage, acting as the town square. Cats curled among the tiny makeshift shanties and apartments that crowded together, housing four times the number of people the prison was designed to hold. During the year that I worked there, I learned that the inmates had to provide their own housing. Officials pocketed big money renting space for prisoners to live, work, eat, and sleep.

A prisoner's position was determined by money and power. If he had the money, anything could be had at La Peni. For the right price, drugs and weapons and prostitutes—but also bicycles, satellite dishes, *pan dulce,* servants, even their own family—could be brought in.

Wives with scuffed black shoes balanced babies on their hips as they bought batteries or toilet paper at the grocery store run by Señor Obregón. An entrepreneurial inmate from Sinaloa made a small fortune in his video-rental shack, a white iron grill protecting the movies of Steven Segal and Bruce Lee. A *taquería* with a hot-pink sign advertising Negro Modelo served the best tacos I've ever eaten. The proprietor would slap a smoky slab of grilled meat down onto a wooden chopping block and hack it with a sharp, curved cleaver. The block was worn down in the center, where he pounded and scraped the most steak. He heaped palm-sized tortillas with steaming carne asada and then added fistfuls of cilantro, onion, and chilies. Each plate was garnished with green triangles of lime to clean your fingers with after your meal.

In my classroom, on day one, I set a rule: "We leave our prejudices outside," I told my students in my best Spanish. I didn't want to know why they were locked up. I knew that I'd treat a molester differently than I would an embezzler, and I didn't want my life complicated by any of that. "And I ask that you don't hold your *prejuicios* about young American women against me either."

I handed out paper and pencils as each student told me his name. I scratched my name onto the board. "Can any of you write your name?"

One of them snickered behind a comic book. A guy with a gold tooth cleaned his nail with the pencil tip. A hand went up. "*Maestra? What should we call you?*" one of the inmates asked. He used the formal *usted*.

"My name's Susana." I said, hearing the sound of it vibrate off the unadorned walls. "And please, let's use *tú*."

We talked about vowels and consonants. "Give me a word with the *ee* sound," I said, chalk poised. "*¡Híjole!*" someone blurted out. One guy snorted. I didn't know exactly what it meant, but I'd heard men use it in exasperation, kind of in the way you'd curse Jesus Christ after stubbing your toe. I wrote it out on the chalkboard, then turned around.

"Good. *¿Qué más?*" What else?

"*Hijo de la chingada.*" Lovely. Son of a bitch. I wrote it on the board.

I smiled a lot. I asked to borrow the comic book, and we talked about the sounds in some of those words. At the end of that first class, I thanked them all and told them how happy I was that they'd made the choice to learn to read. When they filed out, I looked around the empty room, beaming.

After the first day of classes, Bonnie and I boarded the decrepit, lurching bus and headed for home. "Did you see that fat guy with all the rings?" Bonnie asked, her voice cracking. "He looked at my body the entire time," she whispered as we were jostled along over potholes.

Three days later she told me, "I just can't stand it." In the kitchen we shared with eight other coworkers, she dished up muddy pinto beans. "We're just sex objects, just women from the other side to them."

I sighed. "Well, Bonnie, maybe if you thought of yourself as a teacher and not just a sex object, you wouldn't feel so damn vulnerable." I grabbed a plate and sat down at our table, which was covered in red and pink oilcloth. Yeah, it could be unnerving working at the prison. But that was part of the thrill. It was titillating living on the edge of the country, the edge of safety, the edge of my own comfort.

"But they're always watching me," Bonnie said, her chair scraping across the linoleum tiles. When annoyed, Bonnie seemed weak and whiny. But it was also because she insisted on pointing out things I preferred to be blind to, things that threatened to spoil my fun. "I'm not going back," she said. Bonnie quit after her third day at La Peni. I shrugged and stabbed into the chicken breast drowning in *salsa verde*.

At the prison, I felt like a queen. I was proud to be teaching literacy, to be mastering a new language, to be adapting in a dangerous place. I was shedding my skin of insecurity, snaking my way into the powerful world of adulthood. I peeled back the scales of my past life of privilege and coiled up on my own turf. I was trying to find where my own power lay, pushing on the boundaries, testing to see if it was safe. And, like a child, I hoped someone would be there to protect me if I ventured in too deep.

My coworkers and I shared a house in southern Tijuana, a nondescript, poorly built cinderblock building squatting among thorny cactuses, old tires, scrounging dogs, and loudly clucking roosters in the outskirts of town. We all worked at our various nonprofit projects, bought *pan dulce* at the local bakery, got our water from the weekly supply truck that rolled through the neighborhood blaring a distorted *"¡Aaaahhh-gwaaaaa, aaaaaguiiiiiii-taaaaa!"* We played guitar and drank beer, argued about the policies of President Miguel de la Madrid in 1988, and traded paperbacks by Carlos Fuentes and Octavio Paz. Our dramas were minor: winter without hot water, shitty cars that constantly broke down, disagreements with our bosses. We had the typical squabbles and romances that you'd find inside any group house filled with left-leaning, college-degreed do-gooders.

The prison was a microcosm of Mexico: The light-skinned, power-ful *ricos* (rich) got most everything they wanted, and their darker, poorer, less-educated brethren lived crammed together in unimag-inable poverty and filth. I taught the poorer, illiterate men, who squatted within the prison walls, scrounging for a few coins. Many of them lived in a fog of heroin and violence, some slept on the sticky asphalt of the basketball court, but all showed up at my class each afternoon.

"How do you spell 'coyote'?" asked a student who was always talking about his plans to head north someday, to work in Modesto with his uncle.

"Hey, *maestra*," said another, after a stuffy afternoon filled with vowel sounds *(mama, meme, momo, mumu)*. "Translate 'Hotel Califor-nia' for me," he demanded, thrusting an Eagles album into my hand. I helped them to scratch out their own names on paper, to read a bus schedule. I brought in a map of Mexico, a timecard, comic books.

It was easy to feel powerful in front of such a captive audience. Many of the inmates slipped me scraps of paper with a phone num-ber. *"Un favor, señorita,"* they pleaded, hoping I would make a call for them. I could throw my sunshiny weight around by tossing a smile one way or paying a tiny bit of extra attention to a student. I could choose to wave my wand and provide attention, friendship, some connection with the outside world for those trapped in La Peni. I felt powerful for the first time in my adulthood. It was heady, and although I didn't misuse the power, I drank it up. In class one afternoon, I stood over

Kuko, a tall, brooding Oaxacan man. He was hunched over his gritty paper, dirty fingernail moving across the page as he slowly sounded out the words. *"El gato es . . . es . . . negro."*

"Muy bien, Kuko," I said, patting his shoulder. He looked up at me, dark, bloodshot eyes just inches away.

"Gracias, maestra," he said, too close, too hungry, the clammy funk of his breath settling on my face. I removed my hand quickly, quietly, and shoved it down into my pocket.

Another day a student slipped a letter into my bag, saying he dreamed about me, asking for money for a lawyer, promising we could live happily ever after in his brother's Chula Vista apartment. I read it all the way through before it dawned on me that this guy was obviously literate. He had only been going through the motions so that he could hang out in the classroom.

Sometimes I felt inundated by the needs of those surrounding me. Suffocated by the poverty, injustice, loneliness, boredom, and edgy danger that surrounded many of my students, some evenings I left the prison gates behind, gulping in air, staggering toward the crowded bus that would deliver me home. I arrived drained, starved for jokes in my own language and the companionship of people who were not desperate.

I invited Bonnie to the class Christmas party at the end of the first semester. When I met her at the front gates of La Peni, she frowned, staring at my crimson silk tank top. "I can't believe you're wearing that," she hissed. "Don't you even care that they're all checking you out?" Exasperated, I waved her paranoia away. She was just pissed off that I could handle the chaos of the prison and she couldn't. I couldn't allow her criticism to penetrate my thickening skin, to pull me back to a place of insecurity. I was just beginning to find a place inside myself that felt strong. I wouldn't let her drag me over to her side.

Tijuana pulses with the seamy friction caused by the richest country on earth rubbing up against one of the poorest. And it attracts those who gravitate toward the heat. Since the 1950s, when it was built, La Peni has housed those who have gotten burned.

There were nearly five thousand inmates in the prison, both Mexicans and foreigners. The majority were in for attempted drug smuggling, arrested before delivering their American-bound cargo. One of them was a Scotsman, John, who had a lilting accent and spoke horrendous Spanish, even though he'd already been in for four years. He was worn down from his years in the place, his faded belt cinched to the last hole. He'd been busted at customs with a few pounds of pot in his spare tire and got the standard seven-year sentence in La Peni.

Favio was a sweet, cherubic-looking boy from Colombia. A star player on one of the prison soccer teams, he charmed me with his impeccable manners and long, curly eyelashes. I helped Favio pick out tiles for his prison apartment—light blue with photos of water droplets on them. Years later, my mouth dropped open as I watched a Mexican news program: "Cali Cartel member Favio ____ returned to Colombia today after being released from prison in Tijuana, Mexico. He served only four years on trafficking charges. . . ." And there was Favio, still looking angelic, being escorted down the stairs of a private plane.

Adolfo was a pale-faced, sweaty man who made a weekly plea to me: *"Déjame contarte mi caso,* let me tell you my story. . . ." He was desperate to tell me his story. Adolfo claimed that he had been a muckety-muck in L. Ron Hubbard's machine and had uncovered some disturbing news about the legendary leader. The inner circle of the Scientologists was powerful, he said, and they had conspired to hole him up in the Tijuana gulag when he began talking to reporters in Los Angeles.

Victor grew up in Tijuana, where his mother had worked herself nearly blind inserting tiny screws into circuit boards in a foreign-owned *maquiladora* (factory). Victor was branded with an inky tear on the outer edge of his eye and a tiny indigo cross in the webbing between his thumb and trigger finger. A quick study, both of phonetics and of his *maestra,* he reeled in my sympathy. On a chilly December afternoon, he stomped his feet and stretched his worn acrylic sweater over his hands, begging me for a pair of gloves for Christmas. I promptly complied, and a few days later, I spied another inmate wearing the gift. Victor had sold them.

Occasionally I heard about the criminal activity my students had engaged in, but most people knew that I wanted to be blind to it all, and so they kept quiet about it. One afternoon I was chatting about my pal Victor with Silvestre and Chucho, a couple of old guys who, had they been on the outside, would doubtless be nursing sodas and spinning yarns at the local gas station. "So, he's expecting a visit from his lawyer," I told them about Victor's plans. "He thinks that maybe he'll get a reduced sentence, since he was only carrying a couple of joints." They exchanged glances.

"Susi," Silvestre began, "watch yourself with that guy. Victor wasn't busted for drugs. *Ten cuidado*, be careful." They told me he had raped two women.

Soccer was a welcome distraction from daily life at La Peni, just like anywhere in Mexico. The games were every Friday afternoon, and I'd often stay after class and join in the cheering. In the winter, it was dark by 5:00 PM, and the orange vapor lights buzzed on long before I clanged through the gate and caught my bus home. Sometimes I would spring for a round of Cokes and a few tacos while we watched.

One Friday evening, I was leaning against the side of the classroom, watching the last few minutes of the game, my fingers fragrant with dried lime juice, my sweatshirt warming me against the chill of the dry winter night. It was easy to forget that I was in a prison—dogs raced around, nipping each other and sniffing for scraps; a couple of babies cried in the distance; and men strolled through the dirt with their hands jammed into their pockets, smoking and talking. A forward had a long run with the ball, and fans shouted, hoping for a goal in the last moments of the game.

And then it was black. Every light in the prison went out.

Vague shadows crossed in front of me, and the popping staccato of gunshots ripped through the darkness. I heard shouting, scuffling, loud yells I couldn't decipher. My mind tumbled over in a panic, and I stood paralyzed, suspended in the pandemonium. Feet pounded, running toward me, and time sped up. Dust billowed up from the ground; there was more shuffling, shouts, and shots.

And then a body slowly and deliberately pressed up against me. And then another, and another, and another, flattening me against the wall until the stucco scratched through my shirt. I could not move.

A high-pitched roaring clogged my mind as my brain began to scream. I imagined nightmarish scenes of my ripped, twisted body. I saw my parents, choking with grief. An iron door of terror clanged down in my mind. On this side was a wide-awake, fearful foreign woman. The easy, oblivious adventurer was left behind on the other side.

But in the blackness, I realized that I wasn't being shoved or groped or attacked. My breath slowly leaked out. I was only surrounded. The chaos continued for a minute or two more. I remained pinned, eyes wide in the darkness, the copper taste of fear in my mouth. I inhaled and smelled sweat, scalp, bad breath, onion. And then I heard the rumble of a generator. A few orange lights flickered on.

I was ringed by men, all with their backs to me. A small squadron of inmates three deep had backed up against me, guarding me. Some of them were my students; some were other prisoners. All were my protectors for my three-minute sentence in the Tijuana darkness.

When the lights blared out across the compound, my bodyguards immediately disbanded. I had no chance to thank them, they were gone so quickly, and not one of them ever mentioned it again. Favio was one of them. Victor was not. Silvestre and Kuko had been in the group, and John the Scot.

The following Monday, I was taking an icy bucket bath in my tiled Tijuana bathroom. My teeth were still chattering after I dried off and got dressed for class. I hadn't mentioned the prison incident to anyone. I hadn't really let myself think about it at all the entire weekend. But I had dreamed about standing in a wintry ocean, each set of waves commanding me to wade deeper, until I was pulled in over my head, toward the terrifying dark shapes gliding in the depths, the strong currents threatening to swallow me.

I pulled my jeans out of my dresser. An orange T-shirt. Then I lifted out a long, dark skirt. Then a flannel shirt. I went on that way for several rounds, unable to decide what to wear. The longer I stood there, pulling on clothes, the more anxious and self-conscious I became. *That's too tight; these pants are too dressy.* I had never worried about what I looked like in class. *Shit, girl, you're not going to the prom.* I had always fussed over the lesson for the day, not my freaking wardrobe. *Get a grip!*

I climbed down from the bus wearing leggings under a long skirt and a thick black sweater. I threaded through the visitors outside the prison gates, past the guards, into the main plaza of La Peni. I paused, listening to the incessant whistles and shouts. Standing in that caged world, I suddenly realized that I had absolutely no clue about what was going on around me: A cutting motion made with the hand, low across the belly. Right hand grabbing left fist. Long low whistle, followed by two short high-pitched ones.

I squinted into the thin winter sunlight. A short man with enormous biceps jogged into the bowels of the prison, his worn leather sandals leaving tracks in the dirt. An inmate with a stained bandage around his leg hopped by, shooing away a scrawny dog that followed him. A guard crossed in front of me, a thick, black gun jammed into his creaking leather holster. The scene wasn't particularly threatening, but it wasn't benign. It was much more complicated now that I had a taste of how much there was to be protected from.

I folded my arms against the chill and walked straight through the soccer field to my classroom, my skirt whipping around my thighs in the gusty breeze, my head down to protect my blue eyes from the stinging dust.

Sondra Ross Hines

One More Baby

The blacktop road ended with no warning, and we found ourselves bumping along a broad dirt trail, loosely packed in place by the comings and goings of donkeys, horses, foot traffic, and the occasional bicycle. Bits and pieces of parched earth and grit flew up and enveloped the tired Volkswagen sedan. The long winter drought had left its mark on the powdery volcanic soil.

My friend Lucy Averill, a retired but still active social worker from Connecticut, negotiated the holes, bumps, rocks, and errant scrub. A longtime resident of San Miguel de Allende, in north central Mexico, she had been coming the fifteen miles to Atoltonilco—a sparsely populated village with a church and shrine, no paved roads, and one general store—for more than thirty years.

It was the early '90s, and my husband, artist Francis Hines, and I had exchanged our New York City loft one winter for the house next to Lucy's in San Miguel—an elegant, historic colonial town known to be accommodating to foreigners. After settling into the popular expatriate community, we understood why San Miguel was jokingly referred to as "Starter Mexico, no Spanish required." Life here, with the minor inconvenience of rough stone streets and single-lane side-walks, was similar to that of any upscale community in the United States. The rapid gringo influx (now numbering five thousand to seven thousand) had brought with it chic shops, gourmet foods, and a surfeit of international restaurants that required the Mexican staff to speak English—not what I wanted from a second home in Mexico. My interest had begun to shift to the surrounding countryside, what I arrogantly referred to as the "real" Mexico.

So Lucy offered to take me out of town for a day to Atoltonilco. As we approached the center of town, I found myself face to face with the main attraction: a huge, rather formidable-looking church that was built at the urging of an itinerant priest, who determined that this spot was sacred ground. Faithfully following the lines of classic 17th-century Spanish architecture, the structure contained an unusual appendage: Along an exterior wall, past a row of contiguous stalls, we peered through narrow, barred openings into the small, dark, barren cells used by pilgrims and penitents for prayer, fasting, and self-flagellation. Blackened stone walls enclosed each chamber, which were maybe three by four feet in size. I could not bring myself to step inside, let alone imagine what it would feel like to be con-fined in such a space. Yet throughout the year, people arrive in large numbers, not just Mexicans, but North Americans and Europeans as well, to partake of the penitence ritual.

On the way back from Atoltonilco, as we bounced through

clouds of dust, three shrouded figures loomed ahead of us. They were women in long shapeless garments, looking as if they had stepped from a Zuniga drawing of *indígenas*, with their short stocky bodies, wide flat cheekbones, and deep black hair pulled into a single long braid. They shuffled barefoot in the soft earth—chanting, praying, and fingering rosary beads—and ignored us as we pulled up alongside. Lucy stopped the car. There were no houses in sight, and the women looked worn with travel.

"*¡Súbanse!*" I called from the window.

The women exchanged uncertain looks, clearly not used to being offered a lift. But they peered into the windows, obviously tempted. Two gray-haired ladies in a car didn't seem to pose much of a threat.

"*Sí, gracias,*" responded one of the women, and all three climbed into the back seat.

"*¿Adónde van?*" I asked.

The woman in charge simply pointed straight ahead, and Lucy drove directly into the hazy grit shot through with the blinding late-day sun. We learned that the women were coming from a retreat in Atoltonilco. They had gone there to pray for Felipa, one of the women in the group, who had been unable to conceive another child for almost five years. When I heard that Felipa already had four children—two boys and two girls, I thought my Spanish remiss, that I had misunderstood. As a mother of two and committed to women's rights, I could not comprehend her need. It would make much more sense to me if this poor Mexican woman, who appeared to be in her late forties, had been in church giving thanks to God for not raining more children onto her already burdened life.

After driving a few miles, we came upon a compound: half a dozen houses scattered in a large field and surrounded by agave cactus and leafless mesquite trees. The dwellings were squat and rectangular, constructed from adobe brick and topped with corrugated tin roofs. Felipa motioned for us to stop in front of a stick-and-wire fence. The women were barely out of the car when a girl of about thirteen years ran from behind a piece of fabric draped in a doorway. Following close behind came two young boys and a girl of about five. They crowded around their mama, Felipa, happy and relieved to have her home after three days. After lots of squeals and hugs, Felipa managed to free one arm and gestured for us to come over. The two other women murmured *"Gracias"* and retreated to the houses beyond. From our conversation in the car, I had learned they were all part of the Morales family.

On the fence surrounding Felipa's two-room house sat well-tended geranium plants in rusty, discarded paint cans. Looped in and around the plants were some prickly, organic-looking ropes from a plant I didn't recognize.

"¿Qué es?" I asked. *"¿Se puede sembrar aquí?"* ("What's this? Can anything grow here?")

Felipa pointed to the fields of dusty gray agave cactus. With lots of hand motions, she explained that they pulled this sticky, vinelike substance from the cactus and hung it out to dry until it became harsh, scratchy rope.

"After a few weeks," she said, "the children cut the ropes and make them into *sogas.*" Felipa then reached down into a bucket near the fence and pulled up a tangle of ropes. On her own body, she demonstrated how these *sogas* (a kind of cat-o'-nine-tails) were tied around the chest and used for self-flagellation. I then noticed pails of rope soaking in purple and red dyes.

"Why the colors?"

Felipa smiled. "Tourists love to buy the bright-colored ones as souvenirs. They sell quite well on weekends at Atoltonilco. Of course, the pilgrims who come to pray and repent buy only the *sogas* made from raw ropes." Until that moment, I thought the agave plant was good only for producing tequila and gorgeous yellow flowers, never realizing it could also be the source of a thriving cottage industry.

Felipa invited us into the house for *refrescos*. Seated at a small table in the dark, windowless room, we were immediately aware of the family's primitive living conditions. The hard-packed dirt floor was taken up with sleeping pallets, neatly laid side by side. At the far end of the room, a piece of fabric hung, separating the children's space from the parents'. The TV set sat on a stool in the corner.

There was much excited talk about the new room being built alongside the house with the money coming in from recent construction work. A separate kitchen, long dreamt of, would soon be a reality. The new kitchen would include the incredible luxury of a gas stove, for until now, cooking had been done outdoors, over an open fire.

There was no running water and no bathroom. Water, a precious commodity in this drought-prone region, was fetched from a well in the yard. When we "dig a well" in the States, we call in a rig and moan about the expense. Here, "digging" means just that. All the able-bodied men and boys in the compound take up picks and shovels and keep digging down till they hit water—in this case, almost one hundred feet down.

In an isolated *campo* (field) community, where everyone lives in similar conditions, you count on your neighbors to pitch in for everything—childcare, tending the sick and elderly, and home repairs and construction. Interdependence is a way of life and is essential to survival. It was not lost on me that this support system stood in sharp contrast to the highly valued American spirit of self-reliant independence. Our lifestyle would not be a rational concept here.

As I sat listening to Felipa, I became more curious than ever about this woman who wanted yet another child. At the risk of sounding rude, I asked her why. Felipa frowned, and then a puzzled look crossed her face. She stared at me for a moment, then turned to Lucy, who had the good sense to say nothing. Her eyes expressed disbelief as she shook her head and faced me again. Then, opening her hands and thrusting them forward, shaking with emphasis, she replied, *"Porque todavía quiero ser mujer."* (Because I still want to be a woman.)

From her tone of true angst, I knew I was confronting an emotion beyond my own experience. Felipa was younger than I had assumed. She was barely forty. She was the same age as my daughter, Laurie, who had made the decision early on not to have children. For Laurie, there was never a question of defining her womanhood in terms of childbearing. But for this Mexican mother of four, the very core of her being was tied to her ability to reproduce.

Talk about serious differences in the definition of what it means to be a woman. Worse, Felipa was convinced that she was being punished with a terrible illness (she thought cancer) for some unmentionable sin. She may well be dying, she said, and that was why she was unable to conceive.

Her response startled me. Why did she view her inability to produce another child as a punishment? Where did such feelings come from? I could barely grasp her thinking.

"I'm not that old," she said. Her menstrual cycle was still in force, but without the prestige that comes with carrying a child, her pride in being a woman was compromised. She was nothing. A discard. I did not know how to respond. In New York, women suffering from a midlife crisis often try to stave off depression by going on a diet or getting a face-lift, or by taking a lover. All temporary, superficial remedies, but a far cry from Felipa's fatalism. I was staring across one vast cultural gap.

The professional social worker in Lucy sprang to life.

"Felipa, let me take you to the Women's Clinic in town for a gynecological exam." If nothing else, it would allay her fear of cancer. But Felipa rejected the offer with a litany of excuses.

"*No, no es posible.* I have just been away for three days. I cannot leave the children again."

"You won't be gone long," persisted Lucy.

"Ay, no, my husband will be home shortly. And so much needs to be done around the house."

We suspected these were not her true reasons. I believed the crux of Felipa's refusal was an innate suspicion of Western-style medicine. Yet Lucy held her ground, stressing the need to confront physical problems or, at best, eliminate them as a source of anxiety.

I held my tongue. Felipa must have spent days, months, years even, taking herbal remedies, saying prayers, fasting, doing penance. But gradually, Felipa started to weaken under Lucy's patient, persistent urging, and Lucy prevailed. Felipa agreed to go for an exam the following week.

As we left the Morales compound, I found myself thinking about our friends in San Miguel, women who went into the countryside to educate Mexican women about birth control and to distribute contraceptives. Not always welcomed with open arms, they often dealt with open hostility. We Americans are notorious do-gooders, convinced of our superior way of life. When we can't export it, we simply impose it, with little thought to its suitability or whether anyone is even interested. We're quick to blame multiple, unwanted births on the antifeminist attitudes of the church or the macho demands of the men in Mexican society. But Felipa's revelation about her very womanhood being compromised without another pregnancy went beyond religious dogma and issues of machismo.

We picked Felipa up the following week, drove her into town, and stayed with her through the checkup. One of the major achievements of the foreign community in San Miguel de Allende has been the establishment of the Women's Clinic. Thanks to the combined efforts of Canadian and American women with aggressive fundraising skills, a hospital dedicated to women's health and maternity needs exists for the benefit of the Mexican community.

Felipa's doctor was a bilingual Mexican American donating his time. After the checkup and tests, he sat her down and gently explained that there was absolutely nothing physically wrong with her. Not only were there no signs of cancer, there was also no reason she could not have another child. Lucy and I smiled with relief, then watched in confusion as Felipa broke into sobs. I thought they might be tears of joy, but the doctor knew better. He had spent just enough time with her to recognize the symptoms of depression common to many women as they approach the end of their childbearing years. Her reason for being was now acutely in jeopardy. He brought up the subject of depression and suggested that Felipa talk with someone in Social Services. They could refer her to a therapist who might help her through this crisis. (Mexico's healthcare system provides for such services at no cost to indigent patients.)

We left the clinic, each of us experiencing separate degrees of hopelessness. On the ride home, Felipa recovered her composure, which seemed to harden into anger. She made it clear there was absolutely no way she would see a therapist. Lucy and I sensed that we had, with all the best intentions, pushed this trusting woman to a dangerous precipice.

Determined not to abandon Felipa in this state, we returned to her village for several more visits. Slowly, we regained her trust. We visited the two-room schoolhouse, saw the construction of separate boys' and girls' bathrooms completed, and arranged for Random House to donate a box of bilingual children's books. We were even invited to children's birthday celebrations. Often we just sat in the yard, chatting about the family while watching the two piglets, tied to sticklike trees, growing bigger and fatter. They were named Navidad and Pascua for their sacrificial feast days.

It was April when Lucy and I made our last visit of the season to the Morales family. Felipa greeted us with a girlish giggle.

"I will have a surprise for you when you return next year."

"Surprise? Is it a secret? Tell us," we insisted. "We can't wait till next year!"

"*No, no es un secreto—es un milagro*," she stated proudly. "*¡Me estoy embarazada!*"

"You're pregnant!?" we shouted in unison.

"Are you sure?" cried Lucy. "Shouldn't you see the doctor again?"

No. There was no doubt in Felipa's mind. Nor was there any doubt that her good fortune was the result of faith, prayer, and herbal remedies. And who's to say that it wasn't?

When we returned the following January, we found her sitting in the new kitchen, contentedly nursing her newborn son, Maurizio. Because of this *milagro* (miracle), Felipa had come to regard Lucy and me as some kind of spiritual midwives, which left me feeling a little uneasy. But, stealing a line from an old Bette Davis movie, I thought: *Why ask for the moon when you have the stars?*

The occasion of Maurizio's baptism would be my first time inside the *campo* church. Churches in Mexico hold an exotic appeal for me. Whatever the style and wherever they may be, churches have a sense of pageantry and idolatry. With their wildly painted saints, supplicants on their knees praying fervently, and bloody representations of the suffering Christ, it's all a fascinating form of theater to someone born and raised as a Reform Jew in New York City.

On the day of the baptism, Lucy and I, together with the Morales family and their other friends, gathered in front of the church to wait for the special service to begin. The simple structure, built by men in the community, was bare of any architectural features. Only the church facade had been overlaid with stucco and painted a pale yellow with white trim, leaving the unfinished brick sides for a future time, when money and manpower would bring about its completion. When a clanging bell signaled the start of services, we looked on as one of the men near the entryway pulled vigorously on a long rope. The bell was hanging from a high branch, in a leafless tree, alongside the church. Building funds had not been sufficient to include a bell tower.

As we proceeded into the church, I was surprised by the starkly bare interior. Even poor rural churches, simple concrete-block constructions resembling bunkers with a cross on top, usually have a few local saints lining the walls. Except for a faded painting over the altar of their patron saint, San Isidro Labrador, there was no decoration. The place of honor was given over to the saint credited with performing the one miracle that everyone gives thanks for in this parched region, *"Pon el agua y quita el sol."* (He brings forth the water and puts away the sun.) No other visual representation was present; nothing to inspire, attract, exalt, elicit homage, or incite fear; none of the dramatic religious art I had come to expect in a Mexican church.

But looking at the faces focused on the priest as he conducted the service, there was no mistaking the presence of faith and the importance of ceremony among these people. Mexicans live with an intimate knowledge of spirituality. They accept without question the insubstantial, indefinable essence that we in the developed world tend to ignore or overlook. As I left the church with Simon and Felipa, who was smiling down at snugly wrapped Maurizio, I experienced my own little *milagro*. That vast cultural gap had somehow evaporated. The "real" Mexico I was so determined to find had found me.

Kay Sexton

Coyote Hotel

"Of course, around here, you don't need hallucinogenic Mexican cactus to have visions; just looking out of the bus window on the way down was like seeing paradise," I said.

It was meant to be a pleasantry, a way of breaking the ice on our very first day in Cocoyoc, an hour from Mexico City. A hotel there, with a trip into Mexico City most days, had seemed like a good idea when I pondered the capital city's smog and noise from the security of the Oxford college where I'd planned the itinerary for its Department of Plant Genetics interdisciplinary research tour.

What a mistake it was to start the conversation that way. My simple remark was pounced on by the German couple, Herr Professor and Frau Weimer, among the bunch of ethnobotanists, agronomists, and agroeconomists I had gathered at the Mexico City Anthropology Museum to shepherd here. They delivered an impromptu lecture.

"*Anhalonium lewinii* is commonly known as the Mexican cactus," declaimed Herr Professor.

"Although even that nomenclature is now challenged by the recategorization of the genus into *Echinocactus* of the *mammalaria* species, being spineless and flexible," added his lady.

And so they went on. And on. We learned that the original research into Mexican cactus, or peyote buttons, was conducted in Berlin. We were told that an alkaloid, later named mescaline, was extracted. We were informed about the forty experiments conducted by Walter Frederking upon himself, and about the nature and extent of each of his hallucinations. The eyes of every other member of the twenty-strong group had long ago glazed over, and as their guide, I had to remain polite and nod and smile for nearly thirty excruciating minutes of minutiae about the blasted plant that I realized was the focus of their entire lives' work. By the time Herr Professor Weimer announced that even as little as .5 milligrams of mescaline was poisonous, I was already wondering how difficult it would be to obtain the stuff and slip it into their evening cocktails.

Each day, as I led my assorted followers across the baking expanse of Chapultepec Park, my heart sank. Perhaps if they'd been a charming bevy of eager young students I'd have been happy. How had I ever imagined that guiding a cantankerous bunch of hardened field researchers, each with his or her own carefully guarded field of expertise, could be fun? Each was as prickly as a cactus. Not as a Mexican cactus, oh no, because I'd already been put firmly in my place about that subject!

It wasn't a good start. A few years ago I'd have taken this kind of thing in stride. Truth be told, I was getting too old to pull off the balancing act that a good tour guide performs. I'd been in this business for several years now, but Mexico was a new project and another world, and if the regular guide hadn't broken her leg, I'd never have agreed to take over the contract. The only thing I knew about the country was that the chilies were hot, and that to deal with fiery food you had to drink milk, which neutralized the missile strength of the peppers. But I did know enough about the folklore of chocolate, maize, and cane sugar to pass myself off as some kind of culinary expert. Or at least I thought I did until I met the combined expertise of the group and was immediately flattened under their collective pedantry like a pecan under a steam roller.

The only thing that had pulled me through the week was Cocoyoc. The hacienda we stayed at was as beautiful as a Hollywood romance, and when I woke early in the morning I could watch the sun lifting veils of heat from the green surrounding hills as I leaned on my bedroom window and listened to the whoops and whistles from the trees. *Cocoyoc* meant "coyote," I knew that, and although I never heard one call, my dreams were haunted by a strange, coughing bark and small, trotting shapes that slipped between trees in the full-moon darkness. Moths as big as my hand would flit between the dining room pillars even before the group had finished their after-dinner coffee. I would slip between the trees myself, escaping the heavy-footed pursuit of the ethnobotanists to hide in the dark corners of the swimming pool's terrace until I was sure they had all gone to bed. Then I would wander through the hotel grounds, hearing the low thrumming of frogs, and even the beetles traveling through the cane would make their own incessant beat, like maracas at half speed.

Everything in Cocoyoc had a sound, a contribution to the music of the green hills. The hours I snatched from my duties to steep myself in that music were all that kept me going.

I'd hoped that the German couple would turn out to be the exceptions, the two bad apples in a barrel of great guys. Most mornings the group was silent over breakfast, but I didn't take that amiss. I'd recently come to prefer early morning silences myself. The me who liked rock music to start the day had evolved into someone who could hardly cope with a rustling newspaper. It might have been the only preference I had in common with my group, but our shared desire for silence at breakfast made me smile happily on "my" tourists and build happy fantasies in which they were pressing dollars and deutschmarks into my hand at the airport and telling me that their visit would not have been complete without my support and insightful guidance. It was a happy hallucination—possibly I'd been slipped Mexican cactus juice in my hot chocolate. But I enjoyed it for the whole hour, during which they chewed industriously, held out their cups for endless coffee served by equally silent waiters, and read forbidding scientific journals, which they held either close to their noses or at arm's length. It wasn't a pretty sight: scowling scholars sniffing along the lines of text like pigs hunting truffles, or straining their eyes to read the words they held far from them, as though the pages contained a bad smell, but I tried to think magnanimously.

One morning, on the bus down to Mexico City, I mentioned that we would spend the morning comparing the range of domestic technologies held in the anthropology museum, focusing in particular on those that related to the sowing, harvesting, drying, and processing of corn.

"Corn?" It was one of the wider Americans who spoke. "My dear young lady, there's no such thing as corn!" He smirked at me the length of the bus, and his colleagues laughed. I felt my face start to burn, though whether it was anger or embarrassment or just sheer surprise at being called a young lady in my forties, I wasn't sure.

"Well . . . " I began. And that was as far as I got. He held up his big pink hand and waved it at me, as though giving traffic signals in the middle of the road.

"There is either maize or teosinte. Now, it is instructive to compare the history of teosinte's domestication as delineated by contemporary scientists with oral traditions surviving among native Mesoamerican peoples. The maize genus seems to have arrived as a spontaneous genetic mutation, and as such had to be accounted for in some miraculous fashion by the indigenous populations for whom it was to replace teosinte as a staple food crop. . . . " And he was off, telling us all more than we had ever wanted to know about his pet subject.

I glanced at my watch. Seventeen minutes later he wound up his peroration with a description of the genetic markers that separated maize from its great-grandfather, teosinte. I sighed.

It wasn't just boredom that prompted my reaction. The American had just taken a beautiful and funny story—of the arrival of corn in the world—and turned it into something dryer and huskier than the emptiest corncob. Folk stories were my speciality; my freelance career was based on finding the scientific roots in old wives' tales about food and crops. The stories that surround the food of the world were my bread and butter, my corn and lentils, my *bobotie* and honey. Now I was having to endure the desiccation of everything I loved by this bunch of shrunken-souled academics.

"That's very interesting," I said, raising my voice above the rustling of museum guides and maps. "You may wish to know that the Mesoamerican people celebrated the arrival of maize with a tale that combines an explanation for random genetic mutation with a sense of humor about their local environment. The way they tell it is this." I began:

One day a beetle found something. This one had crawled through a crack in a boulder and had come across the sun. Not the great sky sun—the God who demanded blood in return for blessing the people—but a smaller sun, a golden ball, full of goodness and beauty. At first he was content to look at this smaller sun, but eventually, being a beetle, he had to taste it. And it tasted better than it looked.

So the beetle told other beetles, and a constant procession began to travel through the chink to find suns of their own. They became fat, and their carapaces shone with health and power, almost as if the sun food inside them reflected through their bodies.

A lean coyote watched them. He was lean because he had lost a fight with a female coyote some time earlier. He had learned wisdom the hard way and was not inclined to make the same mistake twice. So he watched for a long time and didn't stick his long, hungry snout through the hole until he was sure nothing bad happened to the shiny-shelled ones after they ate whatever lay behind the rock. And when he finally pushed his snout through the gap, he found they were munching on corn. But not the skinny, hard-kernelled corn that grew on his side of the rocks. This corn was golden, as ripe as love, and as milky as a mother's breast.

The coyote ate his fill, then, with crafty movements, he patted and rolled the husks away and pulled the uneaten cobs closer, so that when he returned, he could eat again.

The next day he ate again, once more pushing the empty cobs away and pulling fresh ones toward him with his clever paw. After a while he felt a tapping on his backside. It was a deputation of beetles asking him to move over so that they too could enjoy a feast.

"Of course," he said. "On one condition."

"Which is?" asked the hungry beetles.

"You must move the husks to the back of the pile and bring more fresh cobs forward. If you don't, I shall block the hole with my body and none of us will eat."

The beetles agreed, and so it was organized. Every day the coyote ate, then allowed the beetles through.

It was all going so well that one day he felt ready to show himself to the female he'd been courting—perhaps now she wouldn't bite his nose and savage him. He admired himself in the beetles' shells. He was sleek and fat, his fur bristled with health, and his eyes gleamed. He trotted off to try his wooing again.

"Good riddance," said the beetles.

When he found his beloved's pack, he sat on a high rock and let them admire him. He was delighted when his desired one lowered her head and called him down to talk. He jumped from his high place, and *phoot*—as he landed, a puff of air escaped his rear end. It was the rich food he'd been eating, he told himself. But as he descended the rocks, his journey was marred by the sound of his rear venting air with every stride. By the time he reached the valley floor, the coyote pack was yipping and rolling around with glee.

"I came to share my good fortune with you, as I have found a cache of golden grain in the mountains," he said. "But I can see you are not the kind of people to appreciate it. I bid you farewell." It was an excellent speech, and it would have been perfect if he hadn't parped one last time as he turned his tail for home.

The story was too good not to share. First the coyotes told other coyote packs, who told jaguars, who told jungle birds, who told chickens, and eventually the chickens told the woman who fed them bitter teosinte. The woman told a man, and the man told a headman, who questioned the gods. "Is it right that there should be good food reserved for beetles and foolish, lovesick coyotes when we, who sacrifice to you, make do with inferior grain?"

The gods agreed to look into it.

When they reached the mountains, they found the maize was indeed heaped behind the rocks. Being gods, and a little lazy, for that is the nature of the gods, they decided to smite the boulders with thunderbolts and let the cobs tumble out. When the dust and smoke cleared, the boulders were gone, but so was the heap of golden maize. Instead there was a pile of cobs with multicolored kernels: gold, of course, but also black where cinders from the explosion had landed, red where they had been heat-scorched, and white with dust from exploding boulders—which is why maize cobs have so many colors.

There was a long silence when I finished. "Very pretty," said the American professor eventually, "but rather fanciful."

I wanted to slap his fat face. Okay, I'd taken a bit of a liberty changing the fox in the myth to a *cocoyoc*, but I thought it was allowable, given that we were staying in the coyote's name place. Other than that, I'd recounted the Mexican folktale faithfully enough, and it had always struck me as an amazingly sophisticated and funny story, much more interesting than the sober folktales of Europe or the peculiar myths dreamed up by the American settlers.

When we got off the minibus at the hotel, I hid behind my papers until they'd all gone. I couldn't have coped with another discussion about getting less spicy food, or whether nachos were gluten-free, or how was it that the hotel didn't have a large-screen TV to show the NFL playoffs.

"Good story," said the Mexican driver as I passed him.

"Thank you!" I was more pleased than I should have been; even one tiny compliment seemed likely to tip me into tears of frustration.

"When most people look at Mexico," he said, pulling down the blinds in his cab and settling back in his seat for a nap, "they see themselves." He opened one eye and glanced up at me. "Think about it," he said.

That night, at dinner, while I tried to cope with some of the spiciest tamales ever produced, another academic argument started over the etymology of Quetzalcoatl: Did it mean feathered serpent or bird serpent? It could have been a great debate—if they'd cared about the subject—but all they really cared about was scoring points off each other.

It was then I realized that Mexico was proving too much for them. Despite their decades of experience, they were trying to reduce this vast, ancient, paradoxical culture to something they could assimilate, and that meant turning it into a version of their own beliefs and societies. The economists saw a culture that had indulged in waste and uneconomic behaviors, the agriculturalists saw a society based on staple crops and agricultural monopolies that had led to stagnation, and the social historians saw a militarist hierarchy that limited command to small sections of society and gave no impetus to innovation when a new military threat arrived in the form of the Spanish invaders.

What none of them could see was that the huge, chaotic uncertainty of Mexico was a better mirror than any they could hold up. I could hardly see Mexico myself, but even my fragmented and uncertain understanding was better than theirs. I was buoyed by a sense of superiority for about five minutes, until my tongue informed me that I had just bitten into the hottest chili pepper in the whole of Mexico. I ran from the table to the server stand and guzzled a whole jug of milk. It worked. It really worked! The heat of the pepper didn't go away, but my eyes stopped streaming, and I could speak again.

A waitress took the jug from me, returned to the kitchen, and reappeared with a new jug of milk and a glass. I thanked her, and she smiled at me, and for the first time I really looked at the staff, viewing them through my new understanding. They were older than you usually find in tourist resorts; they were mature men and women, rather than students working on their languages or training for hospitality careers.

I nodded my thanks, and when I'd made sure all my group had eaten and retired back to their rooms or were sitting in the bar sniping at each other verbally, I went back to the restaurant.

The waitresses were setting the tables for breakfast, and when I offered to help by folding napkins, they tried to hide their smiles behind polite refusals. As I watched the speed with which they worked, I could see why I wouldn't have been much help. In my poor Spanish, I asked them to tell me about chocolate and Quetzalcoatl.

"When the last age of the world ended, Quetzalcoatl went down to Mictlan, the world below, and picked up all the bones of the people of the past. There were no humans left. All humans had died, and it was their dead bones he carried back to the empty earth." The speaker was the oldest of the waitresses, a woman who had the flat impassivity of a priestess.

"*Abuela,* tell how he brought us to life," said the youngest waitress.

"Quetzalcoatl sprinkled his own blood on the bones, and a new human race began. To this race the god gave maize and the calendar, so that we could live in plenty and happiness. For this we were to reward him with painting and song and all the things that added beauty to the world he had given us." The grandmother didn't smile. Her eyes seemed to reach back a long way into the past, even beyond my own historical reverie, to a time when the gods walked on the earth. Gods with feathers and serpent tails. Jaguar gods and coyote gods.

"And the chocolate, *abuela?*" prompted the girl.

The older woman put down the flatware she was setting on the tables and came and sat beside me. Her granddaughter joined us, still folding napkins into fan shapes.

"Quetzalcoatl had to leave. Our creator and father was exiled by the other gods, but he left us something to remember him—the cocoa tree." The old woman lifted my hand and looked at my palm, then laid her hand beside mine. I saw how her hand was callused, although the calluses had become softened over time. "Cocoa grows in the shade of other trees," she said. "Each year we pick the pods by hand, they are as big as a little gourds, and we open them with knives and take out the seeds. When they first see the sun, the seeds are white, but they become purple like the dusk, and then they are ready to be fermented."

"Did you pick cocoa?" I asked.

"Many years ago," she said. "When I traveled with my husband, we cut cane, harvested cocoa, stripped corn; we followed the work wherever it went, but then we came home." She nodded toward the darkness, and I saw she felt the hotel belonged to her and her family—not in terms of ownership, but because they had worked here for generations, shaping the place with their labors.

"Tell about Cortés," said the granddaughter gently.

"When Quetzalcoatl was made to leave us, he went across the sea on a raft of snakes," I blinked. Could I have translated that properly? A raft of snakes? The girl smiled and pulled a pen from her pocket. Grabbing one of the paper napkins, she sketched a winged figure in a headdress sailing on a writhing bed of serpents. I nodded, and she tucked the napkin into her pocket.

"He promised to return to his people, and he left us the cocoa tree as the guarantee of his promise—to drink *xocoatl* is to drink the wisdom and strength of Quetzalcoatl. So when Cortés came, with his many ships and his white-faced army, the Aztecs thought that he was the god returning." Both women stared into the dark beyond the pillars, and I shivered slightly. It was as if they expected the winged serpent god to appear, carrying steaming mugs of liquid chocolate.

I wanted to hear a coyote call, to make the moment complete, but all I heard was my German professor, who had emerged from behind the pillars, clearing his throat before insisting, "My wife wants biscuits and tea—now please."

The waitresses smiled politely as they went to meet his demands, and I slipped away, yawning, to my own beehive-shaped room.

The next evening, our last in the hotel, we ate chicken covered with mole, a rich sauce made from peppers, cocoa, and spices.

Everybody else was given a bottle of Corona beer, but when the *abuela* came to me, she brought a cup of frothing, bitter chocolate, flavored with cinnamon, and a bowl of brown sugar.

On one level I understood the sugar hadn't really been grown at Cocoyoc, and I knew the cocoa wasn't the gift of a feathered serpent god, but as I stirred my drink before draining it to its dark grainy dregs, I felt that—just for a moment—I'd finally seen Mexico. Not in a stone carving or a beautiful golden mask in a museum, but as it really was, old and fragmented, one layer of history cracking to reveal another; complicating its past by hiding as much as it revealed. Like the broken color of *cocoyoc* fur, red and gray at once, like the coyote's strange hybrid nature between wolf and dog, Mexico prefers to select more than one reality to present itself in. The myths and the science, the versions of history, the scale of nature were all Mexico, and all were present at the same time. The trick wasn't to choose one Mexico, but to let one choose me.

Reyna Lingemann

If You Bake Them, He Will Come

As a traveler, you inevitably find those places that you are able to pass through unaffected. Sprawling colonial towns that seem foreign and inaccessible, palm-covered beaches that fail to grab you, and ports that, even though beautiful, seem lonely and cold. And then there are those towns that surround you and lure you in—the ones that cause you, day after day, to miss your bus or reschedule your flight home. Maybe it's the sound of giant raindrops hitting your leaky tin roof at night, the early dawn nasal calls of the milkman wailing *"Laay-chaay, laay-chaay, laay-chaay,"* the earthy-sweet smell of burning corn husks in the *ranchitos* outside of town, or the man you meet there who will change your life's path.

I ran out of money late one August, when a spontaneous trip to Mexico stretched from five weeks to ten. At the age of twenty-one, the prospect of being dead broke in a tiny Oaxacan fishing village was surprisingly invigorating. I could have called home to California and asked my parents to loan me money to extend my trip, but I was sure I had the ability to capitalize on the needs of the surfing tourist population I had come to know so well. I wasn't ready to leave, for this town had crept into my soul.

I would walk everywhere barefoot in Puerto Escondido and knew the shopkeepers and hammock salesladies by name. I learned to make tamales from one of the elders by the beach who had seen her town grow up around the family compound—around the mango trees, the picnic table, the tiny cooking stove, and the group of concrete-block cabins she rented to surfers for $20 a week. Carmelita lived next door to the guesthouse I had called home since I arrived, and I made it a point to stop in each afternoon and sit with her on her dirt patio above the beach, practicing my Spanish and teaching her English words to add to her limited repertoire. While we wrapped chicken and masa in banana leaves on Sundays, Carmelita poured shots of clear homemade *mezcal* from a Coke bottle and told me stories about the group of gringo surfers who lived with her for months every summer. Her own children had grown up and moved away, so she thought of the boys as family. She had watched them grow from wiry pale teenagers to strong men who were crazy enough to leave California, her dream destination, to surf in the dangerous ocean she had never set foot in.

One afternoon when I was down to my last $50, I was sitting with Carmelita above the beach that was dotted with blanket vendors who were trying desperately to make a sale, and I realized I was privy to a secret none of the Mexican girls selling pumpkin seeds, jewelry, blankets, or quesadillas could have known: I understood what those skinny, homesick gringos craved. It was sweets—not pink and white puffy, packaged Mexican *dulces*, but freshly baked, chocolaty sweets to remind them of home. Armed with my last few pesos, an empty shopping bag, and the recipe I'd memorized during college from the Nestlé's chocolate chip bag, I walked several miles into town to hunt for ingredients. I would bring a little bit of home to the beach in Oaxaca and, I hoped, make enough money to stay in this slice of heaven for a few more weeks.

At the *mercado*, I wove my way through stalls of fly-covered meat hanging from the ceiling; heaping piles of ripe tomatoes and onions; mounds of red, brown, green, and purple ground chilies; and stalls of embroidered dresses and tablecloths. I found wheat flour in bulk bags and checked it for bugs. I bought fresh eggs, vanilla that smelled like turpentine, perfumey margarine (because real butter was surprisingly absent), a bag of coarse sugar, and some M&M's and a few chocolate bars that would have to suffice for chocolate chips. With my sack full and the midday heat relentless, I used my last few pesos for a *camioneta* ride back to the beach. Sitting on a wooden bench in the back of the covered truck among a dozen women on their way home from market, I felt a strange kinship. I found myself thinking in Spanish and understanding the chatter around me as if it were my language. It seemed that my entire identity had changed since I had come to Mexico, and I didn't remember when or how it had happened.

I remember my first sight of Puerto Escondido—the way the bay seemed to curve into a smile as I looked down upon it from the bus station where I'd been dropped off. I saw the mist rising from giant swells along the southern beach, and I could sense an excitement in the air that I recognized from growing up in a northern California surf town. Loud Mexican pop and *ranchera* music blasted from minigroceries, pharmacies, hair salons, and fabric stores just beyond the rutted asphalt where the driver had left my dusty backpack. I was alone. Not lonely and alone, but solo nonetheless, with nothing more than my *Let's Go! Mexico* book, flip-flops, frumpy blue cotton skirt, and an almost-empty money belt under my oversized T-shirt.

I had been traveling by bus through Mexico for a month, oblivious to the stories of midnight rapes on mountain roads and sweaty-tourist accounts of hepatitis, malaria, and dengue fever. I found another side of Mexico—one of inefficient transportation and alluring siestas, friendly women and overly friendly men, poor yet generous families, roadside filth, and incredible natural beauty.

I met Juan, my bus driver, in the state of Colima. When I boarded the bus, he smiled and said, *"Buenas tardes."* I liked his kind eyes immediately, and he possessed a confidence that suited his fatherly face. I sat several rows from the back with my backpack in the seat next to me—a trick I'd learned that helped keep the young men at bay. Juan watched in his rearview while several men tried to get me to move my pack so they could squeeze into the seat, even though the bus was nearly empty. After a few minutes, he motioned me to the front—the seat where his alternate driver would normally sit. I quickly took his offer.

Our trip was two days along the coast to Oaxaca, traveling some of the most dangerous, winding roads in all of Mexico. For the next forty-eight hours, Juan and I talked in Spanish while he drove. He told me about his wife and grown kids, his pueblo, his dreams of retiring by the beach. "One day," he told me, "I want to build a small house on the edge of a beautiful beach and spend my days fishing, growing a garden, and playing with my grandkids." When he said "grandkids," I remembered for a moment how much older he was than I. His muscular forearms flexed as he cranked the giant steering wheel through kilometers and kilometers of narrow highway. In my college Spanish that improved every hour, I told him about growing up in the country with chickens and goats, how we didn't have a toilet until I was nine, how we grew most of our own food, even still. I never knew how much I would have in common with a fifty-something Mexican man, but our lives were parallel in many ways.

Juan knew all the best roadside restaurants and would invite me to sit with him, much to the chagrin of the young male passengers, who didn't dare say anything but who gave us constant looks. In Michoacan, we would share giant bowls of *caldo de camarones* at outdoor tables by the side of the Mexico 200 highway. Juan told me about the gun he carried under his driver's seat and reminded me to be careful traveling alone.

The second evening, with a dark loneliness in his eyes, he hugged me outside my hotel room and said, "Reynita" under his breath. I looked right back at him in the heavy silence, knowing that I couldn't wrap up this thing we had into a neat little package of words as I could have at home. In the warm breeze that smelled of diesel fumes, standing on the edge of a roadside cliff far from home, I wondered how I could feel so comfortable, as if this country and these people could have been my life.

Just after we entered the state of Oaxaca, Juan and I said good-bye in a dusty red dirt town filled with buses. I knew he was going back the way we came and would drive that same stretch of highway hundreds of times, with hundreds of different people taking my seat. *"Vaya con Dios,"* he said. "Go with God." Our eyes were full, and I noticed an elderly woman with a scarf on her head and a bucket of fish looking at us with a quizzical smile. Juan's hands were greasy like my dad's after working on a truck at our shop, knobby and cal-lused like the men's on the mountain where I lived. As I boarded my connecting bus to Puerto Escondido, I saw, reflected in the young driver's mirrored sunglasses, Juan standing behind me, checking to see, I imagined, if I'd take the first seat up front.

Strange how an unexpected meeting can change the way people see you. I knew that my face was soft and open after spending time with Juan. Women on the buses would speak to me in Spanish, little girls would play peek-a-boo from behind their mothers' jet-black hair, and tourists asked me questions as if I had been on the road for a long time. The protective shell that had always surrounded me at home had begun to slip away.

Sitting on my pack by the side of the road in the evening light, I flipped quickly through my *Let's Go!* book to the short section on Puerto Escondido. I noticed a group of guys in surfer shorts with full surfboard bags talking and looking toward me. Despite my new feel-ing of ease in Mexico, I craved to speak English, and the California slang I heard from the boys was like music to my ears. For the first time in a month, I became self-conscious about my big skirt and unshaven legs. Had I not been so preoccupied, I might have freshened up in the bathroom—at least washed my weary face and run a comb through my hair.

The eldest guy in the group walked over to me. He wore a T-shirt with a wave across the front and carried a small Guatemalan change purse. "Hey, my name is Zen," he said, holding out his hand. "We're getting a cab to this little place on the beach, if you want to join us." *Zen*, I thought. *Anyone with that name couldn't be bad.* I was confident about my instincts now—that beautifully heightened sense of people that traveling alone brings. Without thinking I said, "Okay," and followed Zen over to meet the others, who were loading their boards onto a cab roof.

On the sweaty ride to the beach, past the Corona factory, mango orchards, and the bustling village, Zen and his friends told me they had been coming to Puerto Escondido every summer for fifteen years. In almost perfect Spanish, Zen asked the driver to drop us at Pacololo, a hillside guesthouse with a 180-degree view of the Pacific. They tipped the cab driver well and shook his hand when we gathered our bags, and I knew then that we were kindred travelers.

While they unpacked their boards at their new home, a beautiful little guesthouse that I never would have found, I sat in one of the patio hammocks and watched the bustling beach scene below: burros for hire, young vacationers waxing their surfboards, older tourist men in shorts doing tai chi, and military trucks cruising the dusty road beside the beach.

"Great view, yeah?" Zen asked, already showered, changed, and looking as if he'd been there a week. "I asked Paco, and he said he has an open room for you if you'd like to stay."

"Are you sure you don't mind a nonsurfer girl hanging out with you guys?" I asked.

"No, of course not," he said, smiling. "I get a little tired of hanging out with just surfers."

It didn't take much for me to decide, especially after I found out that my new room with a view was $3 a night. *Just because I live next to the guys,* I thought, *doesn't mean I have to spend all my time with them.* I showered and changed into my least-frumpy shirt and skirt, then lay on my twin bed under the ceiling fan, feeling fortunate to find fellow travelers that felt so quickly like friends in such a remote place.

For the next few weeks, I spent hours with Zen and his friends in our close quarters, lounging in hammocks, watching them surf perfectly hollow waves in the offshore dawn as if they were part of the landscape, and meeting all of the people they had befriended in their fifteen years of visiting there. They took me to see friends in nearby pueblos where they had stayed in the '80s and told stories of the year they had been washed away trying to cross the swollen river to their rooms, of when lightning had knocked them flat on their butts while running up the path on the side of Highway 200. Stories of when they used to slide their boards into the cockpit of the one DC-3 prop plane that transported a few visitors from Oaxaca city to the beach before the airport was built. Every night, while eating lavish meals in local homes and restaurants, they told me how lucky we were. Not many years earlier, the town's menu choices were three: fried fish, grilled fish, or baked fish.

Even though I had grown up around the ocean, it was with this group of guys that I came to truly understand the camaraderie that surfing together in an unfamiliar, wild, and magical place can create. In my hometown I was a fair-weather, small-wave surfer who never graduated from my longboard or ever truly felt comfortable in the ocean. Zen and his friends talked about the swells of summers past as the great moments of their lives, and they looked toward future swells with the excitement of youthful boys. I had dated surfers all my life, but never had I met so many for whom the ocean had been their greatest teacher. For these men, surfing wasn't a pastime or an image, it was a life bound and shaped by nature. In a place where the ocean shook the ground we walked upon and engulfed each day with incredible force, I understood how the setting diminished egos and built powerful friendships that lasted year after year.

In the early days, they would arrive—some by bus, others in old cars driven from the States, some in small groups, but all of them broke. They would live on rice and beans for weeks, or often months, in shacks without running water or bathrooms. They were there for one reason—to surf the unspoiled beach break that loomed high above the Zicatela thorn bushes lining a desolate stretch of sandy beach. Although adventurous guys who preferred to travel solo, they clung to each other just to have somebody with whom to navigate the unknown waves. And all of them had a sparkle in their eyes, not unlike people who claim to have seen God.

With my arms full of pink plastic bags of cookie ingredients, I stepped off the *camioneta* at Carmelita's house and walked the short path home to my single room at Pacololo, thinking about the next challenge: I had to find an oven that worked and a willing host who wouldn't mind the heat my new business would generate. I didn't realize that word of my quest would spread about town quickly. By evening, one of the surfers I barely knew, a guy who lived in an upscale apartment with a kitchen, came forward to offer his oven in exchange for a handful of freshly baked cookies. His name was Evan, and after his room became cookie headquarters, he was known around the beach as "Oven."

The next day, in the 100-degree heat, I carried my heavy bag to his beach shack, donned my bikini, and went to work mixing dough and chopping Hershey's chocolate bars under a lone ceiling fan. Soon, as the unmistakable sweet aroma drifted from open windows into the dusty streets, the surfer boys began to arrive. Afternoon siestas were sacrificed in the name of chocolate—one by one, they shuffled in, their overly tanned, sinewy bodies a testament to many months of surfing giant Mexican barrels and living off fish and tortillas.

I charged the equivalent of fifty cents a cookie and watched the pile of pesos grow far beyond my $3-per-night room rate and the day's food allotment. And I didn't mind the attention, either. Not only was I one of the few tourist girls in town, but I spoke their language—I was the boys' temporary ticket home. I set up shop with a carton of milk on ice, and all of us gringos sat around reveling in the unspoken American bond that is cookies and milk.

One new guy with laughing eyes, a big blond afro, and scruffy shorts seemed to have an insatiable appetite for chocolate. He returned several times that first afternoon and followed me to the outdoor water barrel to help wash dishes. He stayed long after the wind turned offshore and the waves got perfect—a surfer's sacrifice, the magnitude of which I only now understand. I burned my last batch of cookies while we talked, taken by his confidence, his quiet sweetness, and his pure, happy face. That evening, for the second time in a month, I found myself thinking about a man I barely knew as I sat in my room, counting the pesos that would extend my trip.

The next morning, I awoke early while the cool wind still blew from the east and ran down to the sand with a blanket. Pretending to do yoga, I searched the beach for my new friend. As the surfers arrived, waxed their boards, and waited for the perfect lull to paddle out, I kept my eyes peeled. He was nowhere in sight, but the waves were glassy and perfect. When Zen showed up, I asked about him. "If you're looking for Slade, you're not going to find him on the beach," he said smiling. "I guarantee you that he was the first guy out at dawn—the one with the blue-nosed surfboard getting spat out of the heaviest waves." When he talked about his friend, his eyes lit up.

I scanned the horizon for the blue board and noticed what looked like a stick figure dropping down face after face of vertical smooth water. Watching him in the ocean was like watching a well-choreographed dancer with an unpredictable partner. I thought that this guy looked far more graceful out there than he had on land. I secretly hoped that he'd wipe out so he would have to swim to the beach to collect his board. After several hours, I went home alone for breakfast.

That afternoon Slade showed up at my door looking to buy a few more cookies. The way he looked at me, I wondered if Zen had told him that I was on the beach in the morning asking for him. He claimed it was too hot to walk home and instead showed me the proper way to perform what he called "power lounging," a technique of lying in the hammock, cocking your head toward the ocean, and sleeping with one eye open.

I figured that any guy who had spent years perfecting this form of relaxation might not have a job. But to my surprise, I found out that he was an accountant who was in the last few months of a one-year surfing sabbatical. A few more weeks in Mexico, three months in Indonesia, and then he'd be back in a suit and tie, sitting at a desk in a high-rise in downtown Los Angeles.

Maybe it was my youth, but never once did I think that my rapidly intensifying feelings for a globe-trotting, surfing accountant might not be practical. I wasn't the kind of girl who sought out casual encounters with men I barely knew, but when Slade asked me a few days later if I would cut his hair in exchange for a massage, I said yes without hesitation. Before long I was cooking him dinners at his place, the tidiest *cabaña* I'd ever seen. And we would spend long evenings talking about our very different lives back home. When the day approached to leave for Indonesia, I wondered if I'd ever see him again. After only three weeks, would our connection endure for the three months he would be in Asia, or was our relationship just a common case of hot, tropical infatuation?

The evening before he left, while I was trying to decide whether to let him spend the night, Slade and I stood kissing barefoot under the veranda. As he stepped back to lean against a bamboo post that held up the *palapa* roof, he let out a high-pitched yelp and began dancing around on his tiptoes, moaning. When we both realized what had happened, I ran for a flashlight. On the concrete floor, a small scorpion sat poised and stiff, with her tail in the air. For the first time in fifteen summers in Puerto Escondido, he had been stung. As his tongue began to turn numb, we rushed down to the local late-night witch doctor. After looking at the swollen foot, the *brujo*, who had alcohol on his breath, prescribed half a cup of lime juice to be drunk quickly, and then he winked at me and told us to hurry, or Slade might die.

After several shots of lime juice at a roadside bar, the bartender assured us that death by scorpion is rare. Lime juice or no, he said, the swelling should go down overnight. Slade was already feeling better as we left a few pesos, slipped into the night, and walked down the dirt street. The palm trees above us whispered in the dark as Slade leaned against me, limping up the stairs to my room. Every few steps, the waves pounded below us and echoed off the cliffs like a mantra. I pressed my face against him and breathed in deeply, knowing that this moment, and all of the others that we shared in this powerful place, would carry me through until we could be together again. I couldn't help thinking that the scorpion, my astrological sign, had cast her spell. I was quite sure that this surfing accountant would not forget me.

After ten years, I recently returned to that same Mexican village. The surfer with the blond afro and I were celebrating our eighth wedding anniversary, and Zen and the boys were meeting us there. Before the trip, I went to Trader Joe's and bought two pounds of chocolate chips to bring with us. Although the town had grown and was now filled with surf video bars, bikini shops, and tourist restaurants, the spirit of the place was very much alive. Carmelita still made tamales in her outdoor kitchen, butter was sold in only a few specialty shops, chocolate chips were nowhere to be found, and the looks on the boys' faces as they ate my chocolate chip cookies on the dusty curb were just as priceless as they were ten years ago. The only difference? The moment the wind turned offshore, nobody stuck around to sweet-talk the baker.

In the afternoon, while my husband and his friends were surfing, I decided to revisit the bus station where I had first landed in Puerto Escondido. A bit lazier now, I took a cab and told the driver to drop me just beyond the station so I could walk a few blocks down Highway 200. Trucks honked, music blasted, and *tortillerías* filled the air with the aroma of sweet baked corn. With every bus that passed, I imagined that I saw my bus driver Juan as he was ten years before— wise, strong, and vulnerable, taking a young tourist girl under his wing. I hoped that he was living in a quiet house by the water, somewhere far from the highway, and that he had found his dream. In the salty warm air that was still so familiar, I thanked him for helping me find mine, just beyond the place where we said goodbye.

Katherine Hatch

Los Padres of Paraíso

"El respeto al derecho ajeno es la paz," said the great patriot Benito Juárez. Respect for the rights of others is peace. I learned those words when I crossed the border, a terrible and beautiful scar between two countries. I was leaving behind the United States to live and adapt to the rhythms of life on the other side. It was during the presidency of Richard Nixon; I was thirty-six years old.

One night more than three decades later, as I heard music in a garden and laughter, I realized those words still ring true, and I thought again how sweet life can be in Mexico. It was a perfect night, with bright stars and the air perfumed by blooming jasmine. The familiar musty aroma of black earth warmed all day by a tropical sun seeped from the ground, and there was no wind. When I heard the guitars and trumpets softly mellow at the end of a neighbor's party, I stepped out of my living room onto the terrace. As I listened in the darkness, I thought of how lucky I was. I wanted to wrap the music around me, along with the stars in the soft velvety night.

I live in Paraíso, a former Indian village with flowering trees and winding cobblestone streets that follow old footpaths through acres of palms and tropical fruit orchards. It's tucked away in a corner of a city, equidistant from the seedy state penitentiary and a luxurious country-club development and golf course. From a mile up in a cool pine forest, the town rolls down more than a thousand feet through fertile valleys to the *tierra caliente,* the hot land of the Tropic of Cancer, where roses are cultivated by the mile and barefoot boys sell fresh coconuts from the roadside.

Deep ravines, called *barrancas,* cut by rivers tumbling down the mountainsides for thousands of years, crisscross Paraíso. The *barrancas* have transformed driving across town into a ferocious contest. Motorists hurl themselves and their passengers at top speed down potholed switchbacks and around blind curves while the rosaries hanging from their rearview mirrors wildly swing this way and that. Someone told me the motto of one bus line was "Better dead than late." Occasionally, a car or a bus flies through the air and lands with a rolling crash into one of the *barrancas.* In towns, there are two kinds of pedestrians: the quick and the dead.

My view takes in the surrounding Sierra Madre and two snow-capped volcanoes, which are pictured on postcards and in books as lovely, serene, and harmless. The villagers used to picnic on their slopes, and families would crunch through the loose lava sand to stare into the crater of the taller one, Popocatepetl, which rises almost 18,000 feet. Its placid-picnic impression changed abruptly in 1994, when the peak awoke one morning, puffing smoke and throwing up ashes and burning rocks. It's been simmering and acting up from time to time ever since.

Across the street from my two-bedroom house of handmade, whitewashed adobe bricks is the little old Catholic church of San Miguel Arcángel, a neighborhood landmark with high, thick walls and a graceful bell tower. The original church was built by Franciscan friars who followed the Spanish conquistadors to Mexico in the 16th century. Despite changes over the centuries—the addition of electricity, windowpanes, and doors—the little church remains a simple, three-story, rectangular stone structure topped by a symmetrically sloping roof and a belfry where young boys tug the bell ropes to call worshippers and announce momentous events. The church occupies its own grassy yard at the end of a palm-lined walk. During most of its five hundred years, it was the gray color of old stones, splotched with patches of blackish-green moss. I liked to look at it and think about what it had been through. It wore its age with dignity until the 1980s, when some do-gooders decided it needed painting and chose canary yellow. I was happy to see the gray returning almost overnight, streaking its way to the surface before the yellow paint was dry.

It is obvious to everyone that the church was not built with Bingo in mind. It is spare to the point of torture, meant for the conversion of heathens and the hours of rigorous prayer necessary to keep them focused. Walls and floors are of solid stone, ensuring it is always cold inside. Straight-backed wooden pews form stiff rows on either side of the center aisle, and the kneeling boards are hardwood—no sissy, squishy cushions here. A stone altar—unadorned except for a costumed statue of San Miguel with his sword and a painted depiction of Jesus—commands attention at the front.

Side walls hold a half-dozen stone pedestals and niches, all but two vacant. My neighbor, Alma Mendez, said that years ago they all held figures of saints, but one by one the saints vanished, beginning with St. Francis, who was last seen wearing his brown woolen cassock with a poorly stuffed bluebird in his hand. How and when the saints disappeared still fuels local arguments with accusations against one priest or another as the likely culprit who sold them.

At any given moment, half of the parishioners are angry with the other half. Paraíso churchgoers are divided into those who are eager to "share the peace" with their neighbors, smile, hug, and sing the Mass in Spanish to strumming guitars and a tambourine, and people who want to say the Mass in Latin with no singing, no guitars, no tambourines, no touching for heaven's sake, and with the men and women on separate sides of the aisle, where God intended them to sit.

Whenever there was a really big fight, the losers would camp in the churchyard to stake their claim that whatever the disagreement or its eventual settlement, their way would have to be considered too. They would sit in the dust of the dry season, or in puddles of rain beneath sheets of plastic, or under woolen blankets they used to rig tents, cooking their beans and tortillas over open fires until they could regain control or reach an agreement. Sometimes, before either of those was possible, the police would come and toss out everyone, along with their bed rolls, clothes, pots and pans, half-eaten tortillas, and simmering beans.

Police have been called a few times to rescue a priest from the people, even though no one in Mexico ever wants to call the police, not even in life-threatening situations. The "men in blue" are often suspicious brutes—poorly educated, poorly trained, poorly paid, poorly supervised, and very aggressive. Bad combination. The last time they were called to Paraíso, a mob of about fifty had gathered outside the church, demanding to see the priest, Padre Mateo—a young man from the southern state of Chiapas, where he had ministered mostly to indigenous inhabitants. He had darker skin than most of the priests around here, and he was a friend to everyone—Catholics, Protestants, nonbelievers, fanatics, light browns, dark browns, Asians, whites—he always had a smile and time to listen.

One spring afternoon on my way home from shopping, I saw villagers gathering outside the church. It wasn't time for Mass, so I strolled across the street to find out what was going on. Before I reached the churchyard, words came to me from the babble of the ever-growing crowd: "Scandalous," and "intolerable," and the worst, *"sin verguenza"* (shameless). Word was flying through the village that Padre Mateo's housekeeper, a quiet woman with a pretty, round face and soft footsteps, had become his legal wife, and many parishioners were in an uproar. Calmer souls, hanging back on the fringes of the crowd, wondered why he didn't continue living with her and keep the curtains closed.

Someone pitched a small rock at the church's double doors. It was a half-hearted toss, as though the thrower had a change of mind halfway through the windup. But the small sound it made echoed in the church, and it was enough to send the sacristan, fearful in the darkness within, hurrying to the back to inform the priest, who was seeing parishioners in the free clinic. The *padre* told him not to worry, he would look into it. But in a state of panic, the sacristan did the unthinkable. He called the police.

When two beat-up patrol cars arrived twenty minutes later, everyone feared the worst. The collective intake of breath sucked half of the air out of the churchyard. The crowd by then had picked up a couple of balloon salesmen, vendors of steamed bananas and ice cream bars, and three adolescent girls in dresses emblazoned with Coca-Cola who were handing out small plastic cups of Coke. There was always a crowd for anything free, and people jostled one another to reach the head of the Coke line. The police, who looked like sullen teenagers in their wrinkled uniforms and scuffed black shoes, scowled at everyone as they climbed out of their cars. They shoved people out of their way with their nightsticks, looking bored and eager to hit someone. They stopped in front of the closed church doors, whispering among themselves and glaring at the assembled crowd until one of them pounded his stick against the antique door and demanded entry. The door opened, and all four police sauntered through single file before it banged shut behind them.

Nothing happened while the crowd waited and time ticked. Five, ten, fifteen minutes passed, and the people drawn to the drama gradually took on a festive air, as though they were on a day off, a vacation. They bought chocolate-covered ice cream bars for their families, Coca-Cola for themselves, balloons for the babies, and steamed bananas for anyone who wanted them. They talked among themselves and laughed, exchanging jokes and gossip. We didn't know it then, but the priest had phoned the bishop, and they spoke for about ten minutes. He and the bishop got along well, but what they said remains private to this day.

Suddenly, the doors flew open and the crowd hushed. Padre Mateo emerged, smiling, followed by his police escorts. He gave a big, Nixon-style, double-arm "V" wave to the crowd, made the sign of the cross to everyone in general, and, still smiling, climbed into the back seat of one of the police cars. The driver and his partner got into the front seat and slammed the doors. The motor refused to start at first, much to the crowd's amusement. People whistled and laughed out loud. After a few tries, the motor started and both cars chugged away. The priest leaned forward, waving to us behind the closed window. We later heard he and his housekeeper were living happily in a thatched house in Tabasco, a steamy Gulf state below the slope of the Yucatán peninsula—about as far as they could get from Paraíso.

Were they married? Was it true or a rumor? No one knew except the bishop, and he was the only person who wouldn't talk. Conservatives said Padre Mateo had been removed because he was too liberal. Liberals thought he had been removed because he was too married. In the end, the truth didn't matter. Enough people thought he was married; he had to leave.

The next priest was a conservative sent down from Monterrey, a northern city known for its chilly climate, its industry, and the stinginess of its inhabitants. Padre Marcos was tall and light skinned, with a mouth that was straight and thin as a pencil. His wire-rimmed spectacles seemed to go with his whining, nasal voice, and his first official words did not make anyone love him:

"There will be no, I repeat *no*, drinking of alcoholic beverages by the men of Paraíso during the village fiestas this year. There are no, I repeat *no*, exceptions to this rule." He made a quick sign of the cross and, without looking at anyone, he sat down and stared at the tips of his shiny black shoes. The silence was deafening in a vacuum of disbelief, then voices broke out from parishioners:

"What?"

"No drinking at the fiestas? The man is insane!"

"What did he say? What??!!"

"He said no alcohol beverages! Never!"

"He will never last. . . . "

As the murmurs rose and filled the church, the calls and questions raced up the aisles and erupted in a shocked chorus of "No! No!" that rolled from the ancient altar to burst through the church doors. Children riding their bicycles in the churchyard heard the cries and thought they were meant for them—they'd been scolded before for making noise during the Mass. They headed home as fast as they could pedal.

It was no coincidence that the most important fiesta of the year, the one honoring San Miguel Arcángel, was due to begin in a few weeks. Regardless of what else happened during the year, everyone looked to the fiesta to redeem themselves with a lot of praying and celebrating in the name of San Miguel. They knew the fiesta would be glorious and happy and beautiful, and that they would have fun. No one believed Padre Marcos would follow through on his pledge. A fiesta without alcohol? It was sacrilegious. Was this priest out of his mind?

The following Sunday, he said he was not out of his mind.

"There has been too much drinking during our sacred fiestas," he said. "I must stop it, and I will stop it. The dancers and the musicians must learn to entertain us, dance their dance, play their music, without entering an inebriated state. This is the first rule of my new Moral Code, but I see great things for it. Some day, everyone in Mexico will live in a completely sober and moral state forever."

"Is the new *padre* moving to another state?" a deaf woman in the front row loudly asked her neighbor. The idea was picked up, magnified, heads turning, people smiling as they passed along the words to their friends.

"Yes, he's going somewhere, another state, Puebla or Guerrero, I suppose," the neighbor said.

A smile filled the face of her hard-of-hearing companion. "And such a nice young man," she said.

As soon as the bells tolled, announcing the end of Mass, people poured into the churchyard and gathered in small, agitated knots to talk about Padre Marcos and how they could derail his plan for Paraíso abstinence. It wouldn't be easy. Surely, the new *padre* knew how important the fiesta was for San Miguel Arcángel.

Every year, at five o'clock in the morning on September 29, the fiesta for the saint's day began with skyrockets that thundered like bombs. Lest anyone go back to sleep, these were followed by tolling, clanging church bells calling people to a special Mass. The grand celebration ended a week or ten days later, depending on the local economy, with a thirty-foot-tall fireworks display, dancing in the streets, and screaming children pursued by a papier-mâché bull—a *torito* spouting fire. From start to finish throughout the celebrations, there was scarcely a minute of silence, and streets around the church were filled with celebrants. People came when they could and left when they had to in a constant stirring of dust in the streets, with the sound of happy voices calling, laughing, swearing, joking, singing in the night.

The people most affected by the *padre*'s edict—besides the village drunks—were the Chinelo dancers and their accompanying musicians. The masked dancers in long velvet robes and high headdresses were famous for their spirited dancing and music—an accelerated jiggling two-step to a jerky-jivey rhythm. No one could imagine how they would be able to dance for hours at a stretch without something to keep them going—beer, tequila, *mezcal*, even *pulque*—the crude, nasty-smelling potion that had to be consumed the first day, before fermentation caused the bottle cap to blow off.

"What kind of priest would ban liquor from the fiesta of San Miguel?" Don Ángel angrily demanded the next day when I saw him in the street. "What has happened to our church? Doesn't he know that we Mexicans, dancers and musicians, have been raising toasts to the gods since before the Catholics showed up around here? Who are they to tell us what we can and cannot do? And we're running out of time!"

It seemed the fiesta was doomed to silence, or to sobriety, which many people thought was worse. Then, wonder of wonders, another priest, Padre Lucas, turned up on a Saturday before the fiesta started. He was tall and handsome and seemed serious, with a deep frown line between his black eyes. He said it was more than all right for the men of Paraíso to drink while they were performing for God and San Miguel, that it was their sacred duty. He didn't just say that. He wrote it out and read it in a clear, strong voice outside the church doors on Sunday morning. Then he stuck it to one of the doors with a silver thumbtack. Padre Lucas looked older then Padre Marcos, and he gave everyone hope, which is what priests are supposed to do. But the joy of his message was diminished when someone, probably a reformed drunk, tore down his decree, stole the thumbtack, and left a note that said because Padre Lucas was not associated with San Miguel church, he had no standing to issue a yes-drink opinion in the first place—which was true.

At this crucial moment, an attractive widow with a taste for tight dresses and handsome men saw her opportunity, and she took it. She told Padre Lucas she would be happy to turn her house into a church if that would resolve the neighborhood's problem. She had two houses, she explained; the elegant one was on the fiesta parade route. The other, where she could live, was around the corner. Her elegant house already contained a variety of old brass altarpieces, candelabra, large single candlesticks, and angel figures, as well as plenty of expensive furniture and Oriental rugs—all of which could create a very luxurious church.

"How about it, Padre Lucas?" she asked, smiling coyly up at him.

He looked down her low-cut blouse, and his mind was made up. "Thank you very much for your generosity," he told the widow, "I'm sure you will be rewarded one day." He bowed low and kissed her hand.

Because Padre Lucas now had a church in Paraíso, his authority was no longer challenged. The crisis was averted. The fiesta went on as planned and, as usual, with plenty to drink.

When it was time to consecrate the new church, the choice was easy. Because the oldest, most important church in Paraíso was named for San Miguel Arcángel, it was obvious to everyone that the new church should bear the same name. Padre Lucas and the widow agreed with that simple logic. The *padre* telephoned the bishop to ask for his blessing.

"Don't be in such a hurry," the bishop said. "There are papers to sign. Give me the address, and I'll be over." He opened the door of his study and saw a young priest standing in the hallway. "You!" the bishop called, motioning the young man toward him. "Call me a taxi and accompany me. I'm off to see a rich widow."

They pulled up in front of the widow's house, and the driver and priest raced each other to open the door for the bishop, then jostled to ring the bell at the gate. The gate swung open, and the bishop entered. The beautiful widow was there in a turquoise dress to greet him.

"My dear," he said, looking her up and down with a surprised smile, "it is indeed a pleasure." He followed her through the garden and to her house, where Padre Lucas greeted the bishop.

"This isn't going to be difficult to do, is it?" the *padre* asked.

"No," the bishop replied. "I came to meet this lovely and generous woman, who is giving us our new church. We could have signed these papers at my office." Now the bishop gave his blessing, and they all signed the papers. The widow summoned a uniformed maid, who brought three small antique glasses of chilled tequila, and they drank to the health of the new church and the glory of God.

It was done. The new church, formerly the attractive widow's elegant home, was named for the old church, San Miguel Arcángel. The widow moved into her house around the corner, and within a week, her former home became known to one and all as the church of *El Otro*—"The Other"—San Miguel Arcángel.

Camille Cusumano

Las Garzas de San Blas

I had heard that *Playboy* magazine called San Blas a dump, not worth the effort it took to get there. So I made a beeline for that Pacific coast fishing village, located not far north of the fleshpots of Puerto Vallarta. It sounded like just the place for me—low key, authentically Mexican, not overrun with tourists, and a bit time-warped.

It was January 1977, and I was twenty-five. The last six months of my life had been submerged in several centuries of French culture as I crammed to pass exams for my master's in French at San Francisco State University. I looked forward to returning to my senses with the fire of chilies, tequila, Latin sun, and men. I would doze under palm fronds to my heart's desire before I spread my wings for the flyway of life.

I made my nest at the Flamingos, a cheap, sturdy, hundred-year-old hotel on Calle Juárez. A faded reproduction of Our Lady of Guadalupe in my beamed-ceiling room watched over my dreams. The

129

weathered lodging, a former German consulate, was across from the remains of a 19th-century customs house—both of which spoke to San Blas's glory days. The village was once a port center of trade with Spanish galleons passing through. Henry Wadsworth Longfellow's poem "The Bells of San Blas" was inspired by the chimes of a crumbling church now claimed by banana trees.

Adjacent to the morning market—where the flies outnumbered the people and the odors outnumbered the flies—stood the decaying old Templo de San Blas (circa 1810). Constructed of stone and wood, the church is a place of worship as much for faithful humans as it is for fungi and termites. Right next to it, the never-completed newer one—La Apostólica Romana de San Blas, also in decline—stood valiantly like a metaphor for the never fully conquered spirituality of Mexico.

Everything of consequence happened twice daily in this town long governed by sun and sea. The blood-thirsty *jejenes*—mosquitoes the size of poppy seeds—were active in the morning and again in early evening; great-tailed grackles darkened the trees on Calle Juárez and around the plaza then, raising their chatter by noticeable decibels; and most important for someone coming down off her intellectual jag, the Mexicans and the gringos gathered around the town square to practice age-old courtship rituals.

It didn't take me long to deduce that I lacked the essential plumage among the migratory birds: blond hair. Whether trailer-park or cover-girl grade, blond locks were the draw for the *muy guapo* dudes. Which was fine with me. Dead Frenchmen still occupied my brain, leaving my tongue less agile in the small talk that leads to romance.

Besides, there were few secrets in tiny San Blas, and any amorous intercourse was fodder for public consumption.

I felt free to cultivate something less fleeting: friendship. When the *jejenes* bit and the grackles chattered, I gravitated toward the plaza and slowly met the in-crowd. I took pleasure in listening to the guys—Pepe, Hector, Pancho, Fernando, Carlos, Caballo, Julio—pepper their speech (Spanish and fluent English) with American slang.

I met Fernando, whose family owned the *farmacia* where I bought coconut cream and turtle oil for the beach. Gentle and polished, he was dating Lynette from New Zealand, and the word on the street was that he loved to wine and dine her. His sister dated Caballo (which means "horse"), whose real name was Helio. Caballo was only twenty-two and was studying to be an economic lawyer. The first night I met him, he was drunk on homemade tequila and told me he was one of ten children.

"Put it there," I said, extending my hand. "So am I."

"My mother started havin' kids at thirteen," he said.

"Mine started at nineteen," I said.

"Mine had nineteen kids," he said, "but nine of them died."

I couldn't match that.

And there was handsome Julio, who was tall, with long muscular arms, and said "yep" a lot. He liked to kibitz with gringos and asked every one of us, "I look like Gregory Peck, don't I?" He did, but I said, "No, you're much more handsome." One morning he thrust a copy of *Psychology Today* at me—he knew that I had been a psych undergrad.

"Read the story on Plato's Retreat," he urged, a profile of a then-popular public sex venue in New York City. The article, by Sam

Keen, talked of the Love Generation aspiring to have soulmates with whom they could have a communion of "head, heart, and genitals." I wondered if that was what I wanted from life. I never learned what Julio thought of that heady piece—he was always on the run, tending to some mysterious business. But I later learned that he had an earthy side to him too—finding, for a fee, women to sleep with local fishermen.

One morning, I was lying on the surfing beach, Matanchén Bay, reading Katzantzakis, how Zorba the Greek calls his penis the key to paradise, when Carlos appeared. He was the owner of El Mezcalito, a thatched-roof bar, and I admired his radiant, ivory smile and long, curling lashes.

"How's the surf?" I asked, knowing well how bad it was.

"Not very good, it's been bad all year."

"Where did you learn English?"

"I spent a year in San Leandro, near San Francisco, with my aunt, who is married to an American. How do you like San Blas?"

"I wish I could stay."

"Why don't you?"

"Well . . . I feel responsible to people up North, but I know I'd come back."

"Could you live here?"

"For a while, but I would crave those things I left in the city." He was silent, and I went on too long about how we city folk tended to complicate our lives. "I've been conditioned a certain way, you know. I need intellectual stimulation, a movie, play, more education." He listened so raptly that I said, "I can't tell if you understand me."

"Yes, I know what you mean. I live here all my life."

"And you never get bored?"

"No! Never! I can always find something to do. Surfin', soccer, runnin' on the beach. You have the sun and sea always—and good food."

"Yes," I agreed. "I could live off your pineapple, coconut, mangoes, papayas." I made a face of ecstasy and we laughed together. I regretted that he was claimed by a Canadian—a blond.

"But don't you ever want to do anything else with your life?" I asked.

"No. I'm happy now. Maybe someday I gonna get a sailboat and sail."

"I envy you."

"Nah! You can stay here too," he said as he lifted his red surfboard and left me to ponder my state of postgrad, precareer limbo.

As I sat and read, I noticed a man and his little girl approach my spot. The man looked out over the bay with binoculars.

"*Qué ve usted,* what do you see?" I asked idly.

"*Las garzas,*" he told me—herons. The leggy, long-necked fowl congregated on a rocky outcropping just offshore. Then he said very casually, "*¿Te gusta marijuana?*" Before I could answer, he said in English, "Come tomorrow at 11:00 AM here." He whispered, "*Tengo veinte kilos.*" His little girl's eyes studied mine with great interest. "Bring your friends," he continued. "There is plenty of *mota* for all of them." Set up or not, I told him I wasn't interested. He insisted I come, bring my friends. I wondered how much his little girl understood as they backed away.

Evenings, I went to El Mezcalito's. One night I sat at the bar and ordered a coco loco—acrid, tequila-laced coconut milk served in a coconut shell. Idilio, the manager of one of the hotels, sat next to me. He was married with five children, and everyone, surely even his wife, knew that he had a girlfriend. At the reception desk of the hotel he managed, he kept a large framed photograph of Pope John Paul II, with the words "my beloved holy father" emblazoned across the frame. We chatted about his family, and he spoke of them like a loyal husband and proud father. The jukebox was blasting Lynyrd Skynyrd's "Free Bird." All of a sudden, I realized that in the background, where gringos and Mexicans were dancing, several of the male patrons were armed with automatic rifles. They had begun to systematically frisk every male in the place. They came toward Idilio, who said, "Excuse me," and stood up to be patted down even as he kept on talking to me about his family.

"It happens all the time," he assured me. "They search for weapons." The police were dressed casually, in jeans and T-shirts, and after they had done their job, they stood around, looking harmless and bored.

The Rolling Stones' "Beast of Burden" played as I nursed my tropical drink and took in the barfly gossip: Julio had tried to sell yet another young woman to a fisherman at the Playa Borrego; he had turned down the advances of a frosted blond, an actress on the American soaps, and everyone speculated as to why; Hector had been swept off his feet by a fair-haired Aussie in town in just two days; and Caballo was not allowed to see Fernando's sister until he quit drinking.

Idilio left, and Pepe took his barstool next to me and ordered a *cerveza*. He sang to himself, "I never be your beast of burden," and I chuckled to myself. I had mainly known Pepe as the aloof manager at the Flamingos. A few days earlier, he seemed as silently amused as I was by a loud, short Brooklynite, Boomer, who sat in the Flamingos' courtyard, detailing for everyone the nature of his *turista*— "Hehr-shey squehrts," he described.

"Do you get tired of all the gringos?" I asked Pepe.

"Oh no, I like them—they bring fresh blood for the *jejenes*."

Of all the guys, I liked Pepe best. He hid behind an unkempt tangle of curly brown hair and Siamese cat eyes. Although he could party like the rest, he had a serious, retiring side, an artistic temperament. He made beautiful line drawings and airbrushed T-shirts with materials supplied to him by a gringo. I asked him if he dated Mexican women, and he said it had been a long time. He didn't have a girlfriend now. Then he said, to my surprise, "I'm tired of being a machine. I see people come and go, and I get cold. You don't really know me, and I don't really know you," he said. I was touched by his blunt sharing, and behind these pronouncements I sensed losses, but I didn't press him.

I admired how Pepe took care of his close friend, Hector, whom he referred to as "Squirt" or *"mi hijito,"* my little son. Hector, who was irrepressibly childlike with his gleaming, gold-framed front teeth, brought out the old-soul Pepe. I gathered that Hector's susceptibility to the fair gringas was a concern (indeed, a year later, Hector was married to a very pregnant Minnesotan—who was "pretty sure" that Hector was the father).

The torrid days melted seamlessly into each other, distinguished only by some delightful discovery I might make in my wandering—the little bakery where I bought empanadas filled with coconut cream or pineapple. I lived simply on coffee and papaya in the morning, a seething slab of chili lime–spiked jicama from a street vendor during the day, and one full meal at night at one of the restaurants: Amparo's, Diligencia, Torino's, Las Islas. I found their simple interpretations of the fresh local shrimp, oysters, lobster, red snapper, pampano, or butterfish to be revelations worthy of *The Book of Gastronomy*.

In a matter of weeks, I had fulfilled my own prophesy to Carlos. I needed a stimulation not available at El Mezcalito's or on the beach; I returned to San Francisco. But I was met with disappointment: I failed to nail one of three spots in Stanford's French doctoral program. I found a job I liked on a French publication but had to cocktail waitress at night to pay down debt. I was thrilled when Pepe and Hector, traveling to the States like Mexican Huck Finns, visited me briefly that summer, when I lived in the Haight-Ashbury. I introduced my friend Deborah to Hector. The chemistry wasn't quite right, but by winter, she and I, both uncertain about our futures, headed south of the border. Several long bus rides through the state of Chihuahua and we were in San Blas, where little had changed except for a wave of new gringos. The grackles and the *jejenes* and the plaza hummed on schedule. The unfinished church was still in a protracted state of decay. The *mercado* pulsed. El Mezcalito's was a den of alleged scandal in progress. Matanchén Bay throbbed with surfers. *Las garzas* held court on their rocks.

Little children played in the packed-dirt streets. Young people went on giving their hearts away in the square. Deborah gave hers to lanky, hood-eyed, and sad-faced Pancho, whom everyone called Champion. I gave mine, like before, to everyone and everything.

On our first Sunday, a day that was always festive, the village emptied as Matanchén Bay became carpeted with Mexican families. At the plaza, a dozen of us squeezed into someone's car and drove the five miles to the beach, laughing all the way. Julio bought freshly caught shark from a fisherman, and Hector and Pepe roasted it on a grill under a *palapa*. Breaking off pieces of the succulent flesh with fingers, everyone shared in a communion that reminded me of those best of times, simple and spontaneous, in my own family. As I watched the ingenious Mexicans stave off the afternoon attack of sand fleas by burning green coconut husks, I thought this was the communion I longed for, not the one described by Sam Keen. I watched beachgoers throw back *cerveza* after *cerveza* and shrimp cocktails in the shade of grass-hut canopies or under *palapas*. I drank Presidente brandy. The party revved. Life felt good, contained, in the present tense.

I went for a swim in the warm bay, then felt the need for solitude.

"I'm going to walk back to town," I announced to Pepe.

He made such a hissing sound, I got chills. He said, "Are you crazy? You can't walk!"

"Of course I can walk." I was taken aback but stood my ground.

"Listen to me, it's dangerous!" His narrow black eyes raged with some inexplicable fire, and his usually impassive countenance became disturbingly restive.

"I can walk if I want to," I said calmly. I had loved these Latin men who treated me as a peer.

"Eets dangerous, you don't know!" I knew he was upset with his accent more emphasized. My madness rippled through the throng—*She wants to what? Walk home?!* Julio, Hector, Pancho, and Carlos bore down on me, saying I absolutely could not walk. I'd be totally *loca*. But when I asked why, not one of them would say. I had ridden over the route several dozen times in the bus, and it seemed perfectly pastoral and harmless.

We piled into the car back to town. Everyone went to El Mezcalito's for more beers and margaritas. I said goodnight and went to bed early. I was wide awake at 6:30 AM. The sun was bright. A chambermaid's disco music sounded reveille from a boom box. I stuffed my net bag with a book, towel, and lotion and slipped into long, gauzy pants to protect me from the *jejenes*. I covered my head with a paisley scarf and left a note for Deborah, who was asleep in Pancho's arms. I started down San Blas's only paved road to Matanchén Bay. Two or three vehicles passed, their occupants yelling something in Spanish.

San Blas was practically an island, with liquid boundaries on all sides—ocean, lagoons, or mangrove swamp. On my first trip there, I glided in a motorized *panga* through San Cristóbal, one of the jungle-smothered estuaries. It crawled with crocodiles, coati (which look like a cross between raccoon and anteater), iguanas, and geckoes. More than three hundred species of birds flitted through mangrove, coral vine, gumbo limbo, and soft-shell fig trees. I watched crows drop from their roost the fruit of a sour custard tree, feeding turtles below. I saw swarms of dragonflies, butterflies the color of papaya, and carnivorous plants that awaited flies. I knew that just beyond the tropical lowland I was walking through, there was habitat where I would be prey to predators. But I felt content on the unshaded macadam, even as it began to boil.

I never saw where he came from. He was just there all of a sudden, slowly pedaling his bicycle. I was deep in thought.

"*¡Hola!*" I blurted out, so startled by the presence of the man, who had a thick pelt of shiny black hair.

"*Hola,*" he said calmly.

"*Hola, señor. ¿Cómo estás . . . hoy?*" I repeated, trying to hide my slipped composure. *Where were the cars now?* I thought.

"*¿Adonde vas, señorita?*"

"*A la playa, señor.*"

He peered at me through unblinking eyes so dark I didn't dare hold his stare for long. He asked if I lived in Mexico. I said no.

"Climb on my bike, señorita. I'll take you to the beach," he ordered cordially enough. His Spanish was a strange, musical dialect, of which I understood about half. His diction was not that of Pepe and friends. "Oh, no, no," I laughed hoarsely. The clunker certainly could have carried us both.

"I love to walk . . . *me gusta mucho caminar,*" I said, sweat dripping from under my scarf.

My pulse quickened as I searched my repertoire for diversionary conversation until we reached the beach—which seemed so distant. Was this the unpronounceable danger my friends warned me of?

He asked my name and I told him. His was Rogelio.

Silence again. He stared. He jumped off his bike and walked alongside me, his two hands on the handlebars. He adapted his gait to mine, which was brisk, economical, and straightforward. An observer might've thought we were in competition.

With a start, I noticed a machete as long as one of his legs swinging from his belt. I hugged my net bag to my torso.

"Ah, sí, me gusta caminar," I repeated. I babbled on in broken Spanish how in America, I run four miles every day, but here it is *mucho calor*, so I walk only. I walk fast, very fast, because it pleases me. *"Me gusta caminar rapido."*

Rogelio smiled. He asked a few questions. After each, I said, *"¿Cómo?"* He might have been asking me to walk more *despacio*, slowly, which I ignored. I also said *"Claro que sí"* a lot. He asked how old I was, where I was from. Whether I was married. Yes, I lied, very married, and I even produced a left hand with a banded finger. He adjusted his machete, and I swallowed hard. I answered in the present tense, because I knew the present tense best in Spanish. I felt very present and tense.

"Your husband, where is he?"

"He's waiting for me at the beach. Yes, he's definitely there waiting for me. He doesn't like to walk, so I walk alone."

We passed a full set of clothes on the roadside—pants, shirt, *huaraches*, and straw hat lying next to a half-empty bottle of liquor. I wondered where the owner of the clothes was.

I asked Rogelio if he lived in San Blas and was dismayed when he said no. He pointed beyond the jungle. No, he didn't know Pepe, Pancho, Hector, Carlos. . . . He picked oranges. I glanced behind us at the clothes on the road and then at his. They were of similar style. I asked if he were married, and he said no.

"*¿Una novia?*" Surely he had a sweetheart—that would make for good conversation.

No, no girlfriend. And then he said something that translated in my ears as "Mexican women, you know, are not as easy as Americans."

His look was unsettling. I picked up the pace, and at times he had to run to keep up with me. The machete kept swinging, its blade slicing the air like a third arm. He remained oblivious to it, but I kept the distance between his hand and the menacing blade in my peripheral vision.

"Does señor hablas ingles? Even *un poco?*" I pressed. Smiling almost devilishly, he said, "Not even *un poquito.*"

"Haven't you met Americans before?" I asked. He said no, that I was the first one. He said he lived with his parents and that he was thirty years old.

"Do you want a girlfriend?" I asked, sloppily. He of course construed this to mean I was asking if he wanted my help—or me, even.

"Yes, very much," he answered eagerly. "Do you have one for me?" I assumed he was asking to meet a girlfriend of mine and said yes. "*Sí, señor,* I have a friend." His eyes widened. I meant to say *amiga,* but it came out masculine, *amigo.*

"You have a boyfriend too, at the beach? You mean it's not your husband?"

"No, no, there is my husband and our *amigo,* and an *amiga.*" He looked bewildered. *What doesn't he get?*

"Your husband will want to fight me?" *What don't I get?*

"No, he's a nice guy. *Un hombre de honor.*" My voice quavered with exhaustion. We probably had a mile and a half to go. No cars had passed. The beach was so far away.

"*Entonces,* you will give me a woman?" he said. I changed the topic, tried to talk about the weather—a subject on which I could converse eloquently in Spanish.

"How much money will she want?" he persisted.

"Money?" I thought of Julio.

"*Sí.*"

Despairing, I answered, "*Nada.*" But I sensed his skepticism growing. How could I give him a woman—for free no less—if my husband and another male were there?

"What about you and me, señora?" he asked slyly.

"Oh, don't be silly!" I laughed as if I were turning down a generous offer on his part. "*Mi marido,*" I pointed to my ring. But if I were the type who was willing to sell a friend, why would I have respect for a marriage vow?

"*Quiero una americana,* I want an American woman," he said firmly and unequivocally.

"*Hay un problema,*" I answered weakly. There is one problem. I didn't have a woman for him.

The sun pummeled me. Sweat flowed from my turban. "*Hace mucho calor,*" I tried.

"*Sí.*" He had finally conceded to talk of weather. His machete bumped the spokes of his bike, and he adjusted it. My heart beat so fast, I felt dizzy. "Eets toooo dangerous!" ran through my mind to the tune of "I told you so."

He repeated his request for a woman, and I said, *"No comprendo, señor."* A pregnant silence followed.

"Do you care to rest a bit?" he asked.

"Well no, my husband—my *husband*—is waiting."

"Just a few minutes, señora. It won't matter a great deal."

The heat was fierce, but I was losing my cool. He wouldn't take his gaze off me now.

"Let's rest, just *un momento*. I insist, señora," he said. All I needed was a cloud—not a rest—to block the sun and I could outrun him and that swordlike appendage of his.

Suddenly, everything did seem cloudy; my legs were completely rubber. I was leaning back on a pile of hay, staring up in the cool shade of friendly faces. I had run and jumped on the flatbed of the old bus to Matanchén Bay. I saw, through glazed eyes, my good friend Deborah.

"Sister woman," she addressed me by the salutation we started using for each other after watching *Cat on a Hot Tin Roof*, "you're nuts walking in this sun."

"Where's the guy with the machete?" I asked.

"Who?" she asked. My pulse was still racing. "We almost couldn't get the bus driver to stop," she said, "but I guess he felt sorry for you, the way you were running to catch him."

"How far are we from the beach?" I asked.

"Not far," she said. "See right up ahead, where that guy on the bike is turning left? It's just beyond."

There he was, pumping his clunker with his machete at his side. Had he abandoned his hope for *una americana,* or would he continue to search?

I thought of the endings this episode could have had and trea-sured my friends more than they knew. I realized that although they used expressions like "bummer," "dude," "friggin'," and "out of sight" as if they were weaned on American slang, they couldn't quite convey to me the lurking danger of the isolated backwoodsmen. I never told them or anyone about the stranger for years—it gave me a creepy feeling.

Weeks later, Deborah and I stood waiting for our bus in front of the unfinished church. "Forty more years until it's done," said Pepe as he handed me a going-away gift—an ink drawing that he had done, called *Isla de las Garzas* and signed *"para mi amiga Camille, Pepe."* It was a beautiful rendering of the herons at Matanchén Bay, a faint tequila sunrise (or sunset) igniting it from behind.

I framed the drawing and kept it with me through nearly two dozen moves spread over thousands of miles, meanwhile chasing career goals, finding love, losing love. I wouldn't have guessed that it would be twenty-seven years before I saw those herons again. Return-ing for a long overdue visit to San Blas (still dodged by most tour-ists), I called Pepe. We met in the square. He had changed little—his hair was longer. He filled me in on the mostly married gang (Hector to a second blond in Seattle). Pancho, married with a daughter, ran the automotive shop down from the now upscale Flamingos (which was beautifully renovated with marble bathrooms, tiled courtyard, garden, and pool). Pepe had married and divorced a woman from Washington, and he had a twenty-three-year-old son—his age when we met. Not surprisingly, Pepe was best of friends with his ex-wife and her husband. He had a girlfriend whose name—Digna de Virgen de Guadalupe—translated to "worthy of the virgin of Guadalupe." He called her Lupita. Would he marry again? "When the church is finished," he said.

Although damage from the 2002 Hurricane Kenna was visible in the decaying or abandoned buildings (but not the churches—they stood solid), there was a lingering sweetness in San Blas. I found yet another layer of it—in the birds. In two days' time, with the help of a local guide, Armando Santiago Navarrete, I logged fifty-seven species, including many along the jungle lagoon. They were always there, but before, I had lacked the ocular device to see them. I felt great to be back in San Blas, jump-starting a new life list.

Kathy Jo Brisker

Día de Mi Madre

After an exhausting day of travel from LAX to OAX, my father and I finally arrived at Casa Panchita. We had come for Día de los Muertos (Day of the Dead) to honor and build an altar for my mother, who had died the year before.

Driving along the narrow cobblestone road of the Xochimilco neighborhood of Oaxaca, the taxi driver stopped in front of a large metal gate in the center of a tall stucco wall. Although it was dark outside and there were no lights to see by, my father's hand instinctively found the bell high up on the left side of the gate. He pressed the buzzer, and Alejandro, a small man with a dark mustache and smiling eyes, let us in. He welcomed me like family—and in a way, I was.

As Alejandro helped us with our bags and showed us to our rooms, we were greeted by aromas from the kitchen. Mingling with the smell of warm tortillas and chilies was the rich aroma of chocolate. Panchita came out of the kitchen to welcome us and smiled as she embraced my father. Glancing at me from the corner of her eye, she told him in Spanish that I looked like *"la señora."* I knew that she meant my mother and was unable to speak. My first words to Panchita were the tears in my eyes.

Born in Brooklyn, New York, and the daughter of Jewish immigrants from Romania, my mother had a Mexican soul. Her exodus from the East Coast brought her to California, where she settled down and raised my two brothers and me. My own childhood was filled with travels throughout Mexico. Every few years, with Mexico City as our base, we would drive across the country—from the villages on the Pacific coast to the towns and pueblos in between; from Guanajuato and Pátzcuaro to Cuernavaca and Taxco.

With each visit to our southern neighbor, the spirit of the land seeped deeper into my mother's heart. The people of Mexico sometimes mistook her for a *mexicana*. When I was seven years old and we were returning to the States after our winter vacation in Mazatlán—having stayed in what was then the only hotel on the beach—the border patrol didn't want to let my mother across. With her black hair and olive complexion, her dangling silver earrings and brightly embroidered blouse, they questioned my father about the Mexican woman he was bringing into the United States. (Only after they let her pass were we able to laugh about it, and the incident found a place in our family lore.)

The bright colors of Mexico ignited a deep and lifelong passion in my mother. She painted the trims and accents of our home in Los Angeles to reflect these rich Mexican colors. Opening the boldly painted yellow front door of our Spanish-style stucco house, visitors would be greeted by a deep purple wall in the entrance hall. Her dress was always colorful: oranges and reds and pinks. And purple, which was her favorite. The noted Mexican architect Ricardo Legorreta, a colleague of my father and a friend to our family, made the observation that my mother didn't wear brightly colored clothes. Rather, she wore color—just as his country, and the walls of his prized buildings, wore color. As the monarch butterfly migrates yearly to the mountains of Mexico, my mother returned every year to gather the colors into herself and spread her wings with their hue.

My father, also the child of Eastern European immigrants, discovered and nurtured another connection to Mexico apart from the one he and my mother were drawing into themselves. In the latter part of the 19th century, when my father's parents emigrated from Lithuania and settled in Pennsylvania, my grandparents' cousins made a parallel voyage to the New World, settling in Mexico City. Sharing their common roots, my father and his Mexican cousins continue to extend the branches of their family tree across the border to each other.

Long after I decided I was too old for family vacations, my mother and father continued their visits to Mexico—to explore, to work, and to visit their Mexican cousins. Eventually they discovered Casa Panchita, a place that wove them into the fabric of Oaxaca. Panchita, arguably the best cook in a state celebrated for its food, lives at the guesthouse, which was founded as a girls' summer camp more than forty years ago, with her two daughters, her son-in-law, and two grandsons. My mother fell in love with Panchita and her family, and Oaxaca became her second home—the home she carried in her heart—and she would always tell me that I should come, how happy I would be there.

Collecting both her stories of Oaxaca and the crafts she brought back for me after each trip, I folded Oaxaca into a corner of my own heart. But my life had taken a different direction, and it took me thirty years after I first stuck my toe in the river to return for full immersion. Picking up the tether she released with her death, I carried it with me back to Oaxaca. I was now the chrysalis, returning for the wings my mother had shed with her passing.

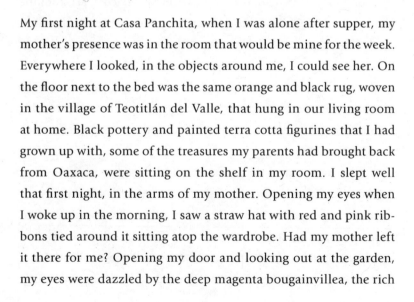

My first night at Casa Panchita, when I was alone after supper, my mother's presence was in the room that would be mine for the week. Everywhere I looked, in the objects around me, I could see her. On the floor next to the bed was the same orange and black rug, woven in the village of Teotitlán del Valle, that hung in our living room at home. Black pottery and painted terra cotta figurines that I had grown up with, some of the treasures my parents had brought back from Oaxaca, were sitting on the shelf in my room. I slept well that first night, in the arms of my mother. Opening my eyes when I woke up in the morning, I saw a straw hat with red and pink ribbons tied around it sitting atop the wardrobe. Had my mother left it there for me? Opening my door and looking out at the garden, my eyes were dazzled by the deep magenta bougainvillea, the rich red roses, and the bright orange and purple birds-of-paradise. My mother lived in color, and her palette was made up of the colors of Mexico. She was in this garden, and not just my lungs but my eyes were breathing her in.

After *el desayuno* of fresh fruit (mango, melon, pineapple with lime, and grapes—why is the fruit sweeter and fresher in Mexico than at home?), *pan dulce,* and *huevos mexicanos,* I sat in the patio, waiting for my father to join me for the day. Alejandro, who was Panchita's son-in-law, came to sit with me and talk. His command of English was slightly better than mine of Spanish, which is *muy malo* (very bad). He told me of the memories he had of my mother.

"She was very elegant," he said. "We are so sad that she is gone."

His two young sons were playing soccer in the yard, and Alejandro called them over to meet me. *"Mucho gusto,"* I said, smiling at them as they stood next to my chair. I remembered how much this family meant to my mother, and that the last time she had seen Paco—the younger of the two brothers—he was still a baby. Now he had grown into a running little boy. Their mother, Irma, who was Panchita's daughter, joined us on the patio.

"We are thrilled that you finally came," she said. "Your wonderful mother talked of you often, and of how much you would like to be here. We all miss her, especially Panchita. But now you are here, and you brought your father. This makes my mother happy," and she gave me a hug.

Later, my father and I walked the mile down to the *zócalo* (square), which was filled with people—tourists and *oaxaqueños*— gathering for the festivities around Día de los Muertos.

Day of the Dead is a celebration in Mexico with roots that reach far back in time, long before the arrival of the *conquistadores* and the Catholic Church. Before Europeans came to Mexico, the distinction between life and death wasn't painted in black and white. The missionaries gave November 1 and November 2 to the native people as All Saints Day and All Souls Day, and the Mexicans wove these holy days into their own world, coinciding as they did with their corn festivals—during which, for centuries, the people had shared their plentitude with the dead.

In every pueblo in Mexico, Día de los Muertos is celebrated on November 2. Altars are built for the dead, and on the altars, loved ones place *ofrendas*—offerings of foods and other things that were part of the dead one's existence. The belief is that soon after midnight on November 1, the crack between the realms opens for one hour, and the two worlds commune like watercolors on a white palette—the red bleeds into the boundary with yellow, and they meet as orange. Families sit at the altars so that they can be ready to receive the spirits of the dead they so loved.

At home I've built altars for my departed pets and left their favorite toys and treats for them. This would be the first altar I had built for Mother, and building it in Oaxaca at Casa Panchita, not at my home in Los Angeles, felt right. I would be building it in the land that was closest to her heart, where her spirit was the strongest. I had brought with me various items for the altar: some photographs and a few pieces of her jewelry. I also brought her reading glasses and a chunk of raw, uncut amethyst—for the purple that she loved. My mother's favorite nephew, my cousin Jefferson, had been killed in a car accident in this year after her death, and I brought his photograph to place on the altar, for my mother to see and to touch.

I was thrilled being back in this country that was such a part of my parents' lives; that was a part of me in ways I'd nearly forgotten. No longer a little girl but a forty-three-year-old woman in the middle of her life, I was still my father's daughter, excited to be on this journey with him. We sat at a table outside one of the restaurants on the *zócalo,* drinking beer and munching on *cacahuates con ajo* (peanuts in the shell, roasted with chili and garlic)—a staple at the bars in Oaxaca. My father—who I thought would be filled with joy by bringing me to this magical place that was so important to the woman he had been married to for fifty-one years—was in another world. Looking into his soft brown eyes, I could see that his sadness was deep, nearly bottomless. Returning to Oaxaca, he was feeling Mother also, but not as a presence like I was. He was feeling her as an absence. For me this had become a voyage of discovery; for my father, it was reinforcing his profound loss. Sitting next to him in the *zócalo,* I thought, *He's fading from this world, he misses Mother so much.* And I wondered if he would be leaving soon to be with her. I was sad for my father and angry that he was living in the past, in his memories, and couldn't be here with me in the present.

"Daddy," I said, "look where we are! Mother would be so

happy to see us here together, and she's here with us. Don't you feel her? Why are you so far away?"

"I'm running out of tape, I don't have many years left," he said (though years later, he's still here, and happy to be so). Looking up, I saw vendors with brightly colored balloons of animals and cartoon characters. Floating high on a string, a blue and silver dolphin caught my eye, and there she was: *mi madre*. She was a swimmer. During her three-and-a-half-year struggle with cancer, when she was well enough to go in the water, my mother told me that she would visualize a dolphin swimming beside her—a dolphin with a sharp golden spear on the end of his nose—and he would attack the cancer cells with his spear. Five months before she died, after she and my father spent a week swimming with the dolphins at the Dolphin Research Center in the Florida Keys, she felt stronger and healthier than she had since becoming sick. A few weeks before she died, she told me that she thought she might come back as a dolphin.

Walking back up the road to Casa Panchita, I held on to the string of my beautiful dolphin balloon as it swam in front of the deep turquoise wall of the house next door, framed with fuchsia-colored bougainvillea growing across the front. My mother brought these colors home, and now I was here, seeing them bloom in the land where they first touched her soul. After I tied my dolphin to the railing outside so that she could float above the garden, my father and I went into the dining room for *la comida*, the big meal of the day. Sitting on the sideboard were the dishes we would serve ourselves: a salad of fresh tomatoes, cold cauliflower and avocados; *enchiladas verdes*; rice with corn, green beans, and carrots; and chicken with a red sauce and *yerba santa*, the native plant that's used as a seasoning (and that's so hard to find north of the border).

¡*Muy sabrosa!* I thought. My husband, Tim, is fond of Mexican food and had been mastering the art of preparing it in Los Angeles. I thought he would do well to come down here and watch Panchita at work. He could learn a thing or two—and bring it home for us.

The next day, my father and I began our visits to some of the surrounding villages, each one known for a particular craft. My parents had been collecting Oaxacan folk art for years, and now not only would my father be reacquainting himself with artisans he hadn't seen in quite a while, but he would be introducing me to the people who had made the gifts he and Mother had brought home for me. Tino was our driver and our guide—although my father was also my guide.

First we went to Teotitlán del Valle, to the home and workshop of Isaac Vásquez. Rugs that were woven by the Vásquez family had hung in my parents' home for years. Stepping into the workshop, I saw three large looms and rugs hanging on the wall or stacked on the floor. The woven pieces varied in size, from individual placemats and pillow covers to table runners and small area rugs, all the way up to the one that now covers the floor of my den at home. They were woven from handspun wool and were dyed in colors from nature: yellow from a type of moss, blue from the indigo plant, black from beans that are grown in the local fields, and red from the cochineal, a dried beetle found on cactus. (Cochineal was nearly as sought after as gold by the Spaniards when they conquered Mexico, and they brought this valuable red dye back to Europe with them.) The human and animal figures and geometric designs woven into the rugs came from ancient sources—the Zapotec ruins in Oaxaca at Monte Albán and Mitla.

As I caressed the rugs that were for sale, my father asked the young man who was helping us whether his father was home. Isaac came into the shop, greeted my father with a warm handshake, and they began talking. Out of my father's mouth, I heard the words: *"mi esposa . . . muerta . . ."* With my limited ear for Spanish, I knew what he was telling the señor. When he introduced me to Señor Vásquez, I could see that both of them had tears in their eyes. Señor Vásquez shook my hand, telling me *en español* that he was pleased to meet me and that he remembered my *"madre muy bonita,"* my very pretty mother.

After buying two rugs from the Vásquez family, we invited our driver, Tino, to have lunch with us at the only restaurant in the village. On the way there, a procession was coming down the road from the church, where there had just been a funeral. They were carrying colorful handmade banners with pictures of saints and were playing drums and horns. Inside the café, Tino asked if I would like to look at all of the business cards he had collected from the many people he'd driven and guide through Oaxaca. Flipping through the pages of his notebook, reading the names of people from all over—some of whom I recognized—my eye, and my heart, paused. There in my lap, in Tino's treasured book, was Mother's card—a card I knew down to the marrow of my bones, not just because of her name but also for the graphic that was her signature. (The visual world—color and graphic—was more than my mother's passion; as an environmental designer, it was also her life's work.)

"My mother," I whispered, and began to sob.

Tino looked stricken at the pain he thought he was causing me. "Kat-tee," he said, "I am sorry," and he put his arm around me.

"No, Tino. This is so beautiful. My mother was here, and you knew her, and she's alive in these pages."

Just as Alejandro and Panchita had touched me where my heart was still raw, Tino told me how he remembered my mother, what a beautiful lady she was.

Since this was my first real trip to Oaxaca (when I was a teenager, I had just passed through), my father had Tino take us to all of the important villages surrounding the city. The last time my mother was in Oaxaca (a few years before she died), she brought me home a real treasure: a hand-embroidered blouse that wasn't bought in one of the many *mercados*, but from the woman who embroidered it, at her home in San Antonino Castillo Velasco. When Tino first introduced my mother to Silvia Sánchez and she saw the woman's exquisite handwork, my mother asked the señora if she would embroider two blouses—one for her daughter and one for herself—with colors of my mother's choice.

My blouse, embroidered with white and pink threads and wrapped in tissue paper, now sits on a shelf in my closet along with my mother's blouse, whose only colored thread is a deep, rich purple. These two blouses, embroidered by Señora Sánchez, keep each other company in my closet, along with the boxes of handwoven *rebozos* (shawls) and *huipiles* that my mother collected over the years in her travels through Mexico. *Huipiles* are poncho-like dresses and blouses woven on back-strap looms by the indigenous women of Mesoamerica. They originated over two thousand years ago and can be found in the Maya communities of western Guatemala and the native Indian villages of southern Mexico. Each village has its own *huipil* design, with traditional motifs that have been passed down through the generations.

I asked Tino to take me to San Antonino Castillo Velasco so I could thank Señora Sánchez for the blouse she had made for me, so I could draw the thread through another stitch connecting me to my mother. Parking his car at the end of the paved road, we walked down a dirt path, stepped through metal doors and into a lush courtyard. Silvia and two of her sisters were sitting at a table, embroidering multicolored flowers and birds on white cloth. After greeting the Sánchez sisters, Tino introduced me to Silvia and told her about my mother. Kneeling beside her, I quietly thanked her, in my halting Spanish, for the beautiful blouse she had made for me.

"Tino," I said, looking up at him, "can you please tell Señora Sánchez that *el amor de mi madre* lives in her stitches?"

My father and I made this pilgrimage to Oaxaca to build Mother's altar, and on October 31—the big shopping day before what is a two-day festival for Day of the Dead—we started collecting the Oaxacan offerings we wanted placed on it. The *mercados* were filled with food and crafts made especially for Día de los Muertos, and shopping was a feast for my eyes and nose. I bought fruits and nuts, and also *copal*—an incense made from the resin of the same trees that are used to carve *calaveras*.

Calaveras—skeletons and skulls—are a strong element of Mexican folk art. What fun I had inhaling the sights and sounds of the markets as I bought *calaveras* for my mother's altar. That night, Tino took some other guests and me to the neighboring village of Xoxo for their fiesta. A *calavera* sitting on a table with *ofrendas* for sale stood out from the others, and my eyes fixed on her. Standing about a foot tall, she wore a yellow ochre skirt and shawl made of crepe paper. Her hair was straight and white, and her eyes were a deep black. Her arms, carrying a green and red watermelon, also held my mother's spirit. I paid for her and brought her back to Casa Panchita. There, I placed her on the altar—between the purple amethyst and a sugar skull I had written Mother's name on—and bowed my head to her as *La Señora*. After I welcomed her at her altar in Oaxaca, Mother now watches over me at home from a shelf high in the kitchen.

On November 1, some other guests of Casa Panchita joined me in building a communal altar, one for all the guests. The day before, Alejandro had constructed a large wooden platform in one side of the garden next to the patio, and now we would be dressing it with a brightly colored cloth, flowers and candles, *calaveras* and *ofrendas*. Coming out of my room in the morning, I saw Becca and Julie stringing *cempasúchil* (marigolds), the flowers of the dead. These two women from San Francisco were attaching the strung-together flowers to sugarcane in order to later form a kind of arbor for the altar. Becca was gaining strength from the bone marrow transplant she recently had for breast cancer, and she had chosen Oaxaca, during Día de los Muertos, as her place to heal. I saw that other guests had begun placing *ofrendas* on the altar for their departed loved ones. Another guest, Wendy, had lost her husband two years prior, and she placed his cigar on the altar, along with a guitar-strumming *calavera*. My mother was part of the web that held Casa Panchita together, and now, by being here and placing her photo on the altar, I was part of the web as well.

Another important offering is chocolate, which stands for something more significant than sweet-tooth cravings in Mexico. Chocolate was sacred to the Aztecs, and they believed the god Quetzalcoatl gave this delectable treasure to the people as a gift. In this way, it became currency in the underworld. On Día de los Muertos, while loved ones wait for the visit from their departed, they place chocolate on the altars and drink hot cocoa while sitting at their graves.

Earlier that morning, Irma had taken cocoa beans, sugar, and cinnamon to the chocolate factory and had it ground up. In the afternoon, I helped her and Panchita make a deep brown paste out of it, and then my father and I got to play with it in the kitchen. The paste wasn't soft and smooth like frosting, but thick and gritty like clay, growing stiffer and less malleable the longer it was out. We pulled it hard and pounded on it, forming it into many different shapes—a moon, stars, a sun, and a heart. My mother's spirit was coursing through my veins, and the love she filled me with was seeping into the chocolate in my hands. I made a dolphin for her. My father became a little boy making mudpies, and he couldn't help but lick his fingers. (He's a fiend for chocolate, and whenever there was a box in the house, Mother would be the chocolate monitor, hiding it high up on a shelf and doling it out at her discretion.) He was missing her so much, and now, in Panchita's kitchen, where Mother's presence was in the air, he could have all the chocolate he wanted. The chocolate became a conduit from our world to hers. I had chocolate under my fingernails for the rest of the day, and I smelled like a chocolate pie. I wanted to sit myself down on my mother's altar, to offer her my sweetness when the crack between the world opened and she came to visit.

After working on the altar, I took a walk down to Santo Domingo Church to sit and reflect. My father stayed at Casa Panchita for his own reflection. On my walk, I visited some of the other altars that had been made in the city. The prevailing color for all of them was the orange of the *cempasúchil,* and the red and yellow of ripe peppers. *Pan de muerto,* the special bread baked for this holiday, was placed beside bowls of *mole negro,* and occasionally *mezcal* and tobacco. Photographs, *calaveras,* and personal items filled the altars. At each one I stopped by, I felt the caring of the family who had built it and the faith they had that their departed would not only visit them tonight but partake of the food and drink that was offered. Stepping into the church and sitting beneath its 16th-century nave, with glittering saints and cherubs soaring above me, I was filled with the certainty that the altar I helped build was a true expression of yearning for connection with the departed.

Then it was time for *la comida,* and as I walked into the dining room at Casa Panchita, I smelled the same chocolate that was in the air the night my father and I first arrived. *Mole negro*—the prized dish of Oaxaca that some travelers focus their pilgrimage on—was the main course for today's feast on All Saints Day. One of the main ingredients of this mole—the one that gives it its dark color and rich flavor—is chocolate.

Just before midnight, I went into the garden to sit by the altar and wait for Mother. Some of the other guests were already there, keeping vigil. Panchita had made hot cocoa for us, and I think it was this—the aroma of chocolate, not the chance to sit at the altar and share with the others—that initially drew my father out of his room. He quietly carried a chair down from the patio and placed it next to mine. Lighting the copal incense that sat on the altar, I heard the church bells ringing to hold open the mystical hour for Mother and me to be together. Sitting quietly, I felt a light breeze, and tears filled my eyes. I reached for my father's hand, and we sat together, not speaking but feeling Mother's presence in the air around us and in our hearts.

The next morning, on Día de los Muertos, I awoke to the sweet smell of *tamales oaxacaños* for breakfast, made with the *mole negro* from yesterday. More of this gift from the gods! My father and I walked down to the *zócalo,* and after the week of celebration—with parades and fireworks, with an abundance of life for the Day of the Dead—the city was quiet. Families were together, at their loved one's graves in the cemetery or at their altars at home. I was with my father, in the city that held my mother's heart.

Melinda Bergman Burgener

Mexican Chocolate

Half my lifetime ago, I was recklessly in love with a wiry, strong-minded short man who chain-smoked cigarillos and spoke fluent Spanish. His eyes, in the sunlight, looked like hot dark chocolate dusted with cinnamon bark. His hair was a cap of gold-streaked brown curls. I thought him beautiful; perhaps he thought the same of me. People mistook us for siblings.

Had it not been for him, I might never have gone to Mexico. A month after we met, in early October—without a plan or second thought—I sublet my apartment, gave up my job at *Rolling Stone* magazine, and moved with Benny from San Francisco to Phoenix, Arizona, a town bursting with big money and eager land speculators. His job was to divest his mother of her consequential Arizona real estate holdings; she counted on his brains and charms to spin her raw acreage into another fortune for herself. My job was to bask in our love and maybe learn some Spanish.

The only dark spot in my life was this mother: a raven-haired, Chicago-born socialite who drank too much. She joined us in Arizona—from her spread in Palm Beach—to oversee her son's negotiations. Grace also had a house in Phoenix but spent every evening at our two-room apartment, enjoying my cooking without taking the smallest notice of me. She didn't dislike me; she hadn't mustered any feelings for me at all. She was dining with her adored only child in order to fashion his strategy for the following day. I was merely dishing up the food.

During dinner one night, she told him she intended to drive to Mexico for the Christmas holidays. Knowing Benny wouldn't go without me, she reluctantly invited the two of us to be her guests at an extravagant resort, Tres Vidas, located on the coast forty-five minutes from Acapulco. I'd ride in the backseat for the five-day road trip, with the fluent Spanish–speaking duo in front. I knew three words of Spanish: the words for "please," "thank you," and "butter." A more astute third wheel might have said, *"No, gracias,"* and spent Christmas alone.

Benny revealed the trip's purpose later that night: to find and land Grace's fifth husband. Until Mr. Right came along, Benny would be her designated escort. Traveling in Mexico after the end of each of her marriages was their tradition. Their inaugural trip was after Grace's first husband, Benny's father (a minor TV personality, also from Chicago), died when Benny was twelve. Mexico brought luck: husband number two (a well-connected, oil-rich Texan) was met and married in Acapulco; husband number four (a nabob from Atlanta) was first spotted in Cuernavaca.

Off went our unholy trinity to Mexico. On the third day of the journey, in the quintessential Spanish colonial town of San Miguel de Allende, Grace treated us to an exquisite two-hour lunch, marred only by the number of margaritas she absorbed and the collateral mood swings they inevitably provoked.

For starters, the moment her second drink was delivered, she palmed a silver object from her purse, fooled with it under the tablecloth, then poured generously from it into the deficient cocktail. Mine were not the only eyes catching her indiscreet, possibly illegal behavior. The manager reacted, quickly sending our waiter over, I imagined, to ask us to leave. But before he opened his mouth to admonish her, she said loudly, first in English, then in Spanish, "Benny, darling, tell this handsome boy to bring me another. I'm counting on him to make sure they don't leave out the tequila this time." Subsequent drinks were no doubt overly fortified. The flask disappeared.

My embarrassed reaction annoyed her and finally, somewhere around the fourth drink, she said, "Benny, darling, tell your Bronx-born sweetie that she's not in Kansas anymore and she can stop gawping at me and at the handsome help."

But before the meal was ruined, before the rich flavors soured in my mouth, I had my first big luscious taste of Mexico, and I was deliciously happy. Each beautifully seasoned, unfamiliar dish sparkled, and, with permission, I dug my spoon into everything on our table: raw fish marinated in lime juice with cilantro, shrimp in green tomatillo sauce with ground pumpkin seeds, thick red piquant crab soup, chicken in mysterious mole sauce darkened with chocolate, pork in tingling-hot adobo, fresh cheese with quince paste, and lime curd.

The good food lessened my inhibitions and loosened my tongue, and I used the lack of butter on the table to try out my entire Spanish vocabulary. *"¿Señor, mantequilla, por favor?"* brought me butter and a warm smile from the waiter. He had struck me as haughty; now we'd become friendly compatriots. *"Gracias,"* I said, gratified by his second smile when he put the huge pat in front of me. Mexico seemed to me a wonderful place to be.

Grace and Benny had visited San Miguel de Allende at least three times before, but after lunch, at my urging, we strolled about. It was easy to grasp why the whole town is a national monument: three-hundred-year-old Spanish colonial architecture, with its elaborately carved heavy wooden doors and its pink gothic cathedral; sinuous narrow streets; Spanish mansions with iron-grilled windows and fountains within courtyards; dozens of crafts shops and art galleries lining skinny sidewalks; vistas and plazas. But most of all, it was the bold colors that thrilled me. They were brilliant without vulgarity. I loitered in the crisp December mountain air, reveling in the surrounding fiesta.

My companions strolled arm in arm behind me. I turned around once and was startled: A woman of a certain age and her perfect young gigolo were following me. Benny saw my astonishment and crinkled his eyes, holding me in their glow until my pang of jealousy evaporated. I'd stop into a church or shop and emerge to find their faces almost touching, so engrossed—perhaps in Arizona land speculation—that they'd hardly noticed I'd been gone.

A small boutique—*Tienda de Ropa*, the sign said—captivated me with its sidewalk display of flowing, ruffled cotton dresses echoing the bright hot colors of the town: glorious hues, completely incompatible with my usual taste for muted functional attire. Like a sparrow bewitched by a parrot, I was drawn inside, where the fantasy continued. A tinny speaker broadcast the half-Spanish, half-English lyrics "Feliz Navidad, Feliz Navidad . . . I want to wish you a merry Christmas . . . " over and over, while two dancing designing women slipped one dress after another over my head and twirled me in front of a broken mirror propped against a chair. If I understood their words ("¡Fabulosa! ¡Preciosa! ¡Perfecto!") and correctly interpreted their pantomime, I was a knockout in every one. The shop was warm, and with the added heat of the colors of Mexico sheathing me, I felt pretty and witty and—certainly—bright.

Half an hour later, wearing an ankle-skimming fuchsia-, scarlet-, and soft pink–striped dress with complementary smocking down the front (my former dim plumage was hidden in a neon-yellow straw handbag), I pirouetted out of the *tienda* to show off my new look. But my audience was gone. I wandered alone, up and down the cobbled hills, cold wind blowing through the thin cotton of my flamboyant apparel, trying hard to believe I hadn't been abandoned in San Miguel.

Around dusk, nearing panic, I finally spotted Grace and Benny in a bar, still engrossed in each other, still tête-à-tête. The conversation stopped when they noticed me shivering outside in what I realized, at that moment, was a ridiculous costume, inappropriate both for me and for the season. From Grace's look, all I needed was a *ristra* of chilies around my neck to pass for a Mexican clown. I came in from the cold.

Benny's eyes registered my misery. He explained that he had thought I would catch up with them as they slowly walked on. He had left Grace in the bar and searched for me. We realized that we had missed each other as we hunted up and down the same alleys, criss-crossed the same plazas, ducked in and out of the same churches and stores. We were like vaudevillians, always a beat away from success as we opened and slammed doors on the other's retreating back.

But I could see that I had finally defined myself for Grace: I was the impediment who also slowed down her trip. "Three has always been an inconvenient number," she snarled, "but you bring a new viv-idness to the equation." She didn't stop there. "And I do mean *vivid-ness:* Whatever possessed you to deck yourself out like an awning?"

For the rest of our trip, I stuck closer to Benny and vexed Grace more each day. We stayed two nights in Cuernavaca with a friend of hers, a European dipsomaniac who also tallied husbands. She was in between marriages just then and lived alone behind high walls in a palatial, baroque spread stocked with maids. The elderly princess, cued by Grace's behavior, treated me excrementitiously. Her maids noticed and took pity. They brought me endless platters of sliced mangoes and pineapples. They encouraged me with their few words of English, telling me not to worry. Early on the second morning, when a skittering scorpion dropped out of my black clog as I held it aloft about to insert my foot, Benny rushed over and smashed it with the wood sole of my other shoe. Maids looked on, shaking their heads, disapproving more of the hero worship in my foolish young eyes than of the scorpion mashed into their sparkling tiled floor.

On the sixth day, we reached Tres Vidas, a membership-only

club for super-rich Americans and Europeans (the only Mexicans I saw were on the payroll). Tres Vidas took its exclusivity seriously: It was rumored that an ex–U.S. president was once turned away because his name wasn't on the gatehouse roster. We were escorted to our haciendas. The one Benny and I were to stay at was far enough from his mother's that we shared neither our pools nor our attendants. We coordinated activities with Grace by phone, meeting for lunch and dinner but breakfasting in our respective private dining rooms, fawned over by our respective private staff.

I built confidence over the following week, having my whims serviced by compliant underlings. Benny felt we could have a day on our own since Grace had just met if not absolutely husband number five, then at least a promising pair of prominent well-heeled single men down from Washington, D.C. Any single man with the requisite credentials of money and an Ivy League background was a contender for her hand. This couple from Washington was of course gay, but we three did not conceive the possibility then. Grace went into flirtation mode whenever she saw their handsome tanned faces and meticulously oiled sexagenarian bodies.

Benny and I took off after breakfast, dispatching a maid to her hacienda to say we'd gone exploring and would return in the evening. We thumbed a ride to the new Princess Hotel, nearer to Acapulco, to see the heralded architecture of its towering atrium. We stayed for a late, drawn-out lunch. Because the day was perfect and we were in love, we decided to walk along the increasingly secluded beach in the direction of Tres Vidas. Eleven slow, voluptuous miles later, we arrived. It was 9:30 PM, the sky was black velvet, and the hotel management, along with the *policía*, met us at the gate. Grace was certain Benny had been macheted by aborigines and had alerted the hotel staff to the possibility hours before we returned. We were both sorry. But she held only me responsible for her upset and for her son's negligent behavior. The drive back to Phoenix was a nightmare.

Two months later, Grace finally returned to Palm Beach, trusting Benny to keep fortune smiling on her in Arizona. One morning, he left as usual after breakfast to continue wheeling and dealing on Grace's behalf, but just a few hours later, he unexpectedly returned.

"*¡Hola!*" he said. "How long do you need to pack your stuff for a few weeks?"

"Theoretically I can do it in about five minutes, *amigo*," I said, playing along, wondering where we were going with this Spanish.

"*Es necesario*, because I've just bought two tickets to Mexico, and the train leaves from Nogales tomorrow morning!" To curb my abundant questions, he added, "You need to see Mexico with just me, just the two of us: flowers, walks on the beach, *mariachis*. . . . Besides, you need another chance to wear your Day-Glo dress."

His spontaneity pulled me along like a magnet. Who could remain measured and ordinary in a whirlwind? Who would want to? We threw our things into a shared duffel bag and gave our food, our goldfish, our plants to a neighbor. We locked the apartment at daybreak. I slid into the bucket seat beside him in the sporty car Grace had given him for his birthday. As we sped to the border town for our train, I looked forward to a different perspective on Mexico—a place I never expected to find myself again so soon.

In our tiny train compartment, we stayed up all night reading Oscar Lewis's *Five Families* to each other. This heartbreaking study of the culture of poverty in Mexico, told through the daily lives of real people, was dramatic. Moved, we vowed together to make a difference, to change lives in the depleted country we were tearing through. Sometimes as we read, we pressed our faces to the black glass, straining to see the real Mexico beyond. And like strobe-lit illustrations for our text, whole families flashed by inside their corrugated shanties, waiting patiently, perhaps, for us to beneficently lift them from their difficult lives. We were on our way.

We sustained ourselves during the journey on these delusions of altruism, and on love, oranges, and tubes of Benny's favorite Marias biscuits, purchased from station vendors. They were dry and almost tasteless, but I mimicked him and soon craved the cookies, nibbling at them compulsively. Finishing one triggered a need for another, until the package was empty, and we'd begin thinking about the next station. We'd get off the train and buy several packets from each poor peasant, trying to convince ourselves that we were already embarking on our good works.

In Mexico City, we rented a car and headed to Zihuatanejo, where Benny and Grace had spent three months some years before we met. I had never heard of "Zihua" until Benny entered my life, but going there together had become another mutual compulsion. There were then—as I remember—only two hotels on the beach. Flowers hung from every balcony of both hotels, but dirt clung to everything else at just one of them. Without Grace footing the bill, the run-down hotel was, by default, our choice. The view was gorgeous, and the cascading blooms of purples, crimsons, and oranges were perfect. The decorating style—down-and-out-in-Mexico—didn't bother me once I had thoroughly cleaned our room. The staff was obliging and served our meals on the pristine beach. I washed my bright dress in the sink and hung it to dry from our balcony. I saw it from the beach as we ate. I liked watching it puff and blow with the flowers: my own Mexican flag.

One morning—it might have been a week after we arrived—Benny said he needed a change of air. He repeated his daily mantra that our run-down hotel would make a good setting for *The Night of the Iguana*. I didn't blame him. He had been spoiled all his life. But he was wrong about the play. The hotel was the backdrop for a more mundane drama, nothing special at all: Without another word, Benny left and didn't come back.

On this second trip to Mexico, he couldn't help measuring both me and his surroundings against unattainable standards. He was seeking a kind of grace that I could never grant him; there is no substitute for the real thing. The cascading blooms and passion fruit in that perfect seaside town hadn't transformed me into his mother. I wasn't his reflection after all. Fitzgerald had it right: "Let me tell you about the very rich. They are different from you and me."

The following day I stuffed my things into the neon-yellow straw bag, leaving only my fiesta-hued flag billowing on the balcony. I boarded a bus for the train to Nogales and made my way to Phoenix. From there I moved back to San Francisco. Benny called once to say he was traveling in Mexico. It was the last time I heard his voice.

Grace's charms nabbed her husband number five. There was even a sixth brief marriage before she died. She left an immoderate fortune to Benny, who is almost sixty now and who has never married. Rumors reach me that he travels widely, always first class, never alone.

A decade after my twin visits to Mexico, I was sitting in Angelina, the pretty prissy tearoom on rue de Rivoli in Paris. It was Christmastime. The waitress set my cup of hot chocolate on the marble table. My mouth watering, I picked up the cup, looked down at its rich dark surface, and saw Benny's chocolate eyes staring back. I watched as they filled with tears. I put the cup down, blotted my face, and stubbed out my cigarillo.

I went quickly through the Tuileries garden, my boots breaking up frozen puddles. Sparrows drank and preened, profiting from the cracked surfaces. I walked back into the streets of Paris. I never returned to Mexico.

Marisa Solís

The Ensenada House

When my mother called to tell me the Ensenada house had been broken into again, I felt a piece of me suddenly rip out, carried into the night along with a coffeemaker, rugs, a crate of tools. Her voice remained calm as she told me how the place was ransacked, how it wasn't two months ago that she had replaced the ancient refrigerator and wiped sea salt and dust from the picture windows. I couldn't help but imagine how the burglars must have hopped the sun-bleached wooden gate to breach my childhood fort, and how the ground outside the gate was all that separated my grandparents' house from the Pacific Ocean.

"Your father and I are going down this weekend to see what needs to be done. We've got to get that door fixed as soon as possible," she continued. Like most mothers, she had already taken matters into her own hands.

"You know," she offered, "you're welcome to come."

As I considered this invitation, I recalled how we had no TV or telephone in the Ensenada house, no potable water, no sidewalks, no garbage collectors. But how we had fun. We sang at the top of our lungs, swam whenever we wanted, and set off firecrackers any time of year. Even as kids we could walk alone to the *tienda* down the road and pay for candy with big coins. We listened to Grandma and Grandpa argue in that house, the way people do when they've been together for more than fifty years. And we listened to them tell stories late into the warm nights.

"Yeah, Mom, I know," I responded quietly. It was my bravest attempt at a polite decline, but it rang coldly into the receiver. As I imagined her disappointedly shaking her head in her kitchen in the San Gabriel foothills, I searched for a way to tell her that asking me to repair the damage to that house was like asking me to tamper with precious memories.

My grandparents, the founders of the house, made the long drive from their homes in Los Angeles every other month or so—as long as they were in good health—to maintain the property. My parents would take that same drive—but only two or three times each year— to relax, read, fish, and soak up some rays. Mom and Dad would pack my three sisters and me into our 1974 Dodge van, a behemoth in three shades of hideous green, designed with most of the engine inside the car and encased in molded plastic that in no way insulated the heat. During the five-hour drive south, with no air conditioning, we amused ourselves singing along to "Louie Louie," braiding each other's hair, and making fun of people in other cars. We watched the landscape change—from the lush yards and sparkling skyscrapers of San Diego, to the dusty hills of Tijuana crammed with tin and scrap-wood shacks, to the sprawling ocean and limitless sky. Freeways became potholed roads; monstrous overpasses became rickety bridges. We saw old men in hats riding rusty bicycles, young men in uniforms and strapped with machine guns. Girls my age carried babies in fabric slings on their backs.

When we arrived in the port town of Ensenada, we'd stop at a *mercado* to pick up several bags of ice, a case of Fanta, toilet paper, and anything else we'd forgotten, and at the best *panadería* in town to stock up on *pan dulce*, sweet bread, for breakfast. Finally, we always visited Josefina's taco stand, a blue wooden trailer with a tin awning in a dirt lot off the highway, just outside of town. Josefina's two gold-rimmed front teeth shone as she laughed and piled carne asada onto two stacked homemade corn tortillas. We shoveled on the chopped onion, tomato, cilantro, and either a spicy avocado or a red chili salsa. I would eat about six of these, the juices of the meat and salsa dripping down my wrist. All of our trips south of the border were inaugurated this way—with us standing in a circle, happy and satisfied, eating tacos together on a dusty roadside under the bright Mexican sun.

Twenty minutes later, we were on an unpaved road, passing through the wooden gates of the Ensenada house. Standing at the far end of a sleepy fishing and senior expat community, the house had an unobstructed view of the faint outline of Ensenada's skyline across the sweeping bay. Grandpa's red Toyota truck was usually parked in the driveway. Sometimes the cars of my aunts and uncles were there too. From the second I set foot onto the cement patio, time—and the sky, sea, trees, and earth—were all mine in the vacation home my grandfather built with his bare brown hands.

My grandmother, still a Mexican citizen, though she had begun living in California by her early teens, would be either in the small, bare kitchen or trying to sweep out the powdery grains of sand that we all dragged into the house. I would always run across the tiled floor, cold under my dirty bare feet, and plop down at the vinyl-covered table.

Dusty spiderwebs clung to the upper corners in almost every room. In the kitchen, fledgling cracks sprouted from the edge of the doorway. I watched the strong, broad backside of my grandmother, with her big belly and large breasts and tightly permed thick hair. Usually dressed in her bright magenta Balboa Island T-shirt and elastic-waistband taupe pants that were tapered at the ankles, she would grab a knife and cutting board. She would deftly slice off the thorns of a teardrop-shaped pad of cactus, all the while smacking away on a piece of gum. Her dexterous knife work on the tender plant always inspired me to pirouette in the center of the kitchen, then relevé to her side.

"What is the cactus for, Grandma?"

"To eat, *m'hija*. Eees good for you."

"You can't eat cactus!"

"Nopales, *m'hija*. And yes, you can eat it. You'll like it."

She would put me to work at some small task while she talked. She told me many times I would become a model and be rich. She gave me advice on foods to avoid in order to stay thin (*"Manteca, m'hija.* Although it adds flavor to everything, you should stay away from lard, or else. Hell, look at your *tías, m'hija,* they're big like me!"). She equipped me with beauty advice I wouldn't need for ten more years ("Use avocado on your face as a—*¿cómo se dice?*—a . . . a mask. Put it on your skin once a week and you will stay looking young forever!").

As I put away the stack of mismatched dishes in the drainer, I stared out the window above the sink, past the worn handsewn curtains that swayed in the breeze, and strained to see the seagulls I never saw back home in Los Angeles. I loved the flash of their white wings across the gentle sky and the breeze coming through the screen that was always cool and smelled like the ocean. I stuck out my tongue to see if I could taste its salty essence.

"Ay, Marisa! Don't stick your tongue out like that! Nice girls don't do that. You want your face to become frozen like that, eh?"

I absolutely knew this warning to be false, but the image horrified me to no end. Grandma's veined hands moved rapidly across each cactus pad, not once getting pricked. She always prepared food without looking down, as if her hands were self-propelled. Her mind seemed to wander, remember, dream. Once she told me about the time before she met Grandpa. I imagined her, a fair-skinned anomaly on the ranch where she grew up, deep in the mountains of Jalisco. I pictured the tall, handsome suitors vying for her attention when she settled in California with her family in the 1920s. As she stared off into space, I smiled, rested my forehead on her wide hip, and listened to her breathe. While drying a plate, I would try to daydream like Grandma, without looking down, but it would inevitably drop.

What I loved most about the Ensenada house was how it offered me long days alone, away from chores and homework and my younger sisters. At home in L.A., my siblings shadowed me and begged me to play house, which I didn't enjoy; outside, we were confined to a rusty swing set and a paved backyard—good for things like chalk and riding bikes, but not much else. We could never play in the street or walk to the corner by ourselves. And we had to be quiet so as not to disturb our neighbors. But in Mexico, I recited limericks at top volume to the frothy waves. I played hopscotch in front of the house until my shadow grew long, 'til my skin turned a shimmery brown. With a washed-up tree limb, I drew pictures in the dirt, which had the consistency of confectioner's sugar. I walked barefoot on the uneven stone retaining wall that separated the road from the narrow, rocky beach, imagining I was on a tightrope suspended one hundred feet in the air. I poked at spiderwebs in the purple bougainvillea that cascaded down a neighbor's fence and chased lizards in the arid scrub that dotted the bluffs at the end of the road.

In the evenings, my mom and dad and aunts and uncles sat on the beach chairs in the dusty front yard, welcoming dusk and sharing jokes, my grandfather the loudest among them. My sisters and cousins ran around the house, playing hide and seek. I ran down to the ocean. I watched the lights of Ensenada flicker on across the bay and the fishing boats, tethered to an anchor, bob forlornly in the choppy offshore waters. A lone truck with one working headlight would inevitably rumble down the road, and its bangs and squeaks would be met by Grandpa's booming voice yelling out to the driver, who would then stop in front of our gate. Grandpa would put one hand on the car door and lean forward, the thumb of his other hand hooked into a belt loop; they talked in Spanish for a long time. Grandpa's dog, Gringo, sniffed his way to me and rested his haunches on my thighs. We sat this way until the mosquitoes came out and fed on my skinny legs.

In the mornings, while my sister's sweaty body snored next to me, I slipped on my bathing suit. From the house next door, roosters crowed—a sound my mother hated but I loved: The call was full of promise and adventure. The house was quiet, except, of course, for Grandma making coffee and organizing her kitchen. I kissed her hello, leaned against her soft frame as she quizzed me on the words for things in Spanish: *taza, cuchillo, hornillo, leche.* I grabbed my pail, stepped off the front porch, and told her I was going to the tide pools. She always said *"Cuidate,* be careful." Grandpa was usually rooting around in his work shed, cussing about something not working: the pump in the well, the power drill, the toilet.

It always seemed to be low tide in the morning. The expanded shoreline allowed me to explore its hidden parts, and the tide pools teemed with dozens of creatures: starfish and sea anemones, sea cucumbers and hermit crabs, black chitons and inch-long fish. I collected seashells and turned over rocks to watch tiny hermit crabs scurry for cover. An occasional pelican sat on the calm surface as fishermen zoomed by in dented boats and cumulus clouds floated lazily across the sky.

"It's time to eat!" my sister yelled from atop the retaining wall.

She hopped from rock to rock to reach me, getting her feet wet and sticking her finger into the belly of a purple sea anemone with lavender tentacles.

For breakfast, my favorite meal in Mexico, we ate fresh *pan dulce*, which Grandpa bought in town in the morning, fresh out of the oven—the only way he'd eat it. There were always eggs and chorizo and corn tortillas from Señora Rosa down the road, as well as fresh salsa and steaming potatoes. After Grandpa wiped his plate clean with a piece of tortilla, he asked who wanted to go into town with him—to visit his friend Pancho or to meet up with the water people or to get some building material. As my sisters and cousins started fighting, I watched Grandma contentedly dish up second servings. I knew she liked having her children and grandchildren around. More of them could fit there than in her home in L.A., which was half the size and surrounded by a chain-link fence, a flimsy barrier against urban living: hungry street dogs, obnoxious car alarms, low-flying helicopters, yelling neighbors, fast traffic.

The last time I stayed at the Ensenada house was 1995, when I was twenty-one and both my grandparents were still alive. A second story had been fully completed, and the entire house had been furnished to its fullest: seven beds, three secondhand couches, dozens of warped beach chairs, two old refrigerators, a couple of battery-powered radios, and four folding tables that migrated to wherever the poker party was happening. Though my grandparents weren't there that visit, I could still smell them in the thick woven Mexican blankets, still see my Grandpa reading the Mexican newspaper by the window with the ocean view and swearing about politics, hear Grandma's rubber-bottomed slippers slide heavily across the smooth tile.

Visits by the rest of my relatives began to taper off after that, too. Grandchildren grew up and moved away. My aunts and uncles didn't have the energy for the commute. When Grandpa died of stomach cancer in 1996 and Grandma succumbed to dementia and a virulent hospital infection eight years later, the house remained empty of its people for longer and longer intervals.

In 2002, when the roof was badly leaking, there was a call for relatives to come and tidy up. And last summer, when the house was broken into the first time, there was another request for family to pitch in and clean, do maintenance, keep it habitable. For two years, a resurgence of relatives went down by the truckload to weed, patch holes, fix leaking faucets, rebuild the crumbling stone fence, repair broken windows, and replace mildewed mattresses.

I never went down to help—only donated money to offset the expenses. I couldn't bear the sight of the house in disrepair any more than I could bear seeing Grandma in her last months. In the hospital she sat, oblivious to the men and women in wheelchairs around her, unrecognizable among the gaping, silent mouths, the uncombed heads of hair, the robotic tapping of fingers. She was sagging at the corners, slumped to the soft earth, decrepit as her beloved house.

If I made the trip south, I would see ghosts emerge from the long cracks in the plaster walls. I would hear Spanish whispering in the night when no one else was in the room. I would hear the sound of the ocean sucking the rocks back into its womb, and that dull sound would no longer comfort me. I would not want to stand at the kitchen sink and hear Grandma's laugh echo off the bare, peeling walls, to hear the scraping of Grandpa's rake as he collected the silver leaves from the olive trees into small heaps to burn later. The setting of the sun beyond the vast, dark ocean would mean nothing without the sharp smell of roasted chilies wafting through the air. I would not want to see broken glass scattered on the dining room floor where the intruders broke in, nor their names etched into the folding table where they sat around, drinking beers.

Like thick, fringed Mexican blankets, the moments of my youth spent at that house are folded and tucked inside a cupboard of memories. And when I shake them out, they are bright and warm as ever—unchanged, undisturbed, comforting. And they don't have an ending. I am afraid to go back to Ensenada, afraid of making new memories. I fear new experiences will replace the old ones. I am not ready to let go of them now. And perhaps not ever.

Laura Fraser

The Food of Love

Every few months, with the changing seasons, I get the bug to go far away. And every few months, for the past four years, I've rendez-voused with a Parisian man I met on Ischia, a southern Italian island, just months after I was divorced. When we met, we had a fantasy four-day fling, but he was married—unhappily—and lived too far away for a real relationship with me. We used travel as an excuse to see each other occasionally, to leave our real lives behind and indulge in our sometime romance. I was single and he was unloved, and so we delighted in one another's company. The last time we had been together, I'd thought it was the end of our affair.

But six months had passed since our last encounter, autumn was turning gray, and I had the urge to be in the sun before winter descended—and to see him again.

So I emailed my friend and casually mentioned I was thinking about a trip. "How about Istanbul?" he wrote right back. Istanbul was apt to be chilly that time of year, and I wanted sun, culture, art, food—I wanted Oaxaca.

Sometimes, I told him, a faraway place just enters your consciousness, unbidden, and stays there until you're compelled to go. This is what happened with this small city in southern Mexico, about 150 miles inland from the margarita-soaked beach towns of Huatulco and Puerto Ángel. Recently, a friend had opened a wooden chest in his house, revealing a pile of area rugs in rich earthen reds, umbers, and yellows—all from Oaxaca. Another friend had flipped through her photo book, filled with images of baroque colonial buildings, sun-weathered churches, banana plants, and courtyard gardens. "Oaxaca," she'd said.

Oaxaca, Oaxaca, *wa-ha-kah*. The word lingered in my mind like a tune or a lover's voice. It's a breezy word, like a children's rhyme, but also the battle cry of a fierce ancient people: *Wa-ha-kah!* (The Aztecs, who ruled Oaxaca City at the time of the Spanish conquest in 1521, were notorious not only for their achievements in art, architecture, and cuisine, but also for their ritual human sacrifices.)

Then I came across a collection of essays by Italo Calvino called *Under the Jaguar Sun*, in which each piece focused on one of the senses. Of all the cities in the world where Calvino had dined—and he was, mind you, Italian—Oaxaca embodied the ultimate fulfillment of the sense of taste. Oaxacan cuisine, he wrote, combines a cornucopia of native vegetables with spices and recipes brought over by Spanish conquistadors. Over the centuries, those cuisines were mixed, enhanced, and perfected by cloistered nuns (for whom cooking was one of few earthly indulgences). Calvino called Oaxacan food "an elaborate and bold cuisine," with flavor notes that vibrate against each other in harmonies and dissonances to "a point of no return, an absolute possession exercised on the receptivity of all the senses."

I realized I didn't just have to go see Oaxaca. I had to taste it.

I sent the Calvino essay to my Parisian friend, and he immediately wrote back with the date he would meet me in Mexico.

I arrived first, happy my guidebook had led me to a room at Las Golondrinas, a charming, inexpensive little hotel with whitewashed walls and lounge chairs in a promiscuous jungle of a garden. I would have been happy to sit there all day, but I instead went out to wander around the heart of the town, around a traditional Mexican *zócalo*, (square). I felt comfortable and safe in Oaxaca, with its clean, grid layout (planned by Alonso Garcia Bravo, who also designed Mexico City), Spanish-style architecture, cobblestone pedestrian streets, and art galleries and museums tucked into unlikely corners.

At the *zócalo*, called the Plaza de Armas, I sat at one of the shaded outdoor cafés and watched the parade of people—small boys hawking huge bunches of colorful balloons, international travelers searching their maps, mariachis in faded tuxedos playing their oversized guitars, street vendors with fruit carts buzzing with bees, and ancient-faced Indians carrying baskets of greens on their heads. The sun warmed the *zócalo*, and beyond it, the Sierra Madre ringed the town. There was no hurry.

My friend arrived, and we fell into each other's arms. He seemed happy, brimming with a secret joy, and explained that he had finally left the wife who didn't love him, and that he'd found a gratifying new relationship. We are sometimes lovers, and he has always been able to tell me secrets about his illicit life. But his excitement about his new girlfriend was dampening my erotic enthusiasm. It's hard, I told him, to be friends who tell each other everything about their love lives, and still be lovers.

"Not for me," he said, leering, but I pushed his hands aside.

"Let's go eat," I replied. Whatever other sensual experiences I'd hoped for on my trip, the food was not going to let me down.

We chose El Topil, a modest place near our hotel, where a young girl in long braids waited on us while her stout mother did wonders in the tiny kitchen. We had dishes that were familiar by name, but they tasted unlike any Mexican food I've eaten. The guacamole was fresher, the tortillas sweeter and crisper, and the dark sauce on the enchiladas and chilies rellenos seemed concocted from an ancient, mysterious alchemy of chilies and spices. By the time we finished our *plátanos con crema*—fried plantains with cream—we knew we couldn't have eaten that meal anywhere but Oaxaca. As Calvino writes, our exotic restaurants at home are counterfeits of the real cuisine—"they are the equivalent not of an actual locality but of a scene reconstructed and shot in a studio."

We finished off our meal with *mezcal*—the smoky alcohol favored in the region and flavored with a little white maguey worm— downing it with lime and chili salt (the Aztecs sacrificed anyone caught drinking alcohol without permission, but fortunately today, the rules have relaxed some). We went back to our hotel and snuggled together like contented old friends, which we were.

The next day, we went to Monte Albán, the nearby Zapotec ruins, to seek the source of this fine and fiery cuisine. The Zapotecs—the Indians who have populated the area since 600 BC—founded Monte Albán on a mountaintop plateau near Oaxaca. They presided over the entire fertile valley and lived there for more than a millennium. Their first invasion was from another native group, the Mixtecs; then the Aztecs took over a few decades before the Spanish arrived in 1521. The early people who built the vast pyramids, palaces, ceremonial ball courts, and monuments of Monte Albán were, to judge from their art, quite a fierce bunch of warriors. Walking around the sun-baked ruins, one can't help but wonder where they performed those human sacrifices.

Alas, the sacrifices have something to do with the cuisine. The bodies weren't simply left to the vultures; the priests, as intermediaries for the gods, had them for dinner. They must have needed a very strong, spicy sauce—a forerunner of the moles Oaxaca is famous for—to hide (or enhance) the flavor. Archaeologists have indeed found fossilized mole ingredients in the tombs at Monte Albán.

Later that day, at lunch, we had our mole with chicken instead, in a peaceful garden restaurant in Oaxaca called El Naranjo. There, under an orange tree, the cook serves a different mole each day of the week. Mole actually mean "sauce," and there are many variations, from the *amarillo* (yellow), with tomatillos and chilies, to the black, chocolaty *mole negro*. All contain a long list of ingredients, some requiring days to prepare. Each bite of mole was a complicated, earthy, mouth-warming experience.

My Parisian friend and I transferred whatever passion we'd once had for each other—at least for now—to the meal. He would sigh, watching me in anticipation of the pleasure of my mouthful, and I would sigh with him, engaged in a ritual that, at that moment, was not a bad substitute for sex.

The next day, I returned to the restaurant for a cooking class. The chef, Iliana de la Vega, who grew up in Oaxaca, teaches several tourists a week the basics of her cuisine—"simple comfort food," as she calls it, though it is anything but. In her bare-bones kitchen, five of us (my companion doesn't cook) learned to prepare some basic Oaxacan dishes. It turned out to be a lesson in the vocabulary of chilies, which grow in the nearby valley and hills. There were smoke-dried Oaxacan pasilla chilies in one salsa; heartier serranos in another; meaty Anaheim and poblano chilies, sautéed with fresh cheese, onions, and crème fraîche; ancho, guajillo, and Anaheim chilies in the *mole amarillo*. Only the vanilla flan didn't have chilies. For each dish, we roasted, peeled, and deveined the chilies; we stung our fingers and blinked back tears from the heat of the vegetables.

As our lunch cooked, we toured Oaxaca's huge food market, with Iliana leading us past stalls with hanging pigs, fresh chocolate, stacks of cactus, and basketfuls of corn, tomatoes, onions, exotic greens, spices, and roasted grasshoppers. Neat piles of chilies stood as tall as we did. I bought a few pesos' worth of pasillas, anchos, chipotles, and guajillos to take home, with every good intention of making mole someday.

My friend and I spent a few more days in Oaxaca, going from chilies rellenos to Aztec soup to chicken tamales wrapped in large green banana leaves. We wandered around the streets for hours, peeking into brightly painted churches, admiring cactus gardens, browsing in art galleries and handicraft shops, and watching street vendors from Guatemala and Chiapas weave their woolen scarves. Over our *mezcal*, satiated by the place, we might not have been through with Oaxaca, but as friends (a transition the Parisian took perfectly cheerfully), we had bigger appetites for culture and change. I wondered aloud whether we might travel again as lovers, or whether our romance was truly over.

"You never know," he said. And then he told me in Italian, our mutual language, *"La vita è bella e lunga"*—life is long and beautiful. We clinked glasses.

And then an idea took hold. There was a place we'd heard of in the south with magnificent Maya ruins, Palenque. Wasn't that in Chiapas, where Subcomandante Marcos hides out in the jungle with his followers? The city of San Cristóbal de las Casas was supposed to be magical.

Chiapas, Chiapas. We rolled that word around on our tongues and liked it. The next day, under the same spell that took us to Oaxaca, we flew on, compelled to taste Chiapas.

Mole Amarillo with Rajas de Chili
Makes 8 servings.

8 pieces	chicken
1	onion (medium)
3	garlic cloves (peeled, medium)
½ lb.	green beans
3	chayotes (medium)
10	husked tomatillos
1	green tomato (large)
½	white onion (large)
4	garlic cloves (unpeeled, large)
2	ancho chilies
4	guajillo chilies
4	chilcostle or chilhuacle amarillo chilies*
4	costeño amarillo or onza amarillo chilies*
8	whole black peppercorns
4	whole cloves
1 tsp.	cumin seeds
3 tbsp.	canola oil
2 cups	chicken broth
½ cup	masa harina
1 cup	water
4	fresh hoja santa leaves (large) or 6 sprigs of cilantro

For the *rajas de chili:*

10	pearl onions
½ cup	lime juice
½ cup	vegetable oil for frying
3	pieces chilies de agua, or 1 jalapeno and 2 Anaheim chilies
1	teaspoon dried mexican oregano, preferably Oaxacan
	salt to taste

Make the mole:

Clean the chicken pieces and place them in a stockpot with boiling water, medium onion, peeled garlic, and salt. Reduce the heat and poach the chicken for about 30 minutes or until tender. In a separate pot, cook the green beans and chayotes in boiling, salted water until al dente.

In a *comal* or thin skillet, dry roast the tomatillos, green tomato, large white onion, and unpeeled garlic. Remove the garlic when black spots start to appear. Peel the garlic, leaving the vegetables until blistered and soft.

Cut open the chilcostle or chilhuacle amarillo chilies and the costeño amarillo or onza amarillo chilies, remove the seeds and stems, and spread the chilies as flat as possible. Roast them in a hot *comal* or thin skillet, and then soak them in hot water to cover for no more than 20 minutes.

In a small skillet, lightly dry roast the black peppercorns, cloves, and cumin until an aroma is released. Process the soaked chilies in a blender with water as needed to blend smoothly. Meanwhile, heat 3 tablespoons oil in a large pan. Pass the chili mixture through a sieve into the pan. It is important that all of the pieces of chili skin are blended or removed to assure that the sauce is smooth. Reduce the heat, and let it simmer for approximately 8 minutes.

While simmering the chili mixture, blend all of the roasted vegetables and spices with enough water to cover. Add this to the chili mixture, let it simmer for about 20 minutes or until it is reduced, then add the chicken broth, letting it gently simmer for 5 minutes. Dilute the masa harina in 1 cup of water, and then add the hoja santa or cilantro to it. Cook over low heat for 10 minutes, stirring often with a wooden spoon. Add the cooked chicken, peeled and sliced chayote, and green beans.

Make the *rajas de chili:*
Make a small slit in the chilies de agua, or jalapeño and Anaheim chilies, fry them in hot oil until all of the sides are blistered, remove from oil, and let them cool down. When cooled, remove the skins of the chilies, discarding them along with the chili seeds and stems. Tear the chilies in strips and place them in a serving bowl. Cut the pearl onions in fourths and add them to the chilies along with the lime juice, oregano, and salt.

Heat the mole through before serving with white rice, hot tortillas, and the *rajas de chili.*

*If you cannot find chilcostle, chilhuacle amarillo, costeño amarillo, or onza amarillo chilies, substitute 8 guajillo chilies instead.

Liza Monroy

An Outsider in a Sinking City

In Mexico City, there's a carnival at the intersection of Reforma and
Esplanada. I still have dreams about it. The curtain goes up when
the light turns red. A man walks up and down between lanes with
individually wrapped bags of cotton candy as an old woman in a
black dress, her gray hair loosely draped by a shawl, sells *chicles* for
a peso. A fire-breather rinses his mouth with gasoline and blows on
his torch, projecting a stream of flames up into the air. A little boy
runs out into the middle of the road. He wears a clown costume
with two inflated balloons on his bottom, held in place by his pants.
In front of the row of cars on Reforma, a main road, he dances and
shakes. The balloons jiggle, creating the illusion that his derriere is
twice the size of his head. Two other boys cartwheel into the street,
and the three of them crouch and jump on each other's backs. They
stand, the biggest kid on the bottom smiling, though his trembling
legs betray the weight on his shoulders. The boys leap to the ground,

bow, and run between cars, collecting whatever spare change drivers hand out. I watch them from behind the tinted glass of a chauffeured car and drop half my lunch money into their plastic cup. When the light turns green, they scatter to the curb.

It was the morning of my first day of high school in a country I'd only lived in for a week.

Seven days before I started my new school, my mother and I flew in over the dusty valley surrounded by mountains. After dropping off our suitcases, we took a taxi downtown to explore El Centro. Mexico's downtown was sinking ever so slowly, especially around the *zócalo*. I'd heard it was the spot where the capital's founders saw the legendary eagle perched on a cactus, the spot where the city should be built—only it happened to be in a lake. So the lake was filled in, and the buildings were then erected on the spot. Today some of the buildings are on a slant, the roofs not parallel to the ground. I walked around the plaza feeling off-kilter too.

My mother was stationed at the United States embassy as deputy chief of citizen services. I'm her only child, and she divorced my father when I wasn't old enough to know him. Since I was three, it had been just the two of us, a world-traveling pair—my mother the cheery optimist, and me, more reserved, an observer. The year she was accepted to the Foreign Service, we left Seattle and lived around the world: Italy, Greece, the Netherlands, Czech Republic. The last four years in Rome were the longest we'd ever stayed in one place until Mexico City, where I was to attend high school. I didn't want to move and swore I would hate it before I even got there. For the first time in my life, I had lived someplace long enough to make friends and form attachments. The idea of having to do it all over again at age fourteen instilled in me a feeling I later learned was known in Mexico as *"hueva"*—a strong desire not to do something, a feeling much deeper than mere laziness. I didn't know that it would take all of freshman year for the D.F., short for "the federal district" and how the locals refer to the capital city, to prove me wrong.

The government took care of housing and school for diplomats serving abroad, and we were assigned to a spacious house in upscale Lomas de Chapultepec (Grasshopper Hills). In Rome, my environment was a mix of kids of all nationalities and ethnicities who effortlessly mingled. Now I was in a city of twenty-five million, where some neighborhoods (mine included) consisted of mansions, while others adjacent had small, squat houses behind plain cement walls with shards of spiky glass on top. The disparate gap between the masses who lived in scarcity and the few wealthy aristocrats was appalling at first. Some houses had satellite dishes but no running water. Some children wore Fendi by age fifteen. Others wore balloons in their pants instead of going to school. But by the end of high school, the economic disparity had been part of my everyday reality for four years, long enough that I could cease to be appalled and begin instead to examine the nuances, seeing the gap as a lens rather than a wall, a stopping point.

My classmates at the private American School were mostly Mexican, sons and daughters of the country's leaders of business, finance, and industry; even the president's son attended. They were tall, lean, and fair in contrast to the greater population of shorter-stature, darker-skinned indigenous people. They lived in Bosques or Polanco, the Mexico City equivalent of Beverly Hills or Park Avenue, while the majority of the population lived in destitution. A middle class existed, but it was barely perceptible. I realized I wasn't just starting high school. I was starting over. I wasn't like them. My mother and I were financially secure, but not enough to acquire the ostentatious possessions they had or to indulge the lifestyle they led. I needed to search for a place to belong, a place to call home, but I wasn't sure where to begin.

In the hall on my first day, a girl said something to me in Spanish that I didn't understand.

"I'm sorry," I said. "I don't speak Spanish. Yet."

She just shrugged, turned, and walked away. It was my first encounter with the icy elite: jet-setting, Prada-clad, fifteen-year-old socialites chattering away in Spanish. I learned these kids were the *fresas* (literally, strawberries), the Mexican equivalent of preppy—only far more chic. They wore designer clothes and leather shoes (with very high heels for the girls). As I went from class to class, I saw them in the halls, standing in their cliques, gossiping, looking perfect. Junior year, a girl in my grade went on vacation with a big nose and came back with a button. She subsequently won the "best-looking" category in the yearbook.

It surprised me that as an American coming to Mexico, I turned out to be one of the "underprivileged" in my school.

My mother, the adventurer, tried to blend in with the culture whenever we moved somewhere new, or at least her version of the culture. Her Mexico was entirely different from the one I'd seen that first day. Her Mexico was a land of tropical colors, upbeat mariachi music, and mole. That night, she cooked yellow rice, warmed tortillas, and mashed up avocados. As we sat at the plain brown U.S. government–provided table, she asked me how my first day of school was. In spite of myself, my eyes welled up with tears that fell straight into the bowl of guacamole.

I was sitting on a bench alone during lunch the next day when a bubbly girl with waist-long black hair bounded over and sat next to me.

"Hi," she said. "Are you new?"

"Yeah, I just moved here a week ago, from Italy."

"I came from Brazil a month ago. I'm Ana."

"Liza. I think we have chemistry together."

She nodded. "I saw you in the front row. Hey, do you have plans this weekend?"

It turned out Ana lived only two blocks from me. Her father was president of a big international bank. She was outgoing and funny, much better at meeting people than I was. In spite of moving around and constantly having to make new friends, I had a shy streak I couldn't seem to shake, no matter how hard I tried.

That weekend, we headed out to the *antros*, Mexico City's nightclubs. Anyone could get in, regardless of their age, and all the *fresas* went, chauffeured in big groups by SUV. We took a taxi. From trendy Mexican clubs like La Boom to the dark rock lounge Bulldog, I recognized people from school. I was surprised by the lack of curfews and the free flow of alcohol, but the teenagers all had drivers who waited for them outside. Though alcohol wasn't forbidden (the legal drinking age was eighteen, but no one followed it), it was very rarely abused. Being drunk was considered low class and unattractive, two things completely unacceptable to the *fresas*.

My mother refused to let me be a part of it all, which led to my rebellion. I would stay at Ana's or sneak out. During the week, the student council organized *cocteles*, cocktail parties that the *fresas* hosted in popular clubs like Coco Bongo and Medusa, the Mexican equivalents of New York City's Bungalow 8 and Lotus. They offered open bars at these see-and-be-seen fiestas. There were also *comidas*, Friday afternoon *barra libre* parties in outdoor spaces or big empty warehouses, where the food was just a sideshow; hired bartenders in black-and-white uniforms ensured that the tequila flowed freely. Girls got in for free, so Ana and I didn't even need to ask for money to go out. The attendees were supposed to be over eighteen, but no one was checking. My mother didn't allow me to attend these affairs, but rather than risk being a social outsider, I went against her wishes.

She wanted me to blend with the culture wherever we moved, but coming home after 3:00 AM when I had an 11:00 PM curfew was not what she had in mind. Toward the end of my freshman year, my mother decided we needed an intervention to control my behavior. She scheduled an appointment with the school psychologist to discuss my difficulty "adjusting."

"She's out of control," my mother told the psychologist. "She wants to go out dancing until all hours."

"Well, you do have to realize that that's part of the social norm here," said the psychologist as I sat in an armchair, not daring to smile.

"Don't you think an eleven o'clock curfew makes sense?"

"Mom, the clubs open at eleven."

"Miss Gennatiempo, I'd say a more reasonable time would be two."

I liked the psychologist. She understood how important it was to become part of the culture, the reality of life in Mexico City. She also understood the divide between my mom and me.

"When you go off to college in a few years and live away from her," she told me, "a completely new side of you will surface." It was true that I wore a defensive shell. Though her intentions were good, my mother was the type to regularly read my journal, pretend she hadn't, then casually mention at breakfast that I should be sure to use condoms.

So for the next three years of high school, as long as my mother knew where I was going and whom I was with, my curfew was officially three in the morning. By the time senior year rolled around, I was navigating Mexico City's club scene like a miniature nightlife doyenne. When I got to college in the States, I couldn't stand the thought of keg parties—the party culture in Mexico City spoiled me for everything that came after.

One warm and hazy Sunday morning, my mother came into my room, pulled up the shades, and told me in a singsong voice to get up and dress.

"We're going to Rosa's for lunch today," she said. I should mention my mother doesn't speak—she chirps.

"We are?" I rubbed the sleep from my eyes and sat up in bed, exhausted from a late Saturday night. I adored Rosa, our housekeeper, who had recently married her sweetheart. She lived with us during the week and went home on weekends. Another fact of Mexico City life: Every house in the upscale neighborhoods had small, adjoining living quarters for the hired help. Rosa would live with us until she had children, at which point the responsibility for earning a living would fall to her husband.

Rosa was pretty and kind. She and I would make quesadillas or bake cakes together and talk about food or relationships—hers with her husband and mine with whoever held my fleeting romantic interest at the time. I knew not to bring up the *fresa* boy at school whose dad controlled the gasoline industry, or my nights of cocktails and irresponsible partying, or the expensive clothes and shoes I bought at Centro Comercial Santa Fe, the upscale shopping mall thirty minutes away. I was ignorant of the American social stigma attached to hired help until we moved back to the United States, where only the very wealthy had live-in help—and some people didn't even like to use the word "maid."

I viewed Rosa as a friend or older sister, not as a maid. In her late twenties, she wasn't much older than I, just in a completely different place in life. She attended beauty school and pierced my ears for me. My mom let her practice hairstyling in our house so often that the living room would reek of ammonia from hair dye.

We drove two hours to Rosa's rural house, not far outside the city. Her family lived in a cement home with two stories, a dirt floor, and handwoven rugs strewn about. By the time we arrived, I was doing a jig, so my mother and I went to find the bathroom, which turned out to be a drainlike hole in the backyard that she helped me squat over. I played makeshift soccer with Rosa's two little cousins in the dusty yard as goats and chickens scurried about, until Rosa's mother and brother came outside. I watched, puzzled at first, as they lunged after a chicken.

"¡Van a matar el pollo!" one of the boys screamed. I understood enough to know that I was looking at my lunch flapping desperately around the yard.

Rosa's mother grabbed the chicken by its neck, waving it around until the head snapped off, the carcass running aimlessly in circles. My mother made me hold the chicken head and snapped a photo in which my nose is crinkled in revulsion. I felt distinctly guilty for enjoying the resulting tacos. I attribute seven years of vegetarianism to this occasion; surely it's haunted my subconscious all this time. But that day I noticed how happy this family was, talking and laughing around the table. I could see it in how their deep brown eyes sparkled, how Rosa's hands guided mine as she taught me to make the tortillas, how her mother smiled as Rosa welcomed us into her home.

Some said Mexico had "the perfect dictatorship," as the same political party had held on to the presidency for some seventy-odd years. The privileged life of the upper class wasn't without its own downside, though. A boy whose father held a high-level government job was pulled out of class one day by the principal. I later learned he'd been rushed to the hospital—to see his dying father, who had been assassinated, shot while giving a speech.

I worried about my mother's safety. She helped troubled U.S. citizens on a daily basis with property thefts. A $50,000 motorhome that was "confiscated" by police in Baja was found at Los Pinos, the residence of the country's president. It was being used to transport military personnel. She also recovered boats, cars, and even a helicopter. A man she dated at one point had been the head of the Mexican prison system, which held several top international drug dealers. He was hospitalized after a poisonous gas was leaked into his home. Then, one morning, he was giving a talk at a local university. While lunching afterward in the cafeteria, quietly reading the newspaper, he was shot in the head and killed. My mother never went out with a high-profile man again.

On my first date, with Manuel, his driver picked me up and brought me to his house. A Picasso hung in the entryway. Ana and I had debated why Manuel had asked me out; all he'd said to me was I seemed "different." I knew he had noticed me early in sophomore year when I caught him looking at me in European History class. It took a year for him to ask me on a date, which I assumed was because my social status was not on a par with his. Manuel was almost six feet tall, with blond hair that flopped into his blue eyes—more like a California surfer stud than a Mexican businessman's son.

"Maybe he's sick of the *fresa* girls," said Ana.

Manuel's driver took us to La Boom, and his bodyguard rode in the front seat.

"You've lived all over the place," he said as we drove by the Ángel de la Independencia, the large golden statue that towered above Reforma. "Where do you consider home?"

"I'm not really sure. My mother thinks it's wherever we're living at the time," I told him. I explained her perpetual cooking of *pollo con mole*, and the day we'd spent at Rosa's.

"She could be killing chickens with her bare hands one day and lunching in Cuernavaca the next," I told him. Cuernavaca was a warmer, pollution-free town about an hour outside Mexico City, with several fashionable restaurants that had huge gardens with peacocks milling about the lawns. "She wants it all."

Manuel laughed. "And you, what do you want?" he asked.

I just looked out the window at the sky, hoping to see a star through the haze. By the time he kissed me goodnight at three in the morning, I knew the allure of dating a *fresa*. At the young age of seventeen, he was already a well-bred gentleman, well traveled and sophisticated. His family had houses in Spain and Valle de Bravo, an exclusive vacation town on a lake. He was educated and attractive, with grade-A genes. But I knew it couldn't last. Manuel was pedigree. I may have intrigued him, but in the eyes of the society he belonged to, I was but a mutt.

When the devaluation of the peso hit, the crime rate went through the ceiling. Things got especially dangerous in twelfth grade, when my mother's work-related horror stories about Americans being kidnapped became more extreme than usual. She came home crying one evening after dealing with a case in which a woman was held at knifepoint in the parking lot of an upscale shopping mall and the mugger cut her breasts, just because he could. Ana and I were forbidden to take taxis, as drivers had started robbing tourists down in the Zona Rosa. The passenger would get in the taxi and it would take off, usually followed by a car of accomplices. The unsuspecting passenger would be driven somewhere remote and robbed.

One Saturday afternoon, Ana and I went with some classmates to the movies. At the entrance, we filled out a sweepstakes form at a booth to win a free vacation to the Bahamas. When Ana and I got back to my house, our parents were huddled around with a man I recognized from the embassy. My mother screamed when we walked in.

"What's going on?" I asked.

"I suspected it was a hoax," said the embassy rep. "We got a call that you had been kidnapped. They demanded a large ransom immediately."

"We just went to the movies," said Ana.

"Exactly," said the man. "You signed up for some kind of sweepstakes or something, right?"

Ana and I looked at each other in shock. We weren't the first kids this had happened to, and soon, word got around. The booths disappeared just as quickly as they'd gone up.

After high school graduation, it was time to move again. I had the same feeling as when I'd left Rome, only amplified, because I spent four of my most life-altering, formative years in Mexico City. Over that time, I'd fallen in love with the city. I was never accepted into *fresa* society, nor did I have a second date with Manuel, but Ana and I still live close to each other, in New York City. Sometimes, as different as the two cities are, Manhattan reminds me of Mexico—late nightlife, rich in culture, an elite ruling class. But during bitter winters, I long for what was the closest thing I ever knew as a home. I want to walk through the *zócalo* and see the sinking buildings. I want to visit the grand old church in Coyoacan, drink tequila with *sangrita*, a spicy tomato juice chaser. I often relive senior prom, which was held in a beautiful old hacienda, and I reminisce about getting drunk that night with the teachers and even the principal. I want to shop in posh Polanco and then eat *tacos al pastor* on a street-front patio restaurant.

I'm reminded of one of my favorite quotes from Salman Rushdie in *Imaginary Homelands*: "It is my present that is foreign, and the past is home, albeit in a lost city in the mists of a lost time." This is not to say that I forget the dark side of Mexico City—the assassinations, the potential dangers, the police corruption. The underbelly of that society broadened my perspective and allowed me to see things that I would otherwise never have understood.

My mother was transferred back to Europe. She's retiring from the Foreign Service soon and still has no idea where she wants to live. The day I left for college, driving through that carnival of an intersection on the way to the airport, I bought *chicles* for the plane from the old woman, and one of the balloon boys waved. *"¡Hasta luego!"* I shouted out the window, just as the light turned green and the cars barreled down Reforma to the start of another day.

Sophia Raday

Panamericano

When I opened the restaurant door, catcalls erupted. In the dusk of the interior, I made out a dozen or so men turning from the television to stare at me, whistling softly and nudging each other, *"Mira, una gringita."* Look, an American girl.

A forty-ish woman with strawberry blond hair and freckles came toward me from behind the counter.

"Hi there. You must be Sophia. I'm Virginia, Gary's wife."

I nodded. Glancing around the room, I suddenly wondered if it was possible to lock the school bus that was to be my new home, according to Gary.

"So, Sophia, did you and Gary talk about what you might do here?"

"Um, no, we didn't get to that."

Gary had spent most of the ride down from San Diego regaling me with his Maoist philosophies.

"Have you worked with children?"

My stomach tightened. I imagined a gaggle of kids swarming around me, running amok.

"I'm sorry, Virginia, I don't have much experience with kids. Plus, you know, my Spanish isn't so hot."

Virginia wiped the sweat from her forehead and sighed.

"Can you cook?"

I stared at the floor. Only tofu and veggies.

Did I know anything about medical care? Carpentry? Painting? Auto Mechanics? No. No. No.

That was how I became the dishwasher at the restaurant in Colonia Panamericano, a squatters' settlement on the outskirts of Tijuana. "Pana" was a random assortment of shacks crowded on a downhill-tilting mesa with ravines on three sides. People held no deeds to their "properties" in Pana, nor was there electricity or running water. I had found an internship with Grupo Primavera Project through a pamphlet entitled "Alternatives to the Peace Corps." The project impressed me because they were helping to start businesses with some of the poorest people in Mexico—plus they would let me do a short internship, just six weeks.

It turned out Grupo Primavera was Gary and Virginia, who had thrown their lot in with the people of Panamericano. They had helped start a metals recycling "plant." The recycling took place in the yard of one of the residents and employed maybe a dozen of the men in the settlement. A water purification plant and a clinic were in the works. Virginia had started a restaurant next door to the recycling plant to cater primarily to the recycling workers.

While dishwashing was a dirty and physically demanding job, it had some benefits. The restaurant was the community's social hub, thanks to its TV, which was intermittently powered by a gas generator. I could be among people and conversation and laughter, but I didn't have to speak too much of my meager Spanish. I listened and picked up little words and phrases, said them softly to myself over and over, and later jotted them in my notebook. The only times I really dreaded were the rare occasions when both Virginia and her assistant, Pilar, left to run errands and I had to deal with customers. That was the worst, and that was how I first met Rafael Ángel.

It was my first Sunday, and Pilar had not yet arrived for work, even though it was close to 11:00 AM. Things were moving slow that morning, probably because the night before, Gary, Cacahuate, Pepe, Manuel, and the others drank and sang until the wee hours. Virginia told me she'd be right back, and I assumed she was going to rouse Gary from his beer-induced slumber so he could help with their baby, Rosita. As soon as she left, I began silently praying that no one would come into the restaurant.

It wasn't that I was afraid of the men anymore. I had come to understand their whistles and calls of "¡Oye, bonita!" as their way of paying me a compliment. The problem was, I couldn't prepare them any food. I had sworn off meat at seven years old, when my father explained to me that meat was animals. *Explained* is a nice way of putting it. He described in detail how mastodon meat had been found frozen in the Arctic Circle and was now considered a delicacy, but with his heavy Hungarian accent, he pronounced it *deh*-lick-*ah-see*. I stared at him and stammered that surely he didn't mean that people eat animals?

"And wot do you tink you ahr eateeng?" was his reply.

While I was now twenty-three, I had no idea how to prepare the chicken, beef, or pork for tacos. The door swung open, and four men walked in. I noticed with surprise that they were clean. The guys I'd seen in the restaurant so far—all workers at the recycling plant—were usually filthy. Their clothes, faces, and bare arms were smeared with soot and engine oil and dirt. And their hands were completely black, as if the dirt had conjoined with their skin cells.

Rafael's blue-black hair was freshly cut and combed, and he was wearing a new white T-shirt. A tiny speck of shaving cream highlighted with a thin white line where one of his sideburns ended. Even his features seemed clean, his nose straight, his chin firm, his eyebrows distinct. His lips were held in a stern straight line, but his brown eyes were playful. A pen hung from his T-shirt at the base of his neck, and I saw the tops of crutches under his armpits.

"*Hola, señorita.*" he said in a mock extra-deep voice and laughed at himself. "*¿Qué hay de comer?*"

"*¿Cómo?*" I asked, my oft-used Spanish equivalent of "huh?"

He made a little bouquet with his fingertips and motioned toward his mouth. I felt my face get warm, and in the realization that I was blushing, I blushed further. That's when I realized why Rafael was on crutches. He only had one leg. The other pantleg was pinned up just above where the knee should be and hung loosely.

The other men were picking up on their poor chances of getting a meal from me. They were shaking their heads. I caught the words *"pinche gringita"* and *"no sabe"* and ultimately *"ay, que pendeja."* *"Pinche"* and *"pendejo/pendeja"* I'd learned on my first day in Pana, since they were the most common words spoken. Everything was *pinche* this and *pinche* that—a working-class Mexican adjective usually connoting mild disdain, but at other times affection, like when it was used before a person's name. *Pendejo* meant anything from goofball to idiot to asshole. I knew the majority sentiment in the room at that point was "Who ever heard of a woman who can't cook?"

"Virginia *venir*," I managed and looked at my watch. Virginia to come.

"Ah, *pinche* Virginia." Rafael said and spoke to the others. They continued shaking their heads but pulled out the metal folding chairs and sat down to wait. Rafael steadied himself against the counter and smiled at me. *"Está bien, señorita, esperamos."* It's okay. We'll wait.

I busied myself wiping the counter. There wasn't much else to do, as I had already gone to the water truck and hauled in three buckets to wash the day's dishes. I glanced now and again at Rafael, who leaned against the counter, mostly joking with the men, occasionally looking over at me. Getting around on crutches had given him shoulders, biceps, and triceps like the weight-lifters at my gym at home. I was trying to make out what the crude tattoo on his right arm depicted, but I didn't dare look at him too long. My misery was interrupted by Pilar, who looked at the men and then at me, and laughed. *"Gracias a Dios,"* I muttered, as Pilar set about frying up chicken and roasting tomatoes, gesturing to me to cut up onions and hot peppers for the salsa.

When the men had eaten and left, I scraped their leftovers into an empty white bucket, then plunged the dishes into soapy water. I was trying to figure out what was odd about how Rafael interacted with the other men. I wanted to ask Pilar more about him, to find out how he lost his leg, but I didn't want my interest in him to be obvious. What must Rafael think about me, a young gringa here in this place, washing dishes? I reflected on my limited cooking skills, my limited Spanish skills, my nearly utter uselessness. Some good my fancy modernization theories did me here.

I swabbed a plate with a soapy gray rag. One thing was sure: I hadn't realized how great I'd had it when I was a student. Everyone thought that it was just sooo wonderful that I was studying at Stanford. It seemed The World was always smiling and nodding at me. But once I graduated, The World started tapping its fingers on the tabletop. *What's she doing with her life? What has she accomplished? Does she carry a briefcase? Does she wear pantyhose?* Suddenly I was expected to do great things.

When all the dishes were rinsed twice, I piled them on a towel on the wooden counter. My first job after college was as an aide to a county supervisor in the Silicon Valley. For the past year I had worked on petty constituent bickering, waved to supporters on behalf of my boss at two or three banquets a week, and dedicated myself to an open-space initiative that was vetoed by the governor. As I dried the dishes, I felt that same little leap of excitement as the day I had quit the aide position. I was flipping the bird at The World.

Wiping down the propane stove, it hit me what was unusual about Rafael. It was the way the men—even the older ones—deferred to him, the way they treated him as the leader. The way he carried himself, so that the pinned-up pantleg came as such a shock. He did not seem diminished, not in the slightest. I wondered where in the *colonia* he lived. I signaled to Pilar that I was going out for a *descanso*, a short break. She nodded.

At that time of day, rusty minivans careened in dusty circles in front of the restaurant, with young men hanging out of their doors, screaming their destinations to potential passengers: "Tlalco!" "Guanato!" "El Centro!" "Rosarito!" "Aquajito!" I skirted the traffic and ducked down the rocky, potholed path that looped through the settlement. Like my school bus sitting on its axles, most of the vehicles that ventured beyond the barren cul-de-sac in front of the restaurant never left. They were cannibalized for roofing or siding, used for shelter or storage, or simply left to molder. I headed away from my bus to the other side of the *colonia*, where I hadn't explored. I wondered how Rafael spent his Sunday, his one free day of the week.

Gary had told me that Pana had once been Tijuana's municipal garbage dump. That explained the smell—rot mingling with exhaust fumes and outhouses. The shacks, with their dust-muted colors, reminded me of patchwork quilts made from used clothing. They were built out of a combination of green corrugated plastic, wood, red brick, blue tarpaulins, tin, sheet metal, and even car doors. Vegetation was nonexistent. Wraithlike dogs skulked in the shadows. Ribbons of garbage tumbled into the ravine. At the bottom of the mesa, I stopped to look out. I was on the rim of a great bowl, with the center of Tijuana below me. Whitish houses with terra-cotta roofs dotted the hillsides around the city center. Up the sides of the bowl, other *colonias* sprawled. No sign of Rafael. I continued along the loop path, passing Gary and Virginia's cement house on the right. Now I was back in familiar territory.

When I had almost gotten back to the *colonia*'s traffic circle, I ducked left between two shacks and came to my bus, which was conveniently located near an outhouse (or not so conveniently, depending on one's tolerance for flies). "It's a composting toilet!" Gary had cried with a smile of pride when I first arrived. It looked like any other outhouse to me. Evidently, others were even less impressed than I. Sometimes I found piles of feces on the floor just inside the door of the outhouse; other times, in the dirt just outside. Then, just as mysteriously, they were cleaned up.

My bus was three-quarters full of random junk—boxes of books, old lamps, broken toasters, and a large pile of clothing. In the less-cluttered part, there was a wooden platform where I had set up my camp pad and sleeping bag, and a little candle lantern for nighttime. Next to my platform lay a Spanish-English dictionary—my evening reading. The bus was a little haven from interaction, from the strain of smiling all the time, of trying to understand but not quite getting it, of having only one role—that of the amiable buffoon. I leafed through the dictionary to the Ts, eventually finding the word that was on my mind. *Tatuaje.* Tattoo.

I didn't see Rafael again for about a week. In the meantime, I gradually became inured to plunging my hands in gray greasy water with chicken bones, tomato skins, and cilantro floating in it. Hygiene in Panamericano fascinated me. I found out that the reason Rafael and the other metals recycling workers were so clean that day was that it was Sunday, their day off, and they all went down to the bathhouse on the main highway. Pilar told me some of the men bathed themselves early in the morning with buckets up by the concrete reservoir, but as far as I could tell, they wore the same clothes all week, clothes that were gradually armored by a thick coating of dirt and oil from dismantling car parts and sifting through garbage.

We had a small bucket and a bar of soap outside the restaurant, but some of the guys ate with their hands totally black. Watching them with dismay, I made a discovery: They corkscrewed their tortillas into a tight roll by twirling it around the end of their forefinger. Then they delicately held the end of the tortilla and used it as we might use a knife, to guide food onto their forks. After eating a forkful of food, they bit into the tortilla, consuming all but the tiny piece they held between their thumb and forefinger, now also black. They threw that piece away.

I found myself following the same pattern as the men, bathing once a week. I changed my T-shirt and underwear each day but wore the same shorts and sweatshirt for several days at a time. I felt like a coconspirator. It made me laugh to think of the contrast between this and how I lived at my father's house in San Jose, a shower in the morning, a dip in the hot tub most evenings, and then another quick shower to rid myself of the chlorine. Life in Panamericano had stripped me to the bare essentials—hard work, good food, frequent laughter—I was surprised to find that I wasn't constantly feeling sorry for the people here. Yes, there was Araceli, a little girl with a cleft palate who needed cosmetic surgery that would have been standard in the United States. Seeing her, I felt the stab of guilt I had expected to fill my days here. Yet more often, I was taken by the easy banter that existed among the restaurant patrons.

Cacahuate was one of the few men who didn't work at the metals recycling plant next door, and to be honest, I never knew how he made his money. He was one of the best off, I knew, because he had one of the few concrete houses—next door to the one Gary and Virginia lived in. He dressed in white slacks and Hawaiian shirts and often sported a tan fedora. When I was introduced to him, I inquired, "Cacahuate?"

Lobo, standing next to him, looked up and said, "Pay-noot."

"Oh, *peanut*," I said, still not getting it.

Cacahuate pointed to his nose and said, *"Por la nariz."* And it was true, his nose was large and pockmarked, closely resembling his nickname. That's one of the things that was different in Pana. There was very little pretense. If you were a chubby guy, your nickname was Gordo. There was no malice in it.

Gary lent me an ancient one-speed bike. I jostled through the potholes and the washboards of the dusty roads to explore the neighboring *colonias*. I was pushing the bike uphill back toward Pana when a beat-up pickup truck with high wooden sides—the kind that haulers used back home—rumbled by. Its cargo bed was packed with standing workers, and I recognized Rafael Ángel among them. The truck bucked along the road. Rafael was holding on to the side of the truck, balancing on his leg, his face tight, frozen. The look on his face arrested me. The truck went right past me with my bike, but I realized Rafael wasn't seeing me or anything else on the dusty road. He looked prepared to endure discomfort forever.

That night in my bus, I took out the old Spanish-English dictionary again. I looked up the verb *terminar*, "to finish," because I'd realized that Rafael's tattoo was an unfinished version of a childlike sun—a circle with triangles surrounding about a third of it. I wanted to be ready for the next time I saw him.

That didn't take long. He came in the next day, my second Sunday, freshly bathed again, wearing ironed jeans and a red V-necked sweater vest. *"Huevos a la mexicana,"* he ordered, and arranged himself on one of the stools facing the cooking area.

By this time, I had learned how to make the salsa, and while Virginia cracked eggs, I blackened the tomatoes and minced onion, *chile de árbol*, and a bit of garlic. I grabbed the blender and began dumping the tomatoes in when Rafael objected, *"No, señorita gringita, no."* I stopped and looked over at Virginia for guidance. She talked to Rafael in Spanish, then turned to me: "Rafael wants you to make the salsa with a mortar and pestle, not with the blender."

I looked at Rafael, who turned his palms up, cocked his head, and grinned. *"La buena salsa viene de molcajete."* Good salsa has to be made with a mortar and pestle. Then he waved to me to bring him the ingredients while Virginia brought him a mortar and pestle. He began with a bit of onion, which he mashed into a liquid, then added a small bit of chili and some blackened tomato. Soon he had a thick chunky liquid going. Finally he handed me the mortar and pestle. *"Ahora, usted."* Now you.

I grabbed the pestle, added some more onion and chili, and

stabbed at my targets. They swam away. Concentrating hard, I managed to catch the chili against the side of the mortar. I pushed on it hard with the pestle and it broke in half. *Victory!* I thought, but the feeling was short lived. I would have to twist the pestle against the ingredients in order to liquefy them. In about sixty seconds, my hand and forearm ached. I looked up at Rafael, who was trying not to laugh. Buying time, I remembered my phrase from the dictionary the night before.

"*¿Por qué no terminastes el tatuaje?*" I stalled, glancing at his right arm.

"*El artista,*" he said, laughing at the word he'd chosen, "*se fue,*" walking his fingertips across the countertop in explanation: The artist . . . went away. Then he reached for the mortar and pestle.

After I'd been in Panamericano for about three weeks, Gary suggested that I go watch the night shift at the recycling plant. Operations peaked at night, because working around a blazing fire in Tijuana's desert sun was unpopular with the workers. The first thing I realized was that the term "metals recycling plant" made it sound a good deal fancier than it was. The plant was mainly a junkyard sprawling along a fairly steep hillside. Car parts, crates of old appliances, broken aluminum lawn furniture, and barrels and barrels of cans were mixed up with a vast variety of general household garbage. The detritus covered the yard in assorted heaps and mounds with an average height of about four feet.

I entered at the bottom, zigzagging through the many obstacles up a meandering path. The path rose to a hummock, off to the right of which was the shack where the recycling plant proprietor lived with his family. On the other side of the hummock, I saw the main recycling area.

How can I describe what I saw that April night in the north Mexican desert? Try to imagine that dusk has turned everything a charcoal color, save for eerie green and violet flames dancing out of garbage barrels. Those strange flame colors come from burning things such as disposable diapers. Folks in Pana burned all sorts of things—plastic bottles, wool garments (if you've ever caught your hair in your blow-dryer, you have some idea of the smell), aluminum foil, you name it. It occurred to me that all the garbage-burning may have spurred the metals recycling idea. As I rose to the hilltop, the gunmetal sky was already ablaze with stars. Then I saw the bonfire, a conflagration about five feet wide. Its sparks exploded above the heads of the workers who fed it. The men were silhouettes, occasionally illuminated by orange flashes. They were all stripped to the waist, and sweat gleamed like orange and red oil in the firelight.

The workers were throwing the random junk from the yard into a great urn, made of either concrete or possibly asbestos, under which the huge fire was kept blazing. There was a small hole off to the side of the bottom of the urn, and out of this trickled the molten metal. It burbled along a short section of metal half-pipe and into ingot molds. This was the plant's end product—aluminum ingots. Here and there along the junkyard path, ingots were stacked, twelve by twelve, on trays to be shipped to the United States.

I sat down cross-legged to watch, a shadow on the hillside.

The men barely spoke, but each seemed to know exactly what was required of him. I recognized Rafael Ángel at the head of the urn, throwing metal items in at regular intervals. I was struck by the rawness and the virility of the activity I witnessed. This was the kind of masculinity that the Marlboro Man tried to capture but couldn't quite—this was authentic. Envy ran through me, and I wondered at it. There was no place where I belonged as perfectly as these men seemed to belong here, to this ritual of breaking down and renewal.

Yet here I was, a dishwasher in a squatters' settlement in Mexico and oddly happy. Sure, I wasn't quite living up to my full potential. But there was something about the place that made me feel like I was inhabiting my skin. My constant self-evaluation, the burden of measuring up to what The World expected of me, had lightened here. I sat for a long time, arms around my knees, surveying this Mephistophelean work shift in the desert.

Finally, beginning to shiver, I commanded myself to take a mental snapshot and rose to go down the hill to my bus. I slowly retraced my steps down the windy path. Night had arrived in earnest, and I picked my way carefully. Descending the hillside, I saw that my way was now blocked by a shopping cart full of car parts. To sidestep the shopping cart, I had to walk on top of numerous milk crates full of metal cans. As I stepped onto the edge of one crate, it pitched forward, and I rode it in slow motion. Cans crashed. I put my hand out to break my fall. There was something at just the right height to steady myself. *Phew*, I thought, *maybe no one heard—Jesus!* I recoiled as pain coursed through my hand. I'd steadied myself on a pile of just-molten aluminum ingots. I grasped my burned hand against my thighs and leaned over, moaning. I didn't hear Rafael come up beside me.

"*¿Qué pasó?*"

"*Me cayo,*" I hissed. (I falled.)

He glanced at my hands, one still clenched in the other.

"*A verla,*" he demanded, with an upward nod toward my hand.

"*No, no, está bien.*"

"*A verla.*"

"No, no, really, it's okay."

"*Déjeme verla,*" Rafael said. It was an order.

When I turned my injured hand palm up, fat, white blisters striped down my three middle fingers, spreading out as we looked at them.

Rafael whistled softly and nodded. "*Eres machita,* Sofia."

I ran down the rest of the hill to the restaurant, hoping I could still get some ice from the cooler. Daggers shot up and down my burned fingers, but I was smiling. Rafael Ángel thought I was tough. I could imagine no greater compliment.

Pilar was just closing up, and we argued over whether to apply ice or butter, but I eventually got my way. I slept in the bus on my platform bed with my hand in a bowl of ice water. Every now and again, I would try to take my hand out of the water. I let the fire build in my fingers as long as I could stand it, and then plunged them back in the bowl. By the next morning, the pain had ceased, but the white stripes prefigured scars, permanent mementos of my night at the recycling plant.

I watched for Rafael to come into the restaurant. But the whole next week there was no sign of him. During this time, I got to be friends with his roommate, whom everyone called Negro. I'm not sure if this was because of his relatively dark complexion, or because he seemed to skip the Sunday bathing ritual. He reminded me of Pigpen from the *Peanuts* comic strip.

On Saturday night, Negro showed up with a six-pack of beer. There was a small group of people watching *Sábado Gigante,* a six-hour-plus variety show that airs from about 3:00 PM till who-knows-when on Saturday night. I was bored, so when Negro invited me to climb to the top of the reservoir above the settlement, I readily accepted. We sat on the edge of the cavernous concrete structure, looked down on the lights of Tijuana, and drank beer.

"And Rafael, where is he?" I ventured casually.

"*Otro lado,*" Negro said with an airy wave. I had heard this phrase many times. For one thing, it is the way that everyone in Panamericano referred to the United States—"the other side"— but I didn't think that was what he meant in this context.

"*¿Cómo?*"

Negro looked over at me. "*Con su no-vi-a,*" he said slowly, meaningfully, watching for my reaction. I was careful to act unimpressed with the news that Rafael had a girlfriend and took another swig of my beer. At least I understood now why Rafael was not seeking me out. I told myself I was leaving in a couple of weeks anyway; what did it matter that he had a girlfriend? But lead sank in my stomach.

Over the next few days, I busied myself with new projects. I painted the fence around the restaurant. I found some rope and fixed the makeshift swings that had dangled from a bare metal crossbeam. When I got home, I decided, I was going to find a job in construction or auto mechanics.

Each time the restaurant door opened, I felt a little gut-skip of hope. But days passed, until I only had a week left in Pana. I worried that I would not see Rafael again. Then one day, coming back from one of my bumpy bike rides, I heard a deep voice call *"Oiga, señorita."* Rafael was calling me from the recycling yard. He held a large knife and struggled with a bundle. As I approached him, I realized the bundle was a skinned pig, and he was dismembering it, blood coating his forearms all the way to his elbows.

"Hola, Güerita. ¿Puede ayudarme?" Hello, Miss Blondie. Can you give me a hand?

I tried to hide my horror. When Rafael motioned to me to hold a hoof, I did so gingerly while trying to look away. But slowly, fascination crept over me, and I began to watch. He was deft with the knife, knew exactly how to cut the animal into usable sections. As he worked, he told me the Spanish names of the body parts he encountered. *Higado.* Liver. *Tripa.* Intestine. *Corazón,* pointing to his own chest at this last. Heart.

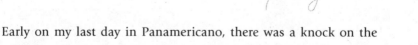

Early on my last day in Panamericano, there was a knock on the school bus door. My backpack was packed, and I was rolling up my sleeping mat. Rafael Ángel leaned on his crutches, avoiding my gaze, and held out a small piece of folded paper. I wasn't sure if the note was from him or if he was delivering it for someone else. As soon as I took the paper, he turned his shoulders and swung away, not even hearing my awkward *"Gracias."*

I sat down on the platform in the bus and unfolded the small notepaper. Glancing down at the signature, I saw "Rafael Ángel" in neat script. My body tingled, the way it did before a big drop on a rollercoaster. My Spanish was still pretty rudimentary, and I didn't understand every word, but I made out one part. "When you leave today, you are taking part of a Mexican heart with you."

I was reading and rereading the note when Gary came to load my gear into his beat-up van. Clutching the paper, I climbed into the passenger seat. As we drove out, the men in the recycling yard gave me their now-familiar catcalls and whistles. I looked for Rafael Ángel's face among them and found it, impassive, enduring. I held my hand up in a goodbye for him alone, and then waved to the others.

Kathleen Hamilton Gündoğdu

Measuring Cups

"¡*Dios mio!* Mom, get them out! I feel like I'm being manhandled by an octopus!" I yell and try to dodge groping hands, but I know I am cornered, with no place to go.

The dressing room is small, but four matronly women have squeezed into it with me. This is not my idea of a vacation: half naked and crammed into a cubicle with only a piece of lightweight cotton hanging down as a door. *Please let this be over soon.*

"Now, honey, just behave. They know what they're doing. It will be over in a few minutes, and we can go to the pool," my mother replies as she continues to browse through the racks of the lingerie store. My already fragile teen body image is being assailed as my breasts are prodded, pulled, pushed, measured, and thoroughly examined by more people than I care to have them exposed to.

We are on my family's annual trip to Acapulco. I have forgotten to pack undershirts, which I still wear because my breasts, much to my thirteen-year-old chagrin, have been slower to develop than those of many of my friends. My mother and I search the shops around the *zócalo* (town square) for undershirts, but to no avail. The dusty plaza stores offer a collection of jewelry, fruits and vegetables, shoes, clothing, and trinkets. We're learning that girls in Mexico don't wear undershirts. After sitting under one of the many palm trees shading the *zócalo* and sipping watermelon juice, we went into the lone lingerie store. It was midday, and many people were home for the siesta, but there were a few women out shopping for the evening meals they would soon be preparing. My mother and the saleswomen in the lingerie shop decided that it was time for me to graduate from undershirts to my first bra.

After this dressing-room experience, I really am looking forward to my usual watered down piña colada with dinner. That may well be the high point of my day.

What has brought me to this? I wonder.

Why, of all places, did my family have to choose Acapulco as our annual Thanksgiving destination? We were the only American family I knew who each year decamped there for an extended stay instead of staying in Texas and having a nice, normal Turkey Day. My friends were home getting ready to enjoy a bird and all its accompaniments, but we would have our usual holiday meal: red snapper served with beans and rice and flan for dessert— eaten as we watched the cliff divers tempt fate with each leap into the surging surf below at La Quebrada. For years I thought that Thanksgiving had something to do with pilgrims jumping off cliffs like lemmings.

Acapulco in the 1960s was still a beachside village. There were two large hotels in town—one on the beach, and the pink and white bungalows of Las Brisas, spread out across one of the hillsides above the sleepy village. We stayed at the Presidente only once. My mother was terrified of the lizards that crawled out of the drainpipe when anyone showered. The scorpions that wiggled inside under the doors were another deterrent. After nights of dodging the wildlife in the rooms, we vowed never to stay there again. The layout of Las Brisas suited our family much better. My parents had a bungalow to themselves, as did my brother and I. The bungalows were grouped in twos up and down the hillside, with a small private swimming pool between every two cottages. The added pluses of staying there were the electric pink and white jeeps provided to guests for trips around town and the surrounding coves.

The fact that Las Brisas was rumored to be a getaway for a few Hollywood jet-setters wanting to soak up the sun and have private rendezvous with or without their spouses was another draw. We would check the large main pool in the morning for celebrity sightings but always came away starless. Acapulco was not yet a destination for the masses of gringos who would one day descend. This was a getaway for families from Mexico City. The bay had no cruise ships disgorging tour groups or private yachts vying for space. Instead, there were a handful of small fishing boats and the occasional Mexican navy ship docked for a few days.

In fact, there was usually only a handful of foreign tourists in town—most came for diving in the shark-infested, crystal-clear waters of a nearby cove, or for deep-sea fishing further off the coast. Many of the gringo tourists were moneyed and wanted to be off the beaten track—but with some degree of comfort. Mexican families drove here over the mountains, risking the roads that washed out in the rains, for a getaway from the hustle and bustle of Mexico City. This was still an exotic destination for foreigners, with an airport consisting of a Quonset hut next to a tarmac strip that was about an hour's drive from town along a two-lane road across a mountain. The trip to the airport could take longer, depending on how heavy the donkey-cart and truck traffic was that day.

Both my parents loved Mexico, but my mother in particular had a soft spot for all things Mexican. At home, outside San Antonio, a city immersed in Mexican culture, we spoke English with Spanish idioms woven into our speech. Our maid, Juanita, from northern Mexico, spoke no English, so our Spanish reflected her northern accent. Our living room was dominated by a huge brass Aztec calendar hung above the fireplace. Flanking the fireplace were two large brass candlesticks bought in Mexico that were more suited to a cathedral than a ranch-style house. The exposed roof beams, painted Pepto-Bismol pink, added to the tropical feel of the decor. The bar off the living room was my father's rendition of a border bar—complete with papier-mâché parrots hanging from the ceiling, a slot machine, and a painting on black velvet of a topless woman we referred to as his "blue-eyed Mexican."

Our Texas home was often the setting for a full-blown fiesta around the backyard pool, complete with a mariachi band blaring away while guests from all over Mexico mingled and sipped margaritas. Many of my parent's friends were wealthy Mexican landowners and bankers who jetted into San Antonio by private plane to pick up the latest fashions, and whenever they were in town, they dropped by for a visit. Professors and their families from the University of Mexico campus in downtown San Antonio were also frequent guests. My mother took classes on Mexican culture and history at the university, all given in Spanish. On weekends, if I were lacking anything better to do, I would join my mother and sit in on classes with her.

I grew up hearing stories of witches who changed into animals, of spells cast against foes or to bring love, of the Virgin of Guadalupe appearing to peasant children, and of conquistadors who tried to conquer ancient, refined cultures with brutality. Mexico, an easily accessible place for vacation—whether in the mountains, deserts, or beaches—was an important part of our lives. We spent large parts of the summer exploring cities and villages in its interior. We often drove through the desert to reach Guadalajara and Guanajuato. The monotony of the dry, brown northern desert was only broken by the sudden appearance of a brightly garbed child by the side of the road, holding up an iguana, tortoise, or large brown desert rat for sale. I never did find out if these were meant for pets or dinner. My parents, knowing that I would want one as a pet, always refused to stop to investigate. Trips to Mexico City and Monterrey were taken in a private plane that my father coowned, with my mother sitting in the front, acting as translator between Mexican air traffic control and my father, who had only learned very basic Spanish.

Thanksgiving weekend offered my mother yet another chance to visit Mexico. Airfares were low, and my brother and I were allowed to miss school for a couple of weeks, promising of course, to bring our books along and do homework to turn in on our return. My teachers thought that it was wonderfully exotic and exciting to have a student who traveled to a place they had only seen in the movies.

A little over three hours by air, and we were away from San Antonio and basking on the beaches. Little did they know that we weren't hobnobbing with movie stars. Instead, my brother and I played in the streets, parks, and beaches with the local children. Because we knew our way around town and knew how to take taxis and buses, we were allowed to roam as we wanted—the only requirement was that we be back at the hotel and dressed for dinner. We were often to be found lying on the beach under the *palapas*, drinking warm sodas bought from passing vendors or eating at our favorite haunt on the beach, Hungry Herman's—a place we were forbidden to frequent after cockroaches crawled up my mother's legs during our first meal there. This, of course, only served to draw my brother and me back, and the owner, Ramón, warmly greeted us. "¡*Mira!* Look who has come back! Sit, eat. Pancakes again you want?"

We would settle in for a meal of gritty pancakes and "bottled" water that had thick swirls of sand floating in it as Ramón filled us in on what celebrities he had spotted recently. "Liz and Dick were at Las Brisas last month. I think I saw them driving past one day. Maybe not, though," he laughed at his "close" encounters with the jet-set.

The shopkeepers remembered us from year to year and measured our growth as if we were long lost relatives. A sort of extended family grew up from our visits. My parents knew that my brother and I could be let loose to roam as we wanted, because everyone would look out for us. If there was a problem or emergency, the village was small, and my parents could be found quickly. So for the most part we were left to spend our days as we chose: swimming at the beach, flying kites with local friends, and nosing around the shops to see if there was anything new that we just couldn't live without—like undershirts!

The decision to fit me with my first bra draws whoops of laughter and comments of encouragement from the sales force about the rate of growth of my soon-to-be-breasts. Suspecting that something interesting is happening inside, other women come in from the *zócalo* to see what the fuss is about. Fifteen or more women of all shapes and sizes surround me. An elderly woman dressed in black cackles with delight at the spectacle of this shy teenage gringa being fitted for her first bra.

"Not to worry, I was the same way, slow to develop on top," one woman tells me.

"And now look at me! *Dios mio*, without support they would hang to my knees!" She laughs, grabbing her breasts and jiggling them for emphasis.

A woman yells across the room, "With those breasts you could feed an entire village, my sister!"

"She has nine children! She did feed a village!" another voice chimes in. The room is filled with laughter at that comment. I am amazed that middle-aged women act this way. My mother certainly would never grab her breasts in public. Mesmerized, I can only watch and listen to this surprising display of female camaraderie.

The realization slowly sets in that to these women, this is not just a form of entertainment, but a rite of passage. *Geez, the first bra must rank up there with First Communion,* I think. As my mother continues to browse, the women compare notes on their breasts— development, ailments, aches, and pains. Every one of these women was once a young girl, shy about her body. They know what I'm going through, and through their stories and actions, they show me that they understand and care. In their eyes, I am entering womanhood, and they—as *comadres,* fellow mothers, who know me from our yearly visits—are bearing witness to my slow but imminent advance into their world. They cheer and encourage me. Teen angst gives way to mutual fascination with the women. My mother continues to browse and listen but doesn't join in. *Is she uncomfortable with her body like I am?* I wonder.

After measurements are taken and approved by all, the selection of an appropriate bra ensues. Even my mother, not one to discuss body parts or functions easily, thought that we could quickly find an under-garment and go back to the pool. However, she too catches the excite-ment and partakes of the ritual. She sorts through the undergarments laid before her for final inspection. "Too frilly, too stiff, too much sup-port, not enough support," she pronounces as she examines and judges each garment before casting it in the "maybe" or "reject" pile.

"Ay, I remember when I was your age. The world waited for me," sighs one old woman.

"*Es verdad*," says another. "All too soon we were wives and mothers. Now we watch our children and grandchildren grow and dream of their futures."

At last, one brassiere finally meets everyone's exacting requirements. It is made of soft cotton, with light padding and a minimum of lace. "The padding will give encouragement to your breasts to grow more," chuckles a middle-aged matron. Before being allowed to put my shirt back on, though, I have to model it for everyone.

"*Ojalá*, God willing, you are now a señorita, no longer a *niña*," sighs a crone dressed in black. Smiling back at her, I wonder if she is remembering her youth.

My mother pays for the purchase as the women hug me to their breasts and pinch my cheeks.

"Just wait until next year," one woman laughs. "You'll be back needing a much bigger size!"

"Yes, my dear, you will soon have bigger *chichis* to try and keep out of the hands of boys!" giggles another matron.

The women adjust their clothes, rewrap their woven *rebozos* around their shoulders, and wipe away the tears of laughter. Dignified, proud, and once again solemn, the women are again ready to go back and finish their errands. Who would suspect that just moments ago these women were jiggling their breasts and laughing so hard they cried? My mother shakes hands with them all and thanks them for their help.

We all leave together, a group of women of all shapes and sizes going about our business. I realize that I don't feel embarrassed any-more. Instead, I feel proud to have shared a common experience with women who know who they are and who are comfortable in their bodies.

Ojalá, I think, *I hope one day I'll have the confidence they do. I hope I can measure up to them.*

Mary Ellen Sanger

A Grammar of Place

I have seen places in Mexico where a sudden shift in the ground opened her up. Simmering lava spewed Mexico's restless heart over a grumbling earth, evaporating streams, erasing fields of corn and worn mountain paths, and leaving behind obsidian shards that glinted in the sun. The new path tore at travelers' feet. Walking on the heart of Mexico hurts.

Mexico has always been seismic and explosive, one of the most active areas of the planet. She is accustomed to colliding with herself. In a land that has never been at rest in her skin, a land where friction and upheaval are commonplace, I fit in. In Mexico the earth is not quiet, and I learned to live and love with the certainty that everything could change tomorrow.

For seventeen years, Mexico was my chosen home. I spoke her language, sang her music, filled my head with her stories, and ate her salsas. My dreams were Mexican. My friends were Mexican. "The stork made a mistake," they used to say. It should have left me south of the border.

In 1986, I moved to Mexico, and through my work in tourism, I promoted Mexico's allure for American tourists eager to experience chipotle and *"mañana"* in situ. From seaside deserts to ruins covered by tangles of jungle, Mexico was home. I could feel her volatile heart quiver—she was not safe and secure. The earthquakes, the hurricanes, and the ash from Popocatepetl were the punctuation in an interrogative clause, reminding me that I lived in a curiously kinetic land.

After fourteen years in tourism, I needed a break from the gloss and diversion, from the beaches and sun of the invented world of vacations. I needed to hear again the accent of the indigenous Mexico I had first fallen in love with, her syllables a result of ancient collisions, metal against stone, blade against bone. At the helm of the operation of Cancún's largest tourism agency, I had to focus on strategic planning and financial statements. I missed the wondrous Mexico that had entangled me.

Accustomed to radical change, I left Cancún behind and took off for rural Oaxaca, an area of striking iridescence and visibly rooted culture. I arrived a week after a strong earthquake shook the city. Downtown, rubble from ancient buildings lined the edges of cobbled streets. Banners throughout the city solicited assistance for those whose roofs did not withstand the jolt. In the small village where I had chosen to live, at the foot of the mountains, the dry corn stalks in rutted fields swayed, and stout concrete-block homes stood unmoved. The locals told me that the only indication of the tremor was the coffee that sloshed out of the pot over the morning fire, spotting the earthen floor. There was more stability in the mountains, where the tectonic slips occur farther below the surface. In the mountains, they just nod and say "Again."

In Oaxaca, I became part of a rural community. I wrote, I lent a hand, drew close to children and elders and animals and plants. I walked and walked over jagged mountain paths. I was shifting under my skin. Oaxaca glistened with rare ambers, jades, and rubies. Indigenous colors. A scarlet bird on a golden cactus bloom. A serpent carved from soft copal wood and painted bright green with topaz eyes. Poised women in crimson blouses embroidered with rainbow geometries that held the history of their family. I filled my pockets with these jewels and sank my toes into a rich, loamy earth. I breathed in the scent of freshly opened ferns and squash blossom soup, set to a score of percolating marimbas and the buzz of cicadas before rain. Everything in Oaxaca was new and exciting. My heart bubbled to the surface, and I collided headlong with myself.

I expected to stay for six months—enough time to detoxify from the corporate world and move on. I stayed for three years. With my world aligned and opening up, I had no reason to leave. Shortly after arriving, I found a home in the village of San Pablo as a live-in caretaker for an elderly man, an expatriate English professor from New York. Russell Ames left the United States with his wife, Jean, during the McCarthy era, finding Oaxaca much more accepting of their somewhat radical voices. The villagers had taken them in forty-five years ago. I was invited by Russell—he had recently become a widower—to assist in the administration of his home, to drive him to the doctor in an old Renault the color of Pepto-Bismol, and to listen to stories of Big Bill Broonzy and songs of the Prohibition. Living with Russell was drenched in its own kind of color.

But I learned well the grammar of place. I was living on a fault line, and I knew that tomorrow everything could change. Three years into my Oaxacan idyll, the earth shifted . . . again.

On that Monday night, I did not make sure that Russell Ames, one week into his ninety-second year, was safely tucked into his book-strewn bed at nine-thirty, as I had every night for three years. I did not ask him where he was in his latest reading of Neruda's autobiography, and I did not bring a biscuit to the dog that slept at the foot of his bed, scratching her tummy and promising her a walk in the mountains early the next morning, as I had done every night for three years. I did not turn off the computer in my writing studio, full of Russell's collection of dusty volumes. Before going to bed, I did not set a place at the breakfast table for Russell, with his pink and white pills on a demitasse saucer, alongside the plate with blue flowers where his Siamese cat would share his bacon. And I didn't ease into my own bed to read Carlos Fuentes before sleep, looking first at the mountain washed in moonlight and framed by the jacaranda tree just outside my window. I did not pull a thick woven blanket around me. I did not smell the age of its heavy wool, as I had every night for three years.

That night I lay on a concrete floor that smelled of insecticide in the Oaxaca State Penitentiary in the town of Ixcotel, on a garish blue Tweety Bird blanket chirping "Pleasant Dreams" in fancy cursive. It was almost midnight by the time I was led down an exterior corridor, following two guards dressed in black and whole families of scuttling rats. They took me to an unused office, with a rusty sink clogged with gray paint chipped off a crumbling wall. There was a half-empty snack-sized bag of chili-lemon corn chips in one corner and that Tweety blanket they arranged for me, which barely fit in the width of the room. Hoarse groans and the sound of a clanging toilet seat came through a barred window high up near the ceiling. The photos and fingerprints were done, the body searches and the medical history. Tired clerks had filled out forms in triplicate, pounding earnestly on tinny manual typewriters. No, I have no tattoos. Yes, I went to college. No, I have no specified religion. Yes, I am in Mexico legally.

Finally alone, I splashed cold water on my face and fell against the wall, sliding to the floor, dripping. *Tranquila*. It will be fine in the morning. Someone will send a lawyer, there will be apologies, and I will go back home. I was worried about Russell. I wanted to sleep so the night would pass quickly; so this would be over. I lay down with Tweety and steadied my breath as I waited for the flood of sounds and images to subside. I bobbed fitfully between dream and reality. The crickets I dreamed that were under my jacaranda turned shrill and sharp as the guards whistled signals throughout the night. I dreamed the lone owl on the branch of the ceiba tree by Russell's tool shed screeched and took off on a great flutter of wings for the dark woods, but it was the guards keeping vigil in the outer corridor, horsing around, playing tag and singing falsetto to the love songs on their radio. There was no small, quiet moment to snuggle into. And no pillow to put over my head to drown out the reality invading my dreams.

Russell was finishing his black bean soup with a square of buttered cornbread. He was telling me again about Wabash College and the A the second-year French professor had promised him but reneged on.

"What happened, Russell? Why didn't she come through with the A?"

At 7:00 PM he was almost ready for his vanilla ice cream with homemade chocolate sauce. Lobo began to bark outside. Lobo was a neighbor's dog, an imposing husky with a gentle heart, one blue eye and one honey-colored. He loved Russell for the dog treats he kept in the pocket of his guayabera, and me for the bones I sneaked out the back door to him when the other dogs weren't around. He sometimes jumped through my open bedroom window at night and settled his big bear of a black dog body where I wouldn't miss him on my way out to walk the next morning. During the day, he slept in the shade of a luxuriant jasmine bush at the entrance and guarded the house as if it were his own, which, to a dog's way of thinking, I guess it was. He had taken possession, but nobody minded.

"Hang on to that answer for a minute, Russell. I hear Lobo making a fuss. There must be somebody coming to visit. I'll be right back."

About thirty feet from the front door, Lobo was jumping in circles around two men swinging at him nervously with branches broken from our ceiba tree.

"Shhhh, Lobo, down. . . . Can I help you?"

"So you speak Spanish. Now call off your dog."

"He's not my dog, and he doesn't like men with sticks. Is there something I can help you with?"

I had not seen these men before and distrusted them for yanking pieces off our tree and greeting me with a command in my own home.

"We need you to answer a few questions with Joe."

"Joe?"

Joe had been Russell's property caretaker twenty years ago. He had long since retired and was living rent free in a small house that Russell provided him at the entrance to his property. Joe was a hermit, and I had little contact with him outside of an occasional wave and having once been summoned by him to twist the wedding ring from the cold hand of his dead wife. "And get her watch too." He was a man of few words, and most of them acid.

"Call off your dog, we said!"

"Lobo, be good." He sat at my feet but didn't take his eyes off the sticks. "I'm sorry. I don't know anything about Joe. Are you sure you have the right person?"

And they said my name. First and last. It sounded like "Moddy Helen Sanher," but it was clearly my name. They were looking at a scribbled piece of paper. I didn't think Joe knew my last name—nobody did. I didn't need a last name in this tiny town of farms and goatherds. I'm not sure even Russell could remember my last name, and I had been his caretaker, staff administrator, and friend for the last three years.

They pulled badges from their pockets and said they were federal "preventive" police. They wore no uniforms. I wondered if the badges were real. I couldn't figure out what they wanted to prevent. I couldn't think fast enough. And what did I have to do with Joe?

"Is Joe all right?"

"We'll ask the questions. Now let's go."

Knowing I had nothing to hide and nothing to be put on the line for, my responsibility to Russell trumped all, and I challenged them with it. I was annoyed by the disruption and anxious to get back to my routine.

"You'll have to wait if you need me to answer some questions, because I left Mr. Ames inside, expecting his dessert. I can't leave him alone. So if you'll excuse me, you can come back in a half hour and I'll try to help you."

They moved closer. "Look, we won't wait a half hour or a half minute. We've asked you nicely. Let's go, and there won't be any violence."

Violence. They might as well have told me they were bringing in circus elephants. Six minutes ago, the biggest question on my mind was why that A in French mattered so much to Russell after seventy-five years. Violence? I didn't dare take my gaze off theirs. I echoed the absurdity of their suggestion.

"No, of course there won't be any violence. I have already told you that I will answer whatever I can. But I will take care of Mr. Ames first. Now you will excuse me. . . . "

And I walked away from them. I needed to serve Russell his vanilla ice cream. It was the only thing that made sense at that moment. I knew I needed to be inside of the house. I let them follow me. Let them see I was not lying. See? Old man, empty plate, quizzical look.

They followed me to the freezer, to the heavy pan with the homemade chocolate sauce, and back to Russell's round table, where he stared out the window at the dimming valley.

"Ho ho! Who are these fine men?" He must not have seen the sticks.

I presented the men to Russell as officials who were trying to help Joe with something. They put their sticks behind their back to shake Russell's hand.

"Russell, these men need my help with some questions about Joe."

"She's pretty smart. You came to the right place." Russell talked to the men, but he looked at me with a question in his eyes.

I asked how long we would be. They were standing too close to Russell.

"Half an hour. That's all it will take. Yes, half an hour or so."

"I'll be back in half an hour, Russell. How 'bout you eat your ice cream in your bedroom?"

I had perceived these two men as one. They came together, both held broken tree branches, both knew my name, both followed me. I remember no details of their individual appearance. They were the collective police with their collective purpose that I couldn't yet grasp. But when I headed to the bedroom with the cut-crystal bowl of softening vanilla ice cream, one official, who was no different from the other, said to the other, who was no different from the first, "Follow her."

He followed me wordlessly as I went to leave the ice cream by Russell's bed, then back to the dining room for Russell. They stood aside watching as I helped Russell out of his chair and positioned his walker. Then we all filed slowly, matching Russell's pace, along the cool red slab tiles that he and Jean had chosen for their garden-edged patio when they built their home here forty-five years earlier, the first Americans to settle in this tranquil village. We walked into his bedroom by the wall of rose-colored river rocks that formed his fireplace.

"Jean and I spent days collecting the prettiest of the pink stones right back there where the stream used to run," Russell said to the men. "And I personally supervised the masons for three days while they were building this, so they placed each one with its best face forward. They were real artists! See? *Muy bonito.*"

Russell's Spanish was dignified and well practiced. He told that story a thousand times, sometimes ending it with "*Fabuloso.*" He went on to show them one of the miniature hand-fashioned books where Jean had left him love notes, and I pulled his drapes shut, reminding him I wouldn't be gone long.

Three years earlier, Russell had awakened here on a Tuesday morning to find Jean still and silent beside him in the bed where they had slept, sung, and told stories together by the rose-colored fireplace. After his many years in Mexico, Russell knew about the fault lines too. How one moment can change your life forever. He got over the death, but he never got over living without her. His world went quieter and darker, and he often spoke of the sunlight illuminating the tiny golden hairs on Jean's arms, and the Shostakovich piece she last played on her century-old piano.

"Let's go, let's go," one of the men snarled.

They stood too close on either side of me as we walked together along the dirt driveway for the hundred feet to Joe's house to see to whatever questions needed to be answered. Three cars and at least five more men blocked the entrance by the hand-painted wooden sign that said CASA AMES.

"Get in the car."

They asked no questions.

In a matter of minutes they had rounded up three Americans who had lived on Russell's property for years. Old acid Joe, melting away from cancer; John, a mild musician and artist who had known Russell for decades and read him poetry after Jean's death; and me. When I refused to get into the car, citing my duty to Russell, they showed me the arrest warrant and a pair of handcuffs. The charge on paper said, "arrest for conspiracy to overtake land." It was issued by the university in Mexico City that Russell and Jean had donated their land to twenty years before.

I read it, I understood the words, and I knew there was a mistake. We all had Russell's permission to be with him on the land. He and his wife had donated the house and property to the university, hoping that an academic institution could put to best use this land where they lived and loved the second half of their lives. It was well understood that the arrangement allowed them to stay there until their death. The entire village knew it. The man who led his tawny oxen to graze in the grassy mountainside knew it. The official who collected the $10 a year for water fees knew it. Russell's long-standing staff of three who cooked, cleaned, and gardened knew it, and so did the town president. The story was repeated like legend. As it was known to the community that Russell and Jean had long ago brought them electricity and water, helped build a school, and distributed candy every year on Children's Day, so it was known that Russell would die in his home, having spent nearly five decades as their friend and benefactor.

An hour later, in the back of an enclosed truck, after the first of many sets of photos and fingerprints, we were being moved from police headquarters to Ixcotel. Joe and John were smoking, and I carved my initials and the year into the layers of green paint that coated the walls, between JOSE LOVES ANA and I AM YOUR MOTHER AND I AM HERE, a reference to the Virgin of Guadalupe, the great protector of Mexicans for everything from athlete's foot to incarceration to crossing the border.

Joe commented on every pothole we lurched over. John and I laughed. There is a kind of rush that comes with facing the implausible—like when the rock-solid ground under your feet quakes, or when you fall in love again. Scary, thrilling, implausible events can make you giddy, wondering what comes next and believing in your invincibility, at least while the rush lasts.

Joe wore a brown plaid shirt. John and I both wore red. I thought of the earthen pottery robins and sparrows on Russell's mantel. As writers, John and I noted our good fortune to be able to add a "one night in jail" story to our repertoires. Joe grumped that he already had plenty of those. We were sitting on wooden benches bolted into the sides of the truck, and there were no windows for us to be able to tell where we were going. It's not far, they had said, though time had already begun to waddle by at a different speed, and our perception of distance was already warped by finding no straight path to link an end with the beginning. We didn't know where Ixcotel was, and I still don't. Out there somewhere past where the owl took off for the woods.

"You think those mug shots they took will come out in the paper? I want to send one home to my mom." John, the entertainer.

"Yeah, they'll come out in the paper, and the kid who sells the *Noticias* on the corner of Chapultepec will open up to the police section, wave it at the drivers caught by the red light, and yell, "Gringos caught squatting!" He'll sell enough to buy himself two *tortas de jamón* tomorrow." Joe, the cynic.

"I should have smiled. I think I was smirking, though. It's still unbelievable, you know?" Me, caught in the sliver of space between one reality and the next, neither one filtering into the close, smoke-filled air in the back of that rumbling truck.

At our arraignment the following day, a fiction unfolded about the three of us and our violent plot to take this land away from the university. Several witnesses had submitted written testimony that we had unloaded furniture with sinister intent from the back of a large truck on a certain night five months prior. I tried to recall when there could have been a truck on the property that could have been mistaken for this conspiratorial truck. I reached for some memory of behavior that could be misconstrued as sinister, some furniture that might have come onto the land improperly. John stopped me.

"Whoa, whoa, whoa! This is no mistaken impression. It's a colossal fabrication. Somebody cooked this up on purpose. Now what?"

With a flash of nausea, I remembered the university representative who used to come by periodically to see if Russell was still alive. She would shake my hand and say, "What a beautiful afternoon" and, "Gee, it looks like Lobo will never leave from underneath that blooming jasmine." Her written testimony in the fat file sewn together with thread lasted several pages. There she stated that she was afraid to ask us why we were violently unloading the furniture. She didn't know what we would do to her. I wondered what this meant. Were we waving floor lamps like spears? Was she afraid for her life?

I remembered the phone call she made several months ago to ask for the spelling of my full name. I gave it little importance, as I had nothing to hide. I thought she must keep thorough records.

Now the university, apparently impatient for their land, was taking us hostage. Like Lobo, we had settled in and taken possession there and were unlikely to leave. The university was worried, we guessed, because none of it made sense. Then, with no coaching from Russell's lawyer, who was quickly drafted into the role of our defense, the three of us were asked for our reply to the charges just read to us. We spoke confidently, trusting the buoyancy of truth.

"We are Russell's friends and have been invited to share his home since . . . "

Our lawyer left early and charged his assistant with telling us that we would be in custody, sleeping on the floor, for six nights while they prepared our defense.

The lawyer was too busy with his own agenda to pull off what should have been a simple defense of three innocents in those six interminable days. After almost a week, we moved from our special quarters into the general population, Joe and John with 1,500 men and me with 150 women. It was six weeks before the university tired of the ruse and the negative press it generated. We were freed on the night of the November eclipse. First we had to ditch the bad lawyer for a good lawyer and pull ourselves free of the twisted subplots gurgling beneath the surface, the hidden agendas and the requisite corrupt government officials on both sides. For six weeks of unerringly faithful daily visits, friends brought us organic lettuce, turkey sandwiches with pickle relish, homemade cookies, and news of Russell. The neighbors were taking care of him and camping at the entrance to his property to keep the university thugs at bay. The press came, and we made statements. They printed that I was sleeping on the floor with forty-five women. I wanted them to print that I slept beside daring, dignified, stoic women who were still hanging on after cataclysms of their own, and we all watched small black birds flit freely through the barbed wire.

The women inside thought I was Mexican. Certainly not for my appearance. Everything about me screamed "gringa" from a thousand paces.

"It's because you didn't cry. You were very calm when they brought you in. Even some of us—some of us who know—we are not calm. We kick and scream and rail at the incongruity. We thought you must be Mexican. You know about this unsettled world."

Yes, I knew. I had been an eager student for seventeen years. My tongue rolled over her crash of consonants. I lived in the subjunctive mood. Mexico's language carried with it a hint of the transitory nature of things. *Ser* and *estar*. To be, and to be for now. I knew about unsettled Mexico. Yet it was not Mexico that shook me out of my comfortable bed and onto the concrete floor—it was greed. Greed takes root anywhere.

We wrung our laundry over concrete tubs lined up against one cracked gray wall and talked of before and dreamed of after. We swept and scrubbed the courtyard four times a day, hauling buckets of water to splash away the footsteps that we counted between one wall and the next. We rolled up our blankets in the morning after emerging from our cocoons at the wakeup signal from the guard tower. It is 6:00 AM. Time to sweep.

There is a metamorphosis in captivity when a cage, however austere and corroded, is the entire world. In that space reduced to minimum, a distilling occurs, a compacting of energies. And when the cage opens to a place you once knew well, it might as well be Jupiter. And you might as well be a serpent, for all the familiarity you feel with the way you look now. With the way you react to the new freedom around you. With the way to find home. You sniff the air for any sign of recognition, but there is none.

Abruptly homeless, I left Mexico ten days after release.

When I tried to say a final goodbye to Russell, the control I had mustered in jail kept me from crying. It kept me from speaking.

I just looked at him and touched my heart. He said simply, "You have gone through a lot."

Now I am in New York. It is stable here, solid. And I struggle to learn the new grammar of this place. The even, unbroken sidewalks trip me up. I am supposed to know this language. I was born here. But Mexico has warmed and warped my voice. Her eruptions have made it hard for me to find balance in stability. I got over leaving Mexico, but I may not get over living without her. I grope for her heart that lies deep below the surface. One day this heart will quiver and spill over a grumbling earth, throwing off sparks that will ignite in me a new accent, wild and uncoiled, just as I remember her.

Karin Finell

El Greco in Mexico

Mexico, August 1958

Only three months had passed since I'd returned from a trip to
Europe, and there I was, homesick again. Not for Germany, where I
was born—nostalgia for Spain, for Latin culture, gripped me. Spain
had bled its vibrant colors into me, and its army of sounds had
invaded my ears with guitars and clapping and castanets; the wail of
gypsy songs still echoed in my memory, the rhythm of stamping feet
found its resonance in my heartbeat. It was too expensive to go back
to Spain, where I had spent three months with friends, but Mexico
was just south of the border and cheap. Two weeks in Mexico had to
satisfy my craving.

In Spain I had fallen in love with the El Grecos, the passionate Renaissance portraits that graced the walls of museums and
churches. But I had not met a living, breathing El Greco in person.
Now, here, in the Hotel Fenix in Guadalajara, someone looking as

though he had stepped out of the frame of one of the paintings I so admired pushed through the glass doors and went straight toward the table in the lobby bar where Sheila and I sat, sipping margaritas. He looked at us, walked past us, then stopped near the elevators and conferred with the concierge.

He was tall and elegantly thin, with anthracite hair and amber eyes feathered by dark lashes. The alertness of his eyes made me think of a falcon watching its prey. His aristocratic nose matched the falcon image—narrow, slightly hooked, and somewhat too long.

Ever since I was a child in war-torn Germany, I had dreamed of a Spanish grandee who would come for me on a white horse and swoop me up; we would soar through the skies and fly to Spain, away from bombs and war. There I would dance flamenco and live with gypsies—by then, my Spaniard had metamorphosed into a bullfighter—as in the third act of *Carmen*.

"My God! They're staring at us, don't look now, but . . . " Sheila whispered. Her pale complexion turned a deep shade of red, as if trying to match her hair.

By then, the raven-haired man was striding across the room and was by our table in seconds. He pointed to his friend, whom he identified as Fernando, introduced himself, and asked if the two of them might have a seat at our table. He snapped his fingers at the waiter for attention and ordered another round of margaritas.

Lucio was Catalan, a Spaniard in Mexico—it was no accident that he looked like one of the models El Greco had used. I had come face to face with my childhood dream in the persona of Lucio Arguello-Burunat.

Lucio invited us to accompany him and Fernando on a drive to Ajijic, by Lake Chapala. It was a sun-drenched Saturday afternoon, and we had no plans until the next day. Sheila was cautious. She had heard rumors of robbers in Mexico. I looked at the two men, Lucio and Fernando, who looked more like well-to-do playboys than robbers. In the end I persuaded Sheila to accept the offer. We excused ourselves in order to change our clothes and grab our bathing suits. To mollify Sheila, I told her we would leave our jewelry at the hotel. It was ludicrous, in retrospect: If we had anything to fear, it would not have been the theft of some silly gold chains or bracelets.

I slipped into a simple dress cut to fit the figure, its iridescent green and blue colors changing on the silk with the light, imitating a watercolor painting. I freed my blond hair from the rubber band that caught it in a ponytail and brushed it so it fell loose below my shoulders. Lucio's eyes lit up when he saw us exit from the elevator. I knew he wasn't looking at Sheila. He later told me that he felt as if he had been shot by an arrow.

While driving to the lake, Sheila and I sat pinch-faced in the back of Lucio's new Buick as he drove at top speed down the highway. (Women at that time sat together when men drove, hence, in the back.) His hands were on the wheel as the tires heated the asphalt below us, but he kept swiveling his head back to talk to me about his family. Sheila and I clutched each other in pure fear when cows suddenly crossed the highway and he had to swing the wheel hard to avoid hitting them, causing us to hit our heads on the side windows.

In between cows, Lucio told me he was born in Barcelona. His father brought the family to Mexico when he was four years old. "But I feel 150 percent Mexican," he assured me, "even though I was born in Spain."

Lucio and Fernando relieved the tedium imposed by Sheila. Her interests in foreign countries were as flat as her face, and her taste in food and curiosity about cultural sites were as insipid as her water-blue eyes. She had slept on the plane and made little conversation. She refused to look at the guidebooks I had brought along or to practice a simple *"por favor"* or *"gracias."* By the first day I regretted having persuaded her to go on this trip with me. I had never noticed how unmotivated she was during our occasional lunches. We both worked in the same engineering office, she as a secretary, I as a draftsperson. I persuaded her to be adventurous and visit Mexico with me, because after all, two could travel more cheaply than one.

Lake Chapala, some thirty-five miles' distance from Guadalajara, is one of the largest lakes in Mexico. The lake was full; its waves lapped whispers to the shore. Blue aquatic flowers bloomed in the shallows, and here and there, the silver dart of a fish flashed, as if it had risen to the surface to greet the sun and thank the sky and the clouds for this day. In the distance, mountains framed the view in a purple haze.

We strolled the narrow cobblestone streets of Ajijic, an artists' enclave four miles west of the small town of Chapala, both by the lake. Many American and European expatriates had made their home there. Scents of cinnamon and coffee wafted in the air. The one-story houses in cream and white and yellow huddled together like the buildings in Spanish villages. Geraniums cascaded from window boxes, and bougainvillea spilled over old stone walls. Boutiques offered exotic clothing and handmade gifts, but alas, it was Sunday, and they were closed.

Lucio took us to visit his friend Jorge at his weekend home, an elegant villa in Chapala. Jorge's house was built at the edge of the lake and had its own boat dock with speedboats for waterskiing.

That afternoon was the first time I water skied. I got up the first try and stayed up, but after a while, when it was Sheila's turn to ski, I could not come down. I would not come down. I saw snakes. Large, black watersnakes slid and slithered in and out of the blue water lilies near the shore. Lucio kept waving for me to let go of the bar. I shook my head, my fists clamped around the piece of metal for all dear life. I pointed as well as I could at the snakes and kept holding on, forcing the boat to go around and around in circles. After a while, Lucio slowed down the boat, making me lose the tension. I let go of the rope, kicked off the skis, averted my face from where I knew the snakes were, and swam the short distance to the dock.

"Why didn't you tell me about the snakes?" I said to Lucio, angry.

"Those little harmless things on the water? You're a German girl. Don't tell me you're afraid of them?"

"What does being German have to do with it? I may not be afraid of bombs, but I sure am afraid of snakes!"

Lucio pointed for Sheila to put on the skis. "Come on. It's your turn."

Sheila shook her head. She didn't even want to get on the boat and preferred to wait on the dock. So Lucio took his turn. He was an elegant skier and later slalomed right to the edge, where he jumped onto shore.

Toward evening we visited more of Lucio's friends. All of them seemed to be wealthy and young. We moved from one party to another, eating quesadillas with guacamole, empanadas, tamales, and enchiladas. We drank different *aguas* (fresh, sweetened juice drinks): *horchata*, an almond-flavored drink made from rice; *agua de jamaica*, made from hibiscus petals and with a reddish-purple hue; and *agua de tamarindo*, made from tamarind pods. I sampled them all, while Sheila stuck to the known: Coca-Cola.

Each of the homes we visited offered another gustatory surprise, each more tasty than the last. We learned to drink tequila straight up—Sheila too. We licked salt from the indentation between thumb and first finger, then took a swallow of tequila and immediately sucked on a slice of lime. There was dancing and laughter, and as the clock moved on, Sheila started to show the dimples in her cheeks. By the time we arrived back at the Fenix Hotel, it was well after two o'clock, and we dropped straight into bed.

Trumpets awakened me. I switched on the light and looked at my watch: four o'clock. We had only slept for two hours. Then the singing began. I rushed to part the curtain and rolled up the blinds. There was a group of mariachis in full regalia beneath our window. Behind them stood Lucio with his arms raised, as if he were the conductor. Then he saw me and grinned, tipped his fingers to his temples in a salute, and threw me a kiss.

I had heard about these early morning serenades. He was presenting me with a *gallo*, given at the time of the rooster's first crow in the morning. I stood by the open window, shivering in the early morning air, while the mariachis played on. I wondered why no one complained, but Mexican businessmen frequenting the hotel were probably touched by the romance of this early concert, and American tourists would more than likely add the memory of this wake-up call to their more tangible mementos and souvenirs.

We slept late that Sunday, called the tour guide, and cancelled our "city and surrounding villages" tour. After all, we now had our very own private guides. However, Sheila was less than taken with Lucio's friend Fernando—a wimpy, mustachioed sort who spoke with a nasal twang and kept honking his hooked nose into an over-sized handkerchief. Fernando seemed as bored with Sheila as she appeared to be with the world. He treated her with respect, as if she were a visiting aunt who had to be tolerated. I felt sorry for her. My wanting to spend every moment of our two weeks with Lucio had left Sheila feeling abandoned.

That night, Lucio and Fernando took us to a private restaurant in the outskirts of the city, in an old adobe house with thick oak double doors. After a discreet knock with the large iron knockers, the doors, which looked as if they might lead to a medieval dungeon, swung open. We entered a miniature bullfighting arena and headed to the surrounding tables and chairs.

Sheila blanched. "They have bullfights here? They kill animals while we eat?" she asked, looking as if she were going to be sick.

"No, no," Fernando said. "Nothing like that. It's just a few of the *chufla* (young socialites with a European background) who'll play with young bulls and cows. No one gets hurt, neither man nor beast."

I questioned Lucio with my eyes, wondering what to expect. Several people were already seated, mainly men. Heavy smoke hung beneath the ceiling. We were the only gringas in the place. The only other females were a few Mexican women wearing heavy makeup and cloying perfume that overrode the ingrained smell of animals and beer.

Lucio pulled a chair for me to sit down. Margaritas arrived. Broiled steaks. Beans and rice, tortillas and salsa, followed by flan. All the while, a mariachi group played. Then trumpeters and buglers entered and blasted a few bars of the *paso doble* that announces the beginning of a bullfight. But this was not a bullfight. Or was it? I was ill at ease. I'd seen a bullfight in Spain—a grandiose spectacle, high-drama theater—and would hate to see a butchery in this small arena.

A young bull entered, then a young man jumped over the barrier and called to the bull, "*¡Toro, olá, toro!*" He waved a red cape and stamped his feet. The young bull looked all around, pawing the sand with his right front hoof.

"Looks like he doesn't want to fight," Lucio said. "When they scrape like that, they're unpredictable."

I was tempted to jump into the arena and pet the bull-calf, to tell him he wouldn't be hurt, that there was no sword. Then the bull had a change of mind. He seemed angry. With lightning speed, he charged the cape. The young man performed his pirouettes and his veronicas as the bull whizzed by him. The animal turned and charged again. The young man seemed exhausted, jumped over the barrier, wiped the sweat from his forehead, and headed back to his table. Everyone applauded. A woman who could have been his mother pulled his head onto her ample bosom and kissed him on top of his curly mop of hair. And all along, the band played *paso dobles*.

I thought the exercise was silly. Grown men playing games of questionable bravery. The night progressed with another little bull, another one of Guadalajara's social-register young men, more tequila, more margaritas, more beer.

I wondered how Lucio would be able to drive us back to the hotel. The spirit of bullfighting seemed to be rising in him in proportion to the tequila he consumed. Quick as a dart, he jumped over the barrier and declared, "I will fight the next bull."

It turned out to be a cow, white and black, with large, curved horns. She was not a calf-cow either. Fernando sat there, chewing his lower lip.

"*Pendejo*, idiot, watch out," he cried to Lucio. "She's more dangerous than the bulls." Lucio had removed his linen coat and used it as a cape. I sat clutching my chair when the cow made a run for Lucio. He soon controlled her with his graceful cape-swinging, his feet planted firmly on the sand, his body swaying with his convex belly and his impossibly curved back. He looked the part of a torero lacking only the *traje de luz*, the bullfighter's sparkling costume. The cow had strafed him close and left stains of dung on his immaculate white linen pants. The cow grew tired of the game and went into a corner, eyeing him suspiciously. Lucio came over to us, grabbed a beer, and gulped it down. We applauded; he smiled. He went back into the center of the arena while holding up his hand as he crossed to the helpers at the other side. Two of them went into the arena with capes. Two more helpers brought in a low table and placed a chair upon it. While the two men near the cow kept an eye on her, Lucio leaped onto the table and sat down on the chair. The men then tied him to the chair with ropes. Everyone but Lucio ran out of the arena, while Lucio shouted, "*¡Toro, toro!*"

This was insane. What sort of game was this? The cow charged the table. Again, "*¡Toro, toro!*" She wheeled and ran toward the table again, this time from a greater distance. The large horns rammed the table, there was a crunch of table legs breaking, and the table, with Lucio tied to his chair, came crashing to the sand. The cow stomped the ground next to Lucio and held her threatening horns over him, dribbling saliva onto his face. I covered my eyes with my hands; I did not want to witness my newfound love being killed by a cow.

Fernando jumped the barrier to help untie his friend, while the men in charge of the animals, using switches and a rope, dragged the cow out.

Lucio was sore and hurt all over his body, but apparently not a bone was broken. "Drunks are like cats," he laughed. "They can fall off the top of a barn and never break a bone." I was not amused.

Sheila and I took a taxi to the Hotel Fenix.

The "cowfight" had left me disappointed in Lucio. But when he appeared the next morning, freshly showered and shaved and looking as if he had never been drunk in his life, I accepted his apology. I told him that Sheila and I had made earlier plans to take a train to Mexico City and view the landscape on the way. Both men decided to take Lucio's car and meet us at our hotel, El Presidente.

They behaved like gentlemen—Fernando because he was not interested in Sheila and only came along to keep his friend company, and Lucio because I made it clear I could not be had as an easy gringa trophy. (Plus, his still being bruised all over his body might have had a part in his restraint.)

In Mexico City, Lucio and Fernando stayed in the latter's house near Chapultepec Park. Fernando's villa, similar to the astounding homes I had seen near Lake Chapala, was built in an ultramodern design. The first and second floors where connected by wide, poured-concrete stairs that were suspended in air as if by magic, curving in a graceful arc without banisters. I wondered if anyone older than sixty had ever climbed these stairs.

Sheila preferred to take a city tour by herself, while Lucio took me to his favorite haunts. There was a courtyard restaurant specializing in a variety of moles and other savory sauces. I opted for the *mole negro,* made with dark chocolate and spices, which proved to be one of the tastiest sauces that ever crossed my tongue. We drank a Mexican red wine with the meal.

After dinner, in an intimate nightclub, Lucio ordered Veuve Clicquot champagne, which was prohibitively expensive in Mexico, and made *fontanas:* Seven glasses formed a circle, and five were balanced on top of them, then three more above, and finally two glasses formed the apex. The maître d' would then pour the champagne, sporting an unctuous mien, the seriousness of which belied the joyous bubbles of champagne flowing in a foaming cascade from the top to the bottom of the glasses. *Fontanas,* a veritable fountain, indeed. Also a waste, since much of the champagne was drunk by the tablecloth.

Sheila told me the next morning that she had changed her air ticket and was returning to Los Angeles. I knew it was my fault. I felt guilty. But I had rights, didn't I? I was not yet twenty-five and selfishly wanted to be with Lucio and make every hour of our time in Mexico count.

I tried to convince Sheila to stay. I promised to see the sights with her and Lucio, said that she did not have to be with Fernando. I attempted one last time to infect Sheila with my love for all things Mexican: I said I was intoxicated with the people of Mexico, the calla lily vendors on street corners presenting a living Diego Rivera tableau. I told her I delighted in the scents of unknown blossoms, of exotic cooking wafting through windows and doors, of the sweet rolls sold on the street. I loved listened to the trilling of parakeets and canaries in cages hanging in open doorways leading to inner courtyard gardens; I loved hearing folksongs streaming from open windows, housemaids singing with lovely voices. I loved it. I loved it all.

"Don't go," I pleaded. "It's a once-in-a-lifetime experience."

It was no use. She took a taxi to the airport that afternoon.

I reviewed the changed situation. The hotel room had to be paid by me alone, but luckily, Lucio paid for dinners and the sightseeing. I would be able to manage alone on my budget and still be able to buy a serape or a clay pot for Mother as a souvenir. But I had to show a firm resolve and keep El Greco with the bird-of-prey eyes from my bed. The sites in Mexico City were grandiose; everything was built on a massive scale, whether it was the pyramids of pre-Columbian times or the cathedral. The streets and buildings reminded me of European cities. Lucio bought roses from every vendor who was selling them at restaurant tables. The flowers' perfume overwhelmed me in the small hotel room, and I put several bouquets in the bathroom. He took me to the Teatro Folklórico, where dances and songs from the different regions of Mexico were celebrated. And he took me to nightclubs, where we danced so close that I seemed to float, held aloft by his arms. I loved him, and I was grateful for the attention that he paid me, but I did not let him share my bed. And then, far too swiftly, it was time for me to return to Guadalajara, to board my plane back to Los Angeles.

"Promise you'll meet me in Tijuana the next time I have to go there on business, *sí?*" Lucio asked. He was employed by Procter & Gamble and was responsible for making sure their products safely crossed the border in Tijuana. He flew to the border city once or twice a month to inspect the incoming shipments.

Lucio: I adored him. He opened a sophisticated world to me. After meeting him twice in Tijuana, an easy trip for me, I flew down to Guadalajara to be with him for Thanksgiving. The air greeting me when I exited the plane was warm and had that peculiar tropical semimoist scent in it. It felt as though I had returned home.

By now, two months later, I was in love with Lucio. And I was broke as well, since my salary didn't allow me to make the many long-distance telephone calls I was making. Not to mention the expense of flying down to Guadalajara again. He usually called me every night, but I was impatient and would often call him in the late afternoon. After celebrating Thanksgiving with Lucio and some of his American friends, he asked me to marry him. I said yes. The next time we saw each other again was in Tijuana, at the office of a judge who married us. Mother gave us a reception, and a brief honeymoon to San Francisco followed. And back we flew to Guadalajara.

But the story does not end here. The little telltale signs I had noticed right from the beginning became more impossible to ignore. I was an independent and professional woman, had made my own money, and was now relegated to sit in the back seat of our life. Lucio changed once he married me. He stayed out late with the young single men of his *chufla*, all more immature than he, playing poker until the early hours and losing money he could not afford to lose. I learned later that he had to borrow money from his brother after we met, since he spent his entire monthly salary of $900 on me in those two weeks. I found tightly wrapped substances in the refrigerator, and when I asked him what they were, he grabbed them and pushed me out of the way, saying, "Don't touch them. It's none of your business." I took lessons in Catholicism, intending to convert so we could marry in a Catholic church with the blessing of his sister and brothers, all the while praying I would get pregnant. I thought that with a baby on the way, Lucio would become responsible. Later I would thank God for not answering my prayer.

After nine months, I knew I had to leave Lucio, but it was hard tearing myself away from new friends (who are still my "Mexican family") and from the city I had grown to love. People speak of a soulmate . . . in Mexico I had found my soulcountry.

The day came when my bags were packed and Lucio drove me to the airport.

"Think it over, Karin. I love you. I'm sure we can work something out. If you were only a little less headstrong. If you want to come back, I'll be here."

Looking down through the smudged porthole window of the plane, onto the familiar layout of the city, the landscape, the mountainous terrain, the lakes sparkling blue below the silver wing, my eyes began to hurt from the tears they shed. Parting is bitter, and I was divorcing not only a man I loved, but also a country.

Adiós, Mexico—or perhaps *hasta luego*. Until we see each other again.

Tania Flores

Across the River

The road to Santo Domingo Tianguistengo is winding, dusty, and isolated. It overlooks desert shrubbery and small poor towns. But when we bump past brittle bushes and cactus plants on the way to my grandmother's town, I am content. When I am on that road, I know that I am going home.

Tianguistengo (called "Tianguis" for short) is nestled in the mountains of northeast Oaxaca, in the area known as the Mixteca region. The people who live there are indigenous and were forbidden to speak their native Mixtec tongue after Spanish became the national language. The younger generations in Tianguis—for example, people like my distant cousin Flor—no longer speak the language of their great-grandparents.

The only picture I have of Flor was taken in the summer of 1998, when I was seven and Flor was eleven. In it, she is holding a bag of candy with green tissue paper spilling out. Her brilliant white smile is carefree, her petite brown face illuminated by the camera's flash. I can still remember the dry heat of that summer night beating down upon us as Flor, her brother, my cousins, and I swung at a star-shaped piñata we made by wrapping newspaper and tissue paper around a cracked clay pot and then filling it with the fruit and candy. It was a perfect night—a night of complete, untouched happiness. We were concerned about nothing but the moment when we would all run to the finally split piñata, jumping and laughing and tumbling over each other in our eagerness.

I was born in Cuernavaca, Morelos, to an American mother and a Mexican father. Two years later we moved to California so we could be near my maternal grandparents. Each year holds the promise of our annual trip to Mexico, usually during summer or winter break. And although I harbor a love for the Mexico City *zócalo*, for the vendors and the colors and the smells and the sights; although I love the house in "el D.F." (or el Distrito Federal, Mexico City), which is always filled to the brim with aunts and uncles and cousins, the part of the trip I always look forward to most is Tianguis.

Visiting Tianguis is entering another realm. It is when you cross the river that you leave behind rushed drivers, road rage, modern skyscrapers, millions of billboards, and people spending hours mindlessly watching television or clicking away at a video game. You cross and you find yourself in a sea of cacti, in a tiny town where no fake faces, no fake lives, no fake people will be thrust in your way. It is a place where no cell phone, no global positioning system will be able to find you. It is a place where you can hide from the world, hide from the superficiality and genocide and ignorance and hate. It is a place isolated from filled-up schedules, long panicky Sunday nights, difficult teachers, insurmountable stress. For me it is a home free of tears; it is a place where I can say, "I am happy," and mean it.

Maybe it's my love for the *pitaya,* a native cactus fruit, or maybe it's the freedom I have there. Maybe it's the sizzle that penetrates all the way to my blood, a feeling of *This is where I'm from.*

The part I remember most clearly of the trips to Tianguis is where we cross the river. I have a perfect image of it in my head—a dark night with millions of stars and the cascades rushing in the background, the water up to our door, our car struggling across the bridgeless Acatlán River, named after the biggest city in the region.

Last time we visited the village, there it was—a long, slender, new bridge. I felt as if it didn't belong there, like somehow it violated the authenticity of it all. It is the only thing that I can recall having changed in my lifetime. Everything else is so reassuringly the same: the town square, with its dried-out "grassy" areas; the benches around the *kiosko;* the Catholic church and the blue general store behind it, with its never-ending shelves of traditional Mexican candy; the playground; the *pitaya* orchards; the hill leading downtown.

As a young girl in California who used to be prohibited from venturing around the block, I feel so free in Tianguis. There my cousins and I can wander around the town square, horse around at the playground behind the church, or go to the general store to buy firecrackers. And it isn't just the freedom I have in Tianguis that I love. There are also the foods that I have never eaten anywhere else.

La barbacoa (barbecue) of the goat is a daylong process. First, it takes several hours for the men to dig a huge hole. Then an enormous *cazuela* (clay bowl) is placed at the bottom of the hole over red-hot coals, and the goat is balanced over the top of the wide brim of the bowl. Leaves of maguey cacti are placed over the goat's body to help flavor the goat broth. The hole is then covered with a *petate*—a woven mat made of palm leaves.

The bowl fills with broth—juices from the cooking goat. The broth has the look and consistency of chicken broth but tastes more sour. The broth is made into a soup that is eaten before the meal. At the end of the meal—which includes goat meat, frijoles, warm hand-slapped tortillas, and an array of salsas—I'm so full I can't move.

But there are still the *pitayas* waiting to be peeled and eaten.

When we describe the *pitaya* to people at home in California, they immediately think of the prickly pear. Perhaps they are related, but if so, it is very distantly. The *pitaya* is a small, round fruit with a prickly outer skin. Starting at the top, you peel the outer skin down, strip by strip. The first strip is done in suspense—you have no idea what color the *pitaya*'s flesh will be. Sometimes it is white, or sometimes it is yellow, or purple, or red, or orange, or a dark fuchsia. The small fruit is dotted with tiny black seeds. When you bite in, it is juicy and sweet. You have no choice but to fall in love.

One summer when we were in Tianguis, my mother got together a group of kids to teach them English. We would sit on the porch of the house, facing the courtyard. Some of us lay in hammocks, some sat on the thigh-high brick wall, others sat around the table. While my cousins learned how to say, "Hello, my name is," we ate ripe *pitayas*, the juice dribbling down our chins. We sang and laughed while my godmother played the violin and the sun drifted down languidly behind the hills. My mother still remembers how Flor and her brother seemed so genuinely interested in learning, so grateful that they had this chance, and determined to get everything out of it that they could.

Until recently, Flor lived in a stick shack about the size of a typical American suburban living room with her grandparents and brother. Her mother, Rosa, moved to New York City twelve years ago, and rarely calls the telephone the town shares. Rosa—smart, restless, and ambitious—left Tianguis looking for a better life for herself. She left in search of the American Dream, perhaps believing at the time that she would one day send for her children. Rosa's children believed—had been told—that their mother would send for them. They would tell my parents that they were going to go to New York one day to be with their mom. But in New York, Rosa, without intending to, made a new life and a new family for herself. She still sends money, but it is not enough. All that's left in Tianguis of her is a legacy—her success in New York and two young adults, trapped in the town that she found a way out of.

Flor has dark medium-length hair, warm chocolate eyes, and tanned mahogany skin. She has a dazzling smile and a cheery personality. She is fun, loving, and very smart. Although she loves learning, after eigth grade, she would have had to travel an hour and a half on a bus over a dusty, bumpy road to Acatlán, the nearest city with a high school. And the commute was too expensive for Flor's grandparents.

Two years earlier, when we had been in Tianguis for only a couple hours, I was walking to the door of my grandparents' house when I saw a woman enter Flor's house across the road. She waved to me. I didn't recognize her, and as I squinted, trying to see who it was, she called out, *"¡Hola, Tania!"* I smiled back vaguely and quickly entered the house.

"Who was that woman?" I asked my father.

He just looked at me and said, "That's Flor."

"What?" I said, looking at my dad as if he was insane. "That was not Flor. Flor is a lot younger than her." I was sure that I had not seen a girl of sixteen, but had seen a young woman—a woman in her twenties, maybe.

My dad just shook his head and laughed gently.

Later, when I went to see Flor, I still couldn't believe it was her. "Why didn't you say hi to me?" she asked me teasingly.

I realized that Flor had been forced to mature much sooner than the girls I knew. She already carried herself like a woman, because she was in a place where that was what she was—by age sixteen. In my California town, girls her age were busy flirting with on-and-off boyfriends, knowing their parents would make them go to college in a few years, feeling that marriage was still a long way off. And because of this, because of the way Flor's childhood had been squished together, because of the fact that she, her grandparents, and the town knew that she was no longer a girl, I did not recognize her as one. I did not recognize her as the playful Flor I knew.

Flor, at sixteen, was trapped. She had a twenty-year-old boyfriend who had become the village mayor. She loved him, and he wanted to marry her, and her grandparents wanted her to marry. But she wanted the impossible—to keep studying, to keep learning. Our last visit with her on that trip was in her dark house, with flies and mosquitoes buzzing around that nobody bothered to swat. Trying to think of ways to help Flor, my dad requested Rosa's phone number. Flor pulled out an old Hello Kitty address book from under a stack of borrowed, worn-out textbooks. Before opening it, Flor blew off dust and a dead cockroach. As she nonchalantly gave my father the number, I think that she knew there was no hope. Even my father, the problem-solver, could not carve a place for her in a picture that she had faded out of. After a while, we left. Flor was sorry to see us go—we were the only people who encouraged her to find a way to continue her education.

Within a year, she ended up married. Her first birth was hard, and her baby did not survive. Even now, she is only eighteen.

That is when *me cayó el veinte*, as my dad would say—that is when I finally understood what had been so clear. I realized what my parents had been showing me all these years. I loved Tianguis and everything about it. But my life, although rooted in the same place as

277

Flor's, was so different from hers—and by pure chance, by pure luck. I had always loved Tianguis, but I had never thought about the fact that I am carted away after a week or two back to Mexico City, and then back to California.

I spend two weeks a year in Tianguis. But my great-grandfather, who is Flor's great-uncle, spent a lifetime there. I can still see him sitting there in his Mexico City bedroom, too old to live by himself in Tianguis, murmuring his prayers fervently. I can see him rubbing lime juice on his bad knee; I can see him eating the food—fruit, oatmeal, frijoles—that his daughter prepares for him every day, the food that has kept him inching nearer and nearer to one hundred years of a hard life. I can see my two-year-old cousin talking in his good ear while he holds her small hand and smiles as she talks. I can see myself sitting next to him, sometimes just holding his worn, leathery, thick hands in my fleshy, soft ones. I never was so aware of my own hands before—my long fingers that type quickly and play the piano and twirl to flamenco music. They are not hands that worked in the fields all day, with corn or cactus fruits, worn by the pricks and sun and desert life. I can see his thin lips curving into a smile, a smile that becomes a deep-belly laugh that crackles gently. I can see him sitting in the filtered sunlight of the house in Mexico City in a plastic chair, straining his eyes, pleading with them to read the paperback book he holds. He is there, he is alive in my mind, but now, having reached a century of life, he is gone.

He lived a hundred years. I have only lived fourteen.

I sometimes feel as if I lead a double life. The Californian version of me is the girl who shops in air-conditioned malls, longs for curly hair, laughs with friends about hot guys, and buys smoothies on hot days. The Tianguistengo version of me is the girl who has ridden a donkey, eats *pitayas*, rides in the back of trucks on long desert lanes, eats Lucas candy, and goes to horse races. I'm as comfortable at salsa parties as I am at junior high formals.

Having an American mother and a Mexican father has permitted me to know the saddest, most desperate poorness and the fanciest, most regal richness. I have been welcomed by those who want to leave their stick shack so badly and those whose houses have marble pillars and plush, expensive sofas.

One night, as I lay in bed at home in California, I realized that my double life goes beyond the material things—it is about circumstance. The villagers are trapped in their town, in dusty fields and working clothes and houses built of sticks, while here I am, with endless opportunities and everything in the world going for me. There is no time for wasting chances, for wasting potential—something that Flor had so much of. All the odds were against her, but they are all in my favor. I have much to be grateful for. And I have a duty to do my very best, try my hardest, not just for me, but for the town and the people who gave me a firsthand lesson in love, difficult work, and hardship.

Charish Badzinski

Sugar Sand

I experienced Mexico first, and most memorably every time I return, through my toes. There is nothing that can invoke an instant state of relaxation like the feeling of Mexico's sugar sand between my toot-sies. The grains first massage, then exfoliate, then take up residence in every piece of clothing I own—which I don't mind a bit. Dirt scat-tered across the hardwood floor in my house will vex me. But way-ward grains of sand that have traveled with me, tucked deep into the folds of my suitcase, will be carefully rescued and held in the palm of my hand while I recall the last time I buried my feet in the embrace of Mexico's beaches.

But sand is a mischievous temptress. She rides waves and erases messages on the shoreline, she rolls on the wind to tap sunbathers on their calves, and she always manages to escape, in little and big ways, no matter how hard you try to contain her.

My first trip to Mexico was by chance, really; a flight bound for the Bahamas had been cancelled because of too few bookings, and my husband, Joel, and I were left to plug the vacation hole. We were devastated at first; the trip to the Bahamas had been scheduled in honor of our five-year wedding anniversary, and it would have been our first beach vacation ever. After wallowing for a day or so, we suddenly realized what this meant: We could capitalize on last-minute deals and go anywhere in the world! We scoured travel ads in the local papers and considered our options. As Wisconsinites just set free from a six-month winter and desperate for summer, we whittled the list down to warm destinations with beaches, preferably with diving and snorkeling—activities that were new to me but old pleasures for my husband. Eventually, Cozumel, Mexico, rose to the top of the short list, and we were on our way.

When we emerged from the plane, we were immediately kissed on the cheeks by the jungle air, perfumed with salt and possibility. We hopped a cab to our modest hotel along a small stretch of beach that faced the morning sun. It was close enough to the city center that we could join the throngs of tourists descending from cruise ships almost daily, and distant enough that we could escape the crowds and find a quiet place for contemplation or a siesta in the shade of a *palapa*.

"¡*Hola!*" We were greeted warmly by the apparent concierge of the hotel, Rogelio, who handed us tumblers of rum punch and motioned to some seats at the front desk, where we would check in to our room.

"Check out that mural," my husband said, pointing across the lobby. Beyond the ceramic tile was a painting of a beach of pristine white sand and a bed of deepest azure, which spread its arms to the horizon. To our color-starved eyes so accustomed to whiteout conditions and dirty slush, this beach simply didn't look real. It took a moment before we both realized the lobby was open, and we were looking at the actual hotel beach.

I stripped off my socks and shoes and stood on the Caribbean's welcome mat. My heels dug into the sand, and I experienced a sense of intimacy with this new country that I had never felt in my own. The land wove itself between the threads of my toes, settled over the top of my nails and pocketed in the valleys. My cheeks flushed in disbelief of this very public pleasure. I dug in deeper, lifting the grains of sand with my toes, burrowing down into the cool of the beach underbelly, as she folded herself around me. I was in paradise.

From our beach chairs, we ordered Dirty Monkeys, a seductive blend of crème de banana, crème de cacao, coffee liqueur, and ice; and as the waves painted the beach with foam, and as the sun pinked our backs, we felt winter drip away. Joel napped in the shade. I grabbed one of the cheap snorkeling sets we'd purchased back home and headed to the water.

I had tried snorkeling once before in an unfortunate incident at a friend's condo pool, where all I could see under the surface were poorly fitted swimsuits and hairy potbellies. This was different. I spit in my goggles, as Joel had instructed me, formed a good seal, and dipped my head under the water. Sound became cotton covered and deeper, as if I were trapped inside a drum. There was an explosion of color: red, gold, yellow, and blue, acrylic paint splatters on a living canvas. Back home, the fish are brown and gray, though sometimes sunfish will have a streak of mustard through them. Here in Cozumel, I saw northern lights, fireworks, champagne, and sun rays, all under the water. These colors darted, waving their fins like flags and cupping bubbles with their mouths. I felt my blood pressure rise. The fish were so close! Some were even bumping against me! I began flailing my arms, grunting and splashing all the while, in an attempt to create some personal space. We Midwestern girls have seen fish—I've seen sizeable walleye and bass—but usually they are battered and simmering in butter, or stiff, coated in frost, and sleeping in the shadow of the ice shack. We know the fish are in the lakes, but frankly, when we're swimming, we don't want to see them.

A dinner plate–sized fish darted near me and I swallowed a mouthful of salt water. When I spied a barracuda hovering near the surface—though small and at a distance—I bolted upright. I decided I would stick to the sand for now.

Rogelio shared restaurant recommendations with us, hailed cabs for us, and encouraged us to take a small plane to Chichén Itzá rather than the tourist bus, a thirteen-hour ride. From the moment we arrived until we went to bed, Rogelio was there—dressed in his white linen shirt, tan pants, and brown leather sandals—cheerfully greeting us, asking us how our day went, and inquiring about our plans for tomorrow. When he wasn't at the front desk, he was walking to the on-site restaurant or talking to the workers who were raking the hotel property and tending the flowers. All of them wore the same uniforms, and as they walked on the beach, sand sifted through their sandals, rolled under their feet, and spilled out the back. I watched them from my perch in the shade as I scooped handfuls of sand and shook the grains over the beach, like powdered sugar on a cake.

Rogelio also arranged for us to take a resort diving course, a two-hour crash course followed by a one-hour dive. Our bronzed instructor, Luis, never strayed from the lesson, even as he surveyed two bikini-clad beauties who joined us on the beach. As I sat there, learning about which doohickeys went into what thingamajiggies, I marveled at the novelty of acquiring new skills while relaxing on the beach and listening to the surf.

Our beach lesson ended, and our diving instructor helped us put on our oxygen tanks. Still not entirely comfortable with the friendliness of the local sea life, I felt pinpricks of nervousness up my spine. I imagined a school of sharks descending upon us, ripping into our limbs, leaving us to choke on the saltwater and finally bleed out and die. My husband was oblivious to my internal panic as he excitedly disappeared under the surface. The three of us floated, hands at our sides, and took in the underwater wonderland. Everything slowed down, and the only sound I could hear was the comforting hiss of my oxygen tank. Our instructor paused time and again to point out sea life, including a lobster making its way across the sea floor, and a starfish, which he placed in my hand, its spiny surface barely touching my palm as the current pulled it into virtual weightlessness. Joel and I were astounded when he showed us a seahorse, so much smaller than I had ever imagined, with an orange sherbet hue.

The dream was near an end; we began to resurface. I felt a twinge in my cheek, and as we came closer to the top of the water, it grew stronger, a persistent pulling at my jaw. We reached the open air, had our photo taken as we stood in our gear, and the sensation grew even stronger, spreading numbness across my chin and a sharp, constant pressure that made me want to yank out my teeth. Our instructor surmised that I had a hole in a tooth, and that it had filled with air and expanded as we surfaced. He scrawled down the phone number of his dentist, just in case the pain got worse. I envisioned myself in a chair at a dentist's office in Mexico and decided to wait out the pain in the hotel. For the next five hours, I fought the urge to vomit from the pain, clutched my face in my hands, and curled on the bed in our hotel room.

While the jaw pain slowly subsided, the pain of being stuck in a hotel room as my vacation time ticked away grew with each crash of the waves on the shore.

To help ease my discomfort, my husband took me to dinner at a second-story Italian restaurant in San Miguel de Cozumel, the only town on the island. As we munched on garlic butter–drizzled bread, he whispered to me, "Charish, look!"

I followed his gaze and saw a young man on his knee, looking intently into his sweetheart's eyes and putting a ring on her hand. The restaurant erupted with applause as the couple kissed, and a mariachi band approached and serenaded the couple. When they were done, Joel waved the band over to our table and explained in broken Spanish that we were celebrating our fifth anniversary. I cried as the band played a ballad while the Caribbean breeze enveloped us. Any pain I'd experienced earlier in the day was forgotten.

Over the next few days, the jaw pain disappeared entirely. In between excursions, meals, and recovery time, we talked with Rogelio about his life and his family. By the end of our stay in Mexico, we had exchanged email addresses and promised to write. Just six months later, my husband and I took advantage of cheap airfare to Cozumel and made the trip again for a quick weekend getaway. With Christmas fast approaching, Rogelio asked us, via email, to purchase some gifts for his family, for which he would repay us when we arrived. He requested a watch for his wife and a portable CD player for his children.

Again, we were greeted warmly by our friend, Rogelio. He eyed the goodies we'd brought him from the States. "I do not have the money today," he said. "But I get paid on Saturday and will give you the money then."

My husband and I exchanged glances. Had we been taken? Sure, Rogelio was nice to us, but maybe it was just the tourist–hotel employee relationship. Had we mistaken his professionalism for something more? We began to doubt our judgment and tried to shrug off the possibility that we might not be repaid for the gifts. With my toes in the sand and the sea set before us, this was relatively easy to do.

On this, our second trip to Cozumel, we planned to do absolutely nothing besides eating, sunning, and swimming. Since we had hit the major tourist sites just six months before, we felt no guilt at the long days of beach-bumming ahead of us. We drank Dirty Monkeys and Sol *cervezas* and chatted with Rogelio.

"You are so lucky to live here. It's paradise!" I chirped.

"It is beautiful, but we work for many hours," he replied. His arms were crossed as he began telling us a story about another tourist he'd met. "He said he wanted to lay on the beach and drink margaritas all day. He said, 'I want to be lazy, like a Mexican.'"

Again, Rogelio was at the hotel when we went to bed that night.

Come Saturday, Rogelio appeared, cash in hand. I suppose it was our reward, or perhaps he felt a kinship with us, but he invited us to join him and his family for dinner Sunday. We would meet at La Plaza, then head to a nearby restaurant. Joel and I were delighted, knowing what a special honor it was to meet a local's family. We accepted the invitation, and the prospect of meeting the people who would enjoy the gifts we'd brought from Wisconsin thrilled me.

Sunday nights in Cozumel are a time of celebration for the families who call the island home. Hundreds of taxis come to a halt along the main road through town. Locals dress in their best clothes and head to La Plaza, at the center of San Miguel. The sound of live music drifts over the crowds, carrying along with it the rich smells of *hamburguesas, frites,* spicy empanadas, and fresh chopped fruit. Dancers in stunning dresses perform for appreciative crowds, artists offer to sketch your image in caricature, and young women painstakingly braid and bead the hair of tourists.

Joel and I strolled among the painters, their canvases spread on the cool bricks, and the vendors peddling food, jewelry, toys, and candies. We bought some churros from a vendor with a cart spewing greasy smoke and the essence of cinnamon. The night air was so thick, it seemed to leave salt on my lips. Eventually, Rogelio approached, accompanied by his wife, Carla, and daughter, Gemma, who was wearing a sweet yellow dress that flared from an empire waist, embroidered in white threads.

"*Mucho gusto,*" I said, using up the bulk of my Spanish-speaking abilities. Carla did not know English, but Gemma knew a little. Rogelio apologized, saying he had to leave to pick up their son.

Together, Joel, Carla, and I sat on a concrete bench beneath a grand, mosaic-rimmed clock, watching the musicians, painters, and the flood of families. We waited, mostly in silence, for Rogelio to return, though we were somehow comfortable together among the festivities. Gemma, meanwhile, twirled and tiptoed around the square, explored the perimeter of the space we'd claimed. In an effort to make conversation, I told Carla all of the words of Spanish I knew, mainly words that tourists need to get by, like "bathroom," "beer," "please," and "thank you." She smiled appreciatively and laughed with us. I discovered, through our broken exchanges, that we both liked tequila. She giggled and blushed, and I could imagine the watch I'd bought for her on her wrist: the loose, gold chain and the mother-of-pearl face on it. It would look gorgeous against her milk-chocolate skin.

When Rogelio returned, he explained that he had only one scooter, and the whole family couldn't ride on it at once. There would have to be multiple trips to and from home.

"Do you live far from here?" I asked.

"We live with my in-laws," he said. "It is what we do so we can afford to send the children to school to learn English."

The swell of music and scents, sea and sand, the place where tourists meet locals to share in simple pleasures, fell from my perspective for a moment. I imagined Rogelio, after a long day at the hotel, driving part of his family around the island and returning to pick up the other half. No doubt they did this everywhere they went as a family: to church, to the *mercado*, to the beach, everywhere. As we walked past the modest homes near La Plaza, homes with doors left open to let in the relief of night, I wondered what his house looked like. Did he and his wife have their own bedroom, a place where they could whisper their hopes for the future of their children while huddled under the blankets? Did they have enough space so everyone could have a seat at the dinner table? Surely it wasn't as small as these little caves with wrought-iron grills over the windows and no yard space. Where would the presents I'd brought from home be waiting on Christmas morning? I looked at his children, just elementary school kids, skipping on the uneven sidewalks, laughing and chattering. They were embarrassed to speak much English with us, not realizing what a life treasure they'd been given and at what cost.

We entered the small family restaurant, which was painted brightly and decorated with traditional blankets and accents of Caribbean blue. It overlooked La Plaza, and the music and laughter wafted up to us through the open balcony and *palapa* roof. We ordered Sol *cervezas*, bottles of Mexican sunshine, and toasted each other. We shared a plate of cheese-covered nachos with spicy *pico de gallo* as Rogelio acted as translator for our conversations. Carla smiled warmly, and we fell into a rhythm of conversation that transcended language and the cultural divide. I was again enveloped by seawater, swimming amid a swirl of smells, ethnic foods, language, and culture, and this time I was unafraid.

Virtually free of the constraints of language, Carla and I teased each other about ordering some tequila. Rogelio confessed that he in fact did not like tequila, and Joel made a face. Though we never ordered it, we felt drunk with new friendships and laughter. The teasing, too often relegated to the halls of longtime friendship, quenched a thirst far deeper than any physical need.

The privilege of dining with Rogelio and his family was not lost on us. Joel and I marveled at how kind and welcoming they were, at the naked honesty of their lives, of living with their family and saving for the children's education. While many travelers will at best walk the cultural water's edge and dip their toes in, we were allowed to dive in and see treasures far beneath the surface. By meal's end, it felt as if we were the only people in the restaurant, old friends who'd come to the table to savor the feast of commonality.

The next morning, I gathered a bit of the beach and poured it into a plastic bag, watching my bounty sparkle, then blend. My husband gave me a quizzical look, and in truth, I had no idea what I'd do with three pounds of sand when I got it home, I just wanted to take a piece of Mexico with me.

We spent the last of our hours in Cozumel at the hotel restaurant, watching the crabs snap at each other on the rock cliff that trimmed the water's edge, and the strung-out black birds puff up to scare the competition away from fallen breadcrumbs. Waiters threw day-old bread into the sea, and fish leapt into the air in an attempt to catch it, while others dove down, down into the brine. The scene was captivating. We finished our Sol *cervezas*, but as we turned to go, two dolphins in the distance shot into the air, arched, and plunged into the waves. We stood, spellbound, until they disappeared from sight.

I know I was barefoot as I walked across that beach for the last time, and I'm certain some teasing sand grains stuck between my toes as I hugged Rogelio goodbye. I envied him in some respects, knowing that he could see the majesty of this real-life mural everyday. But I also knew that he and I were caught in the same snare of unrequited love, a romance in which both of us struggle to contain a small part of Mexico, to make her ours, but are forced to watch helplessly as her jewels slip through our fingers.

Susan McKinney de Ortega

Maestra

In the plain concrete classroom, a wolf whistle broke the deadly calm. My hand, writing with chalk at the blackboard, stopped. I was suddenly conscious of the seat of my jeans hugging my ass. "E-Y," I wrote. "McKinney," I said, turning around.

Eighteen Mexican young adults stared at me.

"Here are some word cards," I said in English, shuffling the stack so nobody would notice my trembling hands.

"You say the English word first, then the Spanish," I explained. "Let's do it with a partner."

Nobody moved. I'd expected my English Now! students to be adults, responsible people with cars in the parking lot, ambitiously taking down my every word, but facing me were girls with freshly scrubbed faces, boys who looked like they'd begun shaving only weeks before. There was no parking lot, and there were no cars. Before class, the director explained that most of the students had only finished middle school. That instead of continuing with secondary education, they enrolled only in English classes, hoping it would liberate them from futures as maids and gardeners and win them positions as hotel clerks, travel agency representatives, tour guides. I admired their goals yet still felt I was facing a roomful of adolescents.

"Come on," I chirped. "Try it. Sky. *Cielo*. Sky." I turned to write "sun" on the board and felt the room grow still again. I heard a girl snicker. A manly snort answered her derisive laugh. It was my first day.

If I cried, they'd know I'd never taught before. I lowered the hand that gripped the chalk. I would turn slowly from the blackboard, I told myself, walk out in a dignified manner and never return. I would go back to Philly and bartend again.

In the calm, I smelled chalk dust and heard heels clicking across the floor of the next classroom. I'd seen the other teacher arrive wearing a skirt to her knees, purposely carrying a load of books. I wore Levis and had debated my footwear: motorcycle boots, Doc Martens, or leather sandals? The classroom was hot and breezeless; I was glad I'd decided on sandals. I'd dressed up my uniform—jeans and a T-shirt—by choosing a peach-colored top with scalloped neck and sleeves.

I took a breath and forced a steely look into my eyes. "How old are you people anyway?" I said, turning around. The students were no longer laughing. I had never run away from difficult situations before. I'd met television, magazine, and advertising deadlines. I'd handled twenty bar customers at a time. I knew how to work under pressure.

I folded my arms and stood with my legs apart, like my father the basketball coach with a whistle around his neck, all confidence.

"*¿Cuantos años tienen?* We'll learn this. Everybody say it. How . . . old . . . are . . . you?" I pointed my finger into the nose of a kid with stubby chin hairs.

"*Veinte.*"

"Twenty," I said. I stood with my finger in his face until he mumbled "Twenty."

"Nineteen," "twenty-one," came the answers in Spanish. "Sixteen," "seventeen," "twenty-two."

"One," "two," "three," I wrote on the board. "Okay," I said. "We'll begin with numbers."

After class, young "men" surrounded my desk. "*Maestra,* how old are you?" they asked in Spanish. "I'm thirty-three years old," I replied, mindful of the phrases we'd practiced.

"Where are you from? Are you married? Why aren't you married? Want to marry me? Don't you have children? *¿Vive usted sola?*" I said I lived alone. Up close, I could see the director was right—some kids were barely pubescent. Boys elbowed each other and raised their eyebrows. "Can I come to your house?"

Every day the boys waited after class, asking suggestive questions. When I didn't reply, they finally left. I was gathering my books the second day when I noticed that one boy remained, perched on the edge of the front desk, watching me.

Carlos. I remembered his name because I'd noticed him. In the storm of adolescent hormones, he'd sat calmly. The black sunglasses he'd worn the entire hour were off now.

"Ever taught before?"

Was I that obvious?

"No," I sighed. I just spent one of the most exhausting hours of my life. Then I gasped. "You speak English. Why are you in my class?"

"It's a requirement to get a job," he shrugged.

"They don't recognize you already speak the language?"

Carlos laughed. "Older people don't speak English around here. How can they judge my skills?"

Carlos's thick, midnight-black hair was cut short in the back and on the left side. The rest of his hair fell in a long sheet from his part down to his chin on the right side, like some bad-boy wannabe without tattoos or attitude. Apart from the MTV look, his eyes were compassionate. How else could I have admitted my inexperience?

"Where do you live?" Carlos asked.

"Over the river and through the woods," I muttered.

Carlos was looking at me patiently.

"I'm sorry," I sighed.

"They're just testing you to see if you're like the vacation girls that arrive here in the summer."

"What are the vacation girls like?" I asked distractedly, hoisting my stuffed backpack onto my shoulder. (I knew the vacation girls—shrieking and loud, out in the bars until 3:00 AM, hungover, morally on vacation from the correct behavior they exhibited in their towns the other fifty-one weeks of the year. But I wanted to hear what he would say.)

"Easy."

"It's popular to make assumptions about American women, I see."

"I don't make assumptions about people I don't know." We were in the school hall now. Without breaking step, he'd slipped my backpack off my shoulder and lifted it onto his. Carlos kept walking; I hurried to catch up.

How old did he say he was? I thought back to his answer in the age exercise the day before. Nineteen. He was nineteen years old.

I walked up and down the aisles, feeling teacherly. The students were writing forms of the verb "to be" in simple sentences on sheets I'd made up and photocopied, since not a single student bought the book I told them to buy. I bent down in front of Carlos, and with my finger touched a cross of string and black beads he wore at his throat.

"That's very nice," I whispered, then, feeling foolish, looked up. The class had dwindled to some ten students who showed up regularly. All of them were looking at me. I moved on, shocked at my own recklessness, holding my hands together to stop them from shaking. I went to the blackboard to hide my face, picked up chalk, couldn't think of what to write.

Carlos was sitting on a low wall as I left the building. He hopped off and hurried toward me. Removing the cross from his neck in one quick motion, he placed it over my head. My heart raced, my cheeks burned. There were a hundred kids around us. Carlos flashed me a Tom Cruise smile and disappeared.

I walked to the street, feeling the ghost of his hands where they floated past my head and lightly touched my shoulders.

It was the last weekend in September, and classes were cancelled for the feast of San Miguel, a fiesta that began at dawn with a deafening firecracker battle in front of La Parroquia, the town's central church, reenacting the confrontation between St. Michael the Archangel and the Devil.

"Teacher, we're having a party tonight. Come!" the students implored on the Wednesday before the long weekend. They wrote the address on a piece of notebook paper.

At nightfall, I put on a short swingy skirt and cowboy boots. *An evening stroll,* I told myself, and set out. There was the house, not far from where I lived, the patio strung with cut paper flags. Mexican rock music blared, and my students milled about with long-necked Coronas in hand.

"Teacher!" someone yelled. "Teacher's here!" A girl in a denim jacket grabbed me by the wrist. "No, no, I'm not staying. I was just out for a walk," I protested as I passed through the gate. "Act your age," my mother sometimes told me at home, half-joking. I was thirty-three years old. If I acted my age, I would be having children.

Carlos was by the grill, holding a paper cup and talking to a taller guy who looked like him. His eyebrows shot up when he saw me.

I watched him come toward me. He walked like my brother. An athlete's walk.

"Rum and Coke?" I asked, pointing to his cup.

"*Coca.* Want one?"

"Sure." He reached into a cooler.

"Teacher, come dance," said one of my second-hour students, a curly-haired boy with a wispy mustache. Carlos returned then, handed me my Coke and glared, and the boy slunk away.

The lookalike came over. He was a tall Ray Liotta type—smoldering good looks and pockmarked cheeks.

"This is Javier, my brother," Carlos introduced. Javier wore a Guatemalan cap. It would have looked ridiculous on half the boys in the moonlit yard, but on Javier it looked good.

"How old is he?" I said out of the side of my mouth.

"Seventeen," Carlos said. "Still going to high school." *My mother should see this*, I thought.

"*Oye, guey*," Carlos's brother said. I heard *parque, rebote, basquet. Basketball*, I thought. *They're talking basketball.*

"Hey," Carlos said a few minutes later, and with a head jerk, he led me away from the crowd to the shadow of a eucalyptus tree. From under the leafy branches, we watched students drinking Coronas.

All my life, I'd wanted a man like my father—kind, strong, doubtlessly sure of the inner rudder that set his path. Few had lived up. What compelled me to follow a nineteen-year-old with his dumb *cholo* haircut into the dark shade?

"There's going to be an earthquake in late winter," Carlos said.

"How do you know?" I asked. Is that how boys impressed girls here, predicting natural disasters?

"You'll see." By the brick grill, a kid in Carlos's class was arguing loudly about a soccer team. "Rodolfo always talks too loud,"

Carlos said, following my gaze. "He doesn't know who his mother is, and, well, nobody teases him anymore, but he's always afraid someone will."

"How . . . ?"

"His mother was the maid. His father is a rich doctor. He got rid of her when Rodolfo was born and kept the baby. So Rodolfo comes to school on a motorcycle, in the best clothes, but . . . "

"But he doesn't know who he is."

Carlos's look told me he was pleased I got it.

I liked his sureness. I stayed where I was and watched him take a step closer to me. Then I breathed slowly and willed him not to move away.

"Let's go to the Jardín," Carlos suggested around one. We stood by the beer tubs. Carlos had suggested we rejoin the crowd when he saw Javier wandering around aimlessly. "The fireworks will start soon," Carlos announced.

And then I was walking toward the center of town with two good-looking almost-men, not wanting to be anywhere else in the entire world. Carlos smiled at me when his brother wasn't looking. Just ahead, the fireworks display begun. Colored lights burst in the night sky. The smoke and lights battle wouldn't take place until dawn, which was hours away, and I wanted to rise in the morning and write. At the door to my apartment I stopped.

"I'm very tired. I live here," I told Carlos. I had moved out of my casita with the goatskin rugs and now occupied a small apartment on the Ancha de San Antonio. "I'm going in." I stepped up one step, turned around, and gave him a quick Latin kiss on the cheek. *Everybody does it,* I told myself. My heart beat rapidly. I fumbled with my keys. Carlos's cheek remained close to mine. "I like your kiss," he whispered.

When I turned, he was walking away, saying something to Javier.

In bed, I read for half an hour, comprehending little, until my heart calmed down and I could sleep.

The following Monday, Carlos waited after class again. "Come with me to Laberintos this Sunday."

"All right," I said, lowering my voice and looking over my shoulder. "I will."

Listen, I can't make it, I'm sure by Sunday night I'm going to have typhoid, I rehearsed in my head. Carlos watched me write *"esperar"*— to wait or to hope—on the board. I thought of the school director and how his face would crumble in disappointment if he knew I'd made a date with a student.

Sunday at nine, I pulled on my motorcycle boots. I was dressed in black jeans and a sleeveless, powder-blue velvet '50s top. *Makeup or no makeup?* I asked the mirror. I twirled on mascara and colored my lips pale pink.

I pushed open El Instituto's door fifteen minutes early to wait for Gussie, whom I'd invited so I wouldn't be on a real date, and found Carlos leaning against the doorway in white jeans, a print shirt, and black boots. At parties, American women whispered that Mexican men were always late, and that they run around on their women. But here he was, not late at all. Carlos greeted me with a nod.

"We have to wait for Gussie, a friend."

"*Bueno.*"

We stood on the steps together. I watched the night wind blow through his hair. I was going to a disco, to stand close to him, covered by darkness and music, not just watch him from yards away. Small talk died on my lips.

Gussie appeared in a Mao Tse-tung T-shirt just as Javier turned onto the Ancha from Orizaba, and the four of us fell into step. The hamburger man was setting up his stand on the street, a naked bulb dangling over stacks of onions and tomatoes, red and yellow plastic bottles. Carlos walked on the outside. *He's being gentlemanly,* I thought with surprise. I tried to imagine a date in Philadelphia protecting me from traffic and could only think of some faceless boy next to me on Spruce, walking hunched against the cold, hands in his jacket packets, until we reached Dirty Frank's (which wasn't called "dirty" for nothing), where he would stride in the door in front of me and order two seventy-five-cent tap beers without asking me if I wanted one.

I drifted over to the curb to test Carlos. I hid my smile when he stepped down into the street and herded me back.

Thumping bass greeted us at the doorway of Laberintos. Labyrinths. What maze was I getting myself into?

Nobody in the disco looked older than fourteen. Girls wore

short shiny dresses, heels, and long bangs that curled on their fore-
heads in enormous half-loops. When I was in high school, girls had
rolled their hair around orange juice cans to get the same effect.

We sat on some carpeted steps. Couples were glued together
in corners. One pair was entwined above us, the girl's patent-
leather, high-heeled foot tapping. From the speakers, Christian
Castro wailed, "Please don't go. Don't go-oooo. Don't go away,"
and I thought of my precarious situation in Mexico—living in a
tiny teacher's apartment to which the teacher would be returning
soon, teaching for little money.

Gussie jumped up. "Let's dance!"

A thrill worked through me to step onto the wooden floor, like
a kid on skates finding an empty parking lot.

"I want more people out here so we can mosh!" Gussie yelled
over the music. The fourteen-year-olds with the big hair loops stared
at her. She danced like she was in Revival at 3:00 AM, eyes closed,
arms swinging around her head. I stomped my motorcycle boots.
Carlos moved across from me, his face a mask, until I caught his eye
and he smiled quickly.

"I'll get this round," I said when we sat. "Coronas!" Gussie and
I told the waiter. Javier and Carlos asked for Coca-Colas. "Make mine
a Coke," I said. "*Una Coca.*"

Shifting around to accept our drinks when the waiter returned,
Carlos's leg pressed into mine. Neither of us moved away. I couldn't
look at him, the thrill was so great. I sat, enveloped by thundering
music, hardly breathing, feeling the warmth of Carlos's thigh.

Gussie pulled Javier onto the dance floor. Carlos and I sat on the carpet, pressing our legs together. I noticed a handsome *cafe con leche*-colored young man dressed in American jeans. He saw Carlos and came our way.

"*Guey*," Mr. Cool and Handsome greeted Carlos. *Guey*—the Mexican version of "dude."

"Memo," Carlos returned. "*Él es* Memo," he told me.

"*Te presento a Susana*," Carlos said to his friend. Carlos had never called me anything other than "*maestra*" before. My name on his lips had an exciting intimacy.

Memo eyed our legs smashed together. "*Rayando el sol, oh-wee-oh*," a group called Mana sang over the speakers. Carlos and Memo began to sing. Memo spread his hands and mouthed the words to me. He turned to Carlos, cocked his head, and crooned to him. Carlos sang back.

Carlos turned to me then, and Memo dropped to one knee. "*Es más fácil llegar al sol que a tu corazón*," they sang to me. It's easier to reach the sun than your heart.

The lights went down and the music slowed then. Carlos put his hand on my back, and we stepped onto the dance floor. He held my right hand and encircled my waist like a ballroom dancer. *Another slow song*, I prayed. The following song was, and Carlos dropped my hand and put his arm around my neck. Next to us, Gussie and Javier shuffled cozily around in a tight circle. As we moved, Carlos slid both arms around my shoulders.

My cheek was precariously close to Carlos's face. I took discreet gulps of air to drink him in. Then his cheek touched mine. It was completely smooth, like no man's cheek I'd ever felt before. At nine-

teen years old, he had no facial hair. It was like a baby's skin, like butter, like air after a rain. We moved in a circle, touching at the waist,
the shoulder, the cheek. The world was pure sensation—music, glit-
tery light from the sequined ball above, and Carlos's skin.

Our cheeks slid until our lips touched. We kissed, slowly,
slowly, suspending the moment into one long taffy pull of time. In
that moment, I did not foresee a wedding during which our parents
would try to make small talk without understanding each other's
languages. I did not predict registering a child's birth with both the
governments of Mexico and the United States. I felt only the softest,
sweetest sensation I had known in my adult life.

Acknowledgments

As with the first two books in this series of "Love Stories," I am thankful to the many writers who sent me their painstakingly crafted work for consideration in this collection. I, at least, am a better, more informed person for having read so many essays on Mexico. And I offer the same lament—that space precludes my including more of the wonderful personal accounts I received. I also thank the writers whose work appears in this book. I feel blessed to be working with authors who are talented and willing to tweak, rework, and rewrite their precious words upon demand. I am ever grateful to Seal Press, small in size but big of heart when it comes to championing women's writing—and most especially to managing editor Marisa Solís, whose guidance in assembling this anthology (and the previous two), assuring its quality, and moving it seamlessly through production was indispensable. Thanks are also in line for the people who provided invaluable support throughout the book's life, pre- and post-production: Denise Silva, editorial assistant; Domini Dragoone, who located the book's captivating cover image; and our ace copy editor, Wendy Taylor.

About the Contributors

Charish Badzinski is a freelance writer and editor of *Coulee Region Women* magazine, in La Crosse, Wisconsin. She and her husband, Joel, have now made four trips to Mexico, and each time they return, Charish brings home a little piece of the beach.

Kathy Jo Brisker lives in Los Angeles with her husband, who fills her belly, heart, and soul with the best homemade Mexican food she can get when not in Oaxaca. They share their home with two dogs and the crafts and spirit of Mexico.

Melinda Bergman Burgener was born in New York City. She began writing after working twenty years as a graphic designer, and her stories have appeared in magazines, newspapers, and books, and on the Internet. Her memories of Mexico are like the chocolate she loves—strong and bittersweet. She and her husband leave their San Francisco home each year to travel in France. She can be reached at writemelinda@mac.com.

Fran Davis lives in Summerland, California. She is a freelance writer, a newspaper columnist, a winner of the Lamar York Prize for Nonfiction, and a Pushcart Prize nominee. Her work has appeared in numerous journals, periodicals, and anthologies. She contributed an essay to *Italy, A Love Story*. Her fiction has been dramatized onstage at Speaking of Stories, a Santa Barbara–based actors' equity performance group. She is currently working on a nonfiction book for baby boomers.

Karín Finell has won literary prizes for nonfiction and poetry. Her work has appeared in *Community of Voices*, newspapers, and literary magazines, including *Merian, Poetry Therapy Journal, Cafe in Space,* and the anthology *Yellow Slippers*. She teaches poetry and personal-essay writing at Santa Barbara Community College. She has discussed her literary work on National Public Radio and other radio shows. Her memoir, *Goodbye to the Mermaids—Memories of a Childhood Lost in Hitler's Berlin,* will be published by University of Missouri Press in 2006.

Tania Flores is a freshman at a northern California high school. She writes poetry and fiction for herself and for publication, and has published Harry Potter book reviews. She is bilingual and attends a Spanish for Native Speakers class at her high school. Once a week, she leads an advanced Spanish conversation hour at the Chico Peace and Justice Center. She spends as much time as she can in Tian-guistengo. When in California, she satisfies her *pitaya* cravings with the fruit's jam.

Laura Fraser is a San Francisco–based journalist and the author of the best-selling travel memoir *An Italian Affair*. She fell in love with Mexico when she lived in San Miguel de Allende for a summer as a child. You can read her Italian recipes, travel tips, and handy romantic phrases at www.laurafraser.com.

Kathleen Hamilton Gündoğdu, a displaced Texan by choice, has been a chef, roofer, secretary, bookkeeper, international meetings planner, editor, fundraiser, and textile dealer. She has traveled extensively throughout the world—her son, born in 2001, had stamps from three continents in his passport by the age of seven months. She writes articles about the lesser-known historical treasures of Istanbul, where she has lived since 1998. She has contributed to *Tales from the Expat Harem*. See her writing at www.travelwriters .com/kathyhamilton and www.expatharem.com.

Katherine Hatch left a good job, good house, good car, and good friends to move from Norman, Oklahoma, to Mexico in 1971. She has had a career as a newspaper reporter, foreign correspondent, and biographer. She cowrote, with Helen Hayes, *Helen Hayes: My Life in Three Acts*, a book that spent the summer of 1990 on the *New York Times* Best Seller List. She still lives in Mexico.

Sondra Ross Hines, born and raised in New York City, was among the first group of women stockbrokers at Merrill Lynch. After marrying sculptor Francis Hines, she left the stock market for the art market. While managing an art gallery, she developed an interest in photojournalism. Her photojournalism has appeared in *Fabric & Tension; Atención*, a bilingual publication in San Miguel Allende; and in a cultural publication in Johannesburg, South Africa.

Suzanne LaFetra is a writer living in Berkeley, California. Her work has appeared in the *San Francisco Chronicle Magazine, Diablo,* and *Asian Week,* and in several anthologies, the *Rocking Chair Reader* and *Whose Panties Are These?* Her story, "El Otro Lado," received honorable mention in the William Allen Creative Nonfiction Prize, appeared in *Rosebud* magazine, and is excerpted from her memoir, *Hecho in Mexico.*

Reyna Lingemann is a travel, food, and fiction writer in Santa Cruz, California, where she lives with her husband, Slade, and their two-year-old son. As an undergraduate Latin American Studies major, she first visited Mexico at age nineteen and fell in love with the language, the people, and her husband. She earned her MFA in writing from the University of San Francisco in 1997.

Susan McKinney de Ortega, born in Philadelphia, is a former television news reporter and daughter of an ex–National Basketball Association coach. In addition to newspapers and Fodor's travel publications, her work has been published in *Salon,* the *San Miguel*

Writer, and on the *Literary Bulls* website, and will appear in *Philadel-phia.* She has aired commentaries for National Public Radio's "All Things Considered" on bicultural living. She lives in San Miguel de Allende in the Mexican central highlands with her husband, the sub-ject of "Maestra," and their two bilingual daughters.

Liza Monroy, daughter of a U.S. Foreign Service officer, grew up in Guadalajara, Rome, Washington, D.C., and Mexico City. She received her BA in Writing and Literature from Emerson College in Boston and is now a freelance writer in New York City. Her work has appeared in *The New York Times,* the *Village Voice, Time Out New York, Nerve.com, CITY* magazine, and other publications. She is at work on a novel loosely based on her years in Mexico, and she hopes to put her love of writing and travel to work as a travel journalist.

Linda Grant Niemann is the author of two nonfiction memoirs about her career as a railroad trainman on the Southern Pacific from 1979 to 1999. The first book, *Boomer: Railroad Memoirs,* was later retitled *On the Rails.* An excerpt from this book is included in Travelers' Tales *America.* Her second book, *Railroad Voices,* is a text and photograph collaboration with Lina Bertucci. Since 1998, she has continued to publish articles and stories in *Railroad History, Trains,* and the *Women's Review of Books,* and her work has been anthologized in *West of the West, Every Woman I've Ever Loved,* and *Tomboys.* She is currently an associate professor of English at Ken-nesaw State University in Georgia, with a teaching specialty in creative nonfiction and feature writing.

Sophia Raday is at work on a book-length memoir of her three-year relationship with Rafael (the subject of her essay, "Panamericano") after he crossed illegally to "the other side." A founding editor of *Literary Mama*, www.literarymama.com, she writes a bimonthly column there titled "Mommy Athens, Daddy Sparta." In the spring of 2005, Forbes.com mentioned one of her columns specifically when it hailed *Literary Mama* in its Best of the Web list. Her writing has also recently appeared in *Stanford* magazine and in the anthology *Using Our Words: Moms & Dads on Raising Kids in the Modern Neighborhood.* She lives with her husband and son in Berkeley, California.

Laura Resau is a writer, teacher, and anthropologist who lives in Colorado. Her first novel, *What the Moon Saw*, is set in an indigenous community in southern Mexico and will be released in fall 2006. Her writing for adults and young people has appeared in a number of magazines, including *Cricket; Cicada; Matter;* and *Brain,Child;* as well as in anthologies published by Lonely Planet and Travelers' Tales. Her essay, "Bees Born of Tears," also appears in the literary journal *Pilgrimage*. Smack in the middle of winter, she usually finds herself missing Mexico terribly, at which time she heads to rural Oaxaca, where something delightfully surprising always happens. Her website is at www.lauraresau.com.

Mary Ellen Sanger, after seventeen years is Mexico, now works in New York City with a Mexican-immigrant support group. Her poetry, fiction, and personal essays have been published online and in print in MexConnect.com, MexicoFile.com, Hackwriters.com,

Delirium Journal, PoetsAgainsttheWar.org, Travelers' Tales, *Human Journey*, and *Writers Weekly*.

Chris Scofield writes, creates art, reads voraciously, and loves to travel. She has studied writing and literature under a variety of authors, including Ursula K. Le Guin and Tom Spanbauer. Her short story "Old Fucker LaVert" won the Lane Literary Guild Prize in 1992. She continues to write short stories and manages a file of flattering rejection notices.

Kay Sexton is an associate editor for *Night Train* journal. Her short story "Domestic Violence" was runner-up in the *Guardian* fiction contest, judged by Dave Eggers; "Acorns and Conkers" was the runner-up in the ESSP short story contest, judged by Sarah Hall; and her work is widely anthologized. She is currently collaborating with the painter Fion Gunn on *Green Thought in an Urban Shade*—a project that explores and celebrates the parks and urban spaces of Beijing, Dublin, London, and Paris in words and images. For more about her work, visit www.charybdis.freeserve.co.uk.

Marisa Solís struggles to find the time, energy, and best ergonomic position to write after long days of editing parenting, women's studies, and travel literature titles. For four years prior, she was writing—and traveling—vicariously as a senior editor of travel guidebooks. Solís turned thirty last year and tirelessly tries to understand the changes within and around her, often with a glass of red wine. She lives and plays in Oakland, California.

About the Editor

Camille Cusumano is the editor of *France, A Love Story* and *Italy, A Love Story* and is the author of many food and travel articles, several food books, and *The Last Cannoli*, a novel. She lives in San Francisco.

Selected Titles from Seal Press

For more than twenty-five years, Seal Press has published groundbreaking books. By women. For women. Visit our website at www.sealpress.com.

Italy, A Love Story: Women Write about the Italian Experience edited by Camille Cusumano. $15.95. 1-58005-143-X. Legendary for fabulous food, persistent men, and a lyrical language, Italy has inspired many great love affairs—with the country itself. In this thrilling and layered collection, two dozen women describe, in loving prose, individual infatuations with a land that is both complicated by and adored for its rich tradition.

Es Cuba: Life and Love on an Illegal Island by Lea Aschkenas. $15.95. 1-58005-179-0. This triumphant love story captures a beautiful and intangible sense of sadness and admiration for the country of Cuba and for its people.

Reckless: The Outrageous Lives of Nine Kick-Ass Women by Gloria Mattioni. $14.95. 1-58005-148-0. From Lisa Distefano, who captains a pirate vessel on her quest to protect sea life, to Libby Riddles, the first woman to win the legendary Iditarod, this collection of profiles explores the lives of nine women who took unconventional life paths to achieve extraordinary results.

The Risks of Sunbathing Topless: And Other Funny Stories from the Road edited by Kate Chynoweth. $15.95. 1-58005-141-3. From Kandahar to Baja to Moscow, these wry, amusing essays capture the comic essence of bad travel, and the female experience on the road.

Solo: On Her Own Adventure edited by Susan Fox Rogers. $15.95. 1-58005-137-5. An inspiring collection of travel narratives that reveal the complexities of women journeying alone.

The Unsavvy Traveler: Women's Comic Tales of Catastrophe edited by Rosemary Caperton, Anne Mathews, and Lucie Ocenas. $15.95. 1-58005-142-1. Thirty bitingly funny essays respond to the question: "What happens when trips go wrong?"